HOME *and* AWAY

A STORY OF FAMILY IN A TIME OF WAR

DAVID AND NANCY FRENCH

CENTER
STREET ®

New York   Boston   Nashville

Copyright © 2011 by David and Nancy French

All rights reserved. Except as permitted under the U.S. Copyright Act of 1976, no part of this publication may be reproduced, distributed, or transmitted in any form or by any means, or stored in a database or retrieval system, without the prior written permission of the publisher.

Center Street
Hachette Book Group
237 Park Avenue
New York, NY 10017

www.centerstreet.com

Center Street is a division of Hachette Book Group, Inc.
The Center Street name and logo are trademarks of Hachette Book Group, Inc.

The publisher is not responsible for websites (or their content) that are not owned by the publisher.

Printed in the United States of America

First Edition: July 2011
10 9 8 7 6 5 4 3 2 1

Library of Congress Cataloging-in-Publication Data

French, David.
  Home and away : a story of family in a time of war / David and Nancy French. — 1st ed.
     p. cm.
  ISBN 978-1-931722-90-2
  1. Iraq War, 2003—Personal narratives, American. 2. United States. Army—Officers—Biography. 3. Families of military personnel—United States. 4. Military spouses—United States—Biography. 5. French, David, 1969– 6. French, Nancy, 1974– I. French, Nancy, 1974– II. Title.

  DS79.766.F74A3 2011
  956.7044'3092273—dc22
                                   2010043422

*To Captain Leonel Brodhead and Captain David ("J-Dave")
Robison, who taught me about friendship and brotherhood.*

*To Colonel Paul T. Calvert and Major Gregory McLean, who taught
me about leadership.*

*To
Major Andrew Olmstead
Captain Thomas Casey
Sergeant Corey Spates
Captain Torre Mallard
Sergeant Phillip Anderson
Specialist Donald Burkett
Mr. Albert Haroutounian
Sergeant Gregory Unruh
Specialist Matthew Morris
Captain Ulises Burgos
Specialist Andre Mitchell
Captain Michael Medders
You gave all that any man could give.*

ACKNOWLEDGMENTS

From Nancy

I'd like to thank the people at Zion Presbyterian Church who were nosy and bossy and concerned enough to love me through the entire year of David's absence. I'd like to thank Arch and Joyce Warren for their spiritual counsel and the Calvinettes (Kim, Jana, Anna, Mary Beth) for putting the T in the Presbyterian acronym TULIP. I'd especially like to thank Jeff Bryant, who fixed my garage door, dishwasher, and car. He also drove to Mount Pleasant to fill my tank with gasoline when I was running low, babysat briefly, and even once (during a low point) pulled my son's tooth when I just couldn't muster the fortitude. When David finally came home, he shook his hand and said, "She's your problem now."

I'd also like to thank the Sweatsuit Mafia (Tabby, Monica, Kris, and Lauren) for their unwavering ability to cheer me up while chatting on the elliptical machine, how they made sure I knew about all major school functions, and gave me a lingerie shower upon David's return.

Thanks to Zion Christian Academy, which not only has amazing academic standing in the state of Tennessee, but also was gracious during the year I showed up late for drop-off every single day. (No jokes from headmaster Don Wahlman about how I haven't improved much since David's return.)

Thanks to John and Jean Kingston, who let me practically live with them in Boston that summer, for their counsel and friendship over the years in good times and bad.

Thanks to my neighborhood book club (Kittye, Nana Joyce, and Arch), who read all the way through *Les Misérables* and *The Gulag Archipelago* during the deployment. (Hey, maybe we could've picked happier tomes?)

To my family, who stepped up in love and support during David's absence... to Mom and Dad for helping Austin cut out and paint the Jeff Gordon pinewood derby car. To my sisters for helping with Send-a-Box and our political adventures.

To my kids, who only now are beginning to understand the value of what they went through, for their obedience and trust.

And to David, whom I love.

From David

Thank you. Those words are just not enough to describe the gratitude we feel toward so many who played such a key role in our lives during our most challenging year (so far).

Thank you to the men of Sabre Squadron and especially to my comrades in "Operation Snakeyes." Long live the bucket! You are the finest men I have ever known.

Thank you to the men and women of the Alliance Defense Fund. It was humbling to come home and see my picture in every office and every cubicle.

Thank you to Zion Presbyterian Church, for all the many, many ways you sustained us in scary and uncertain times.

Thank you, Mom and Dad, for not blinking when your son said he was going to war, for praying every day, and to Mom for giving me the "Joy" pillow that I laid my head on every night.

Thank you, Christina, Angela, and the rest of the Hachette team, for making this book better than we thought it could be. And thank you, DJ, for making it all happen. Your work is brilliant, and we treasure your friendship.

Thank you, Camille and Austin, for understanding why Daddy

had to leave and may yet have to leave again. And to our beautiful adopted daughter, Naomi, who was born the very day that I flew into Forward Operating Base Caldwell and joined our family after I returned, this book represents an important chapter in the history of your new family. We love you with all our hearts.

Most of all, thank you, Nancy, for the steel in your spine and the love in your heart.

INTRODUCTION

David

SOME SIGHTS YOU NEVER FORGET. I can remember my wife's face the instant before our first kiss. I can remember my daughter's tiny little body as the doctor held her up on the moment of her birth. I can remember my son scampering up our stairs as he raced me to the PlayStation before our first (virtual) NASCAR race. And now I can remember the dark Iraqi landscape as I peered over the shoulder of a door gunner in a CH-47 Chinook transport helicopter.

It was Thanksgiving eve 2007 and I was flying to Forward Operating Base Caldwell, in eastern Diyala province, Iraq, with the 2nd Squadron, 3d Armored Cavalry Regiment—into the teeth of the Iraqi insurgency and within sight of the Iranian border. Amid the indescribably loud clatter of the helicopter's rotors, the unspeakable discomfort of hundreds of pounds of gear piled on and around me, and the terror at the thought of facing combat, I had the ultimate Admiral Stockdale moment.

Who am I? Why am I here?

For a time, it had all seemed so dramatic. So storybook. At age thirty-seven, I was a lawyer—a graduate of Harvard Law School—and president of a successful nonprofit in Philadelphia. I had a dream job defending free speech and making various media appearances while the war in Iraq raged unabated and the Army struggled to meet recruiting goals. That's when I realized with shocking immediacy that

I could no longer in good conscience support a war I wasn't willing to fight.

After reading an article about a wounded officer—exactly my age—who'd called his wife and kids on a satellite phone to tell them that he was hurt but not to worry, I felt stricken. How was he different from me? Why was it right for him to sacrifice and not me? After all, he no doubt loved his children as much as I loved my children. He loved his wife as much as I loved my wife. There was simply no good reason—no reason that made any sense—why I should spend my life secure in the knowledge that "someone else" would volunteer. So I turned to my wife, Nancy, and declared I wanted to join the United States Army Reserves.

She didn't blink at that declaration. She didn't say no. She didn't laugh. She didn't immediately declare that I was insane. Instead, she said that she'd think about it. And she did. She thought and prayed and—after a few short days—told me not just that I could join but that I *should*. I changed jobs to one more forgiving of a deployment. I endured my first rounds of training, and then I volunteered to go . . . to Iraq and to the war.

No, actually, *we* volunteered. This book is the story of a family at war. Of a wife who loved me from afar and who lived as a single parent—wracked with worry for my safety—while taking the kids from school to Cub Scouts to Brownies to basketball to piano and working on her own career. Of kids who learned what war meant when they heard "One of Daddy's friends died yesterday," and who began to understand what it meant to live for something more than yourself. And of a balding yuppie sweltering in indescribable heat, sitting knee to knee with al Qaeda terrorists, making decisions with terrible consequences, and weeping at shocking losses.

We don't live storybooks but real—and messy—lives. Nothing is more real than war. As a student of history, I'd read that war brings out the best and worst in human nature. As a soldier, I learned that it does—but it's more than that. There's nothing more absurd, more obscene, more horrifying than war. And—in some truly strange ways—it can actually be comical. Or, more precisely, comical things can happen in war. At the end of the day, our story is not really our story at all, but the story of all those around us who helped, and prayed, and laughed, and fought, and died. We were a family at war, but wars are not fought alone.

But I'm jumping ahead. So let's go back—back to the day I decided to join the fight.

THE DECISION

Nancy

THE WAY DAVID TELLS IT, I took the whole thing in stride. But I remember standing in our apartment in Philadelphia, clutching the back of one of my recently purchased black barstools.

David was standing in the doorway, waiting for my response.

Unable to speak, I glanced down at my white knuckles tightly wrapped around the chair like it was my child's hand on a busy street. The chair looked modern and chic at IKEA but cheap under my bright kitchen lights. Nevertheless, we could now eat breakfast there instead of on the dining room table, which was stainless steel—perfect for games and crafts, but a little cold.

Tears threatened to break the brink of my eyelids as he destroyed my idea of "the perfect family life." I guess everyone has a different image, but in my ideal world, the kids would sit on those barstools and do homework, and then I'd say, "Clean the table off for dinner." And they'd gripe a bit as they ran a wet cloth over the surface, but I'd ignore them, and when I turned around the table would be more or less set and their backpacks would slump on the floor, homework spilling out. I know some people dream of eating off perfectly set tables, the kind made of wood, not Scandinavian or assemble-yourself. While they might envision their kids gently dabbing the corners of their mouths with cloth napkins like Marsha, Jan, and Cindy Brady, formality didn't exist in my vision—just four plates, forks haphazardly laid on them, mismatched mugs, and Viva paper towels. Vivas instead of paper napkins, because when you open napkins up you can see through them and they seem ghostly, frail, and inadequate to the task.

Instead of buying a sports car or vacationing in exotic locales after David made partner at his law firm, he held up a roll of inexpensive paper towels—probably Brawnys or some other form of glorified toilet paper—and tossed them in the garbage can.

"Now that I'm a partner, no more cheap paper towels."

Over the ensuing years, we'd moved from a law firm salary to a nonprofit one, but the Vivas remained—a symbol of "the good life," along with the kitchen nook barstools, two brushstrokes in the picture I was painting of the perfect family life.

What had caused me to reach out to the stool for stability was this.

"I want to join the Army."

It was around five o'clock in the afternoon, and the sun was pouring through the windows that overlooked the Walnut Street Theatre and the Philadelphia Eagles stadium on the horizon. Cars buzzed eighteen stories below us, but I couldn't hear them.

"If I run every day, I can get into good enough shape to pass the physical."

I still hadn't spoken, and David's voice cracked. I was having one of those moments where images flash before your eyes—but instead of my life, it was my relationship.

I remembered how I met him on a sidewalk in Nashville while wearing a blue dress, and I skipped my eighteenth-century literature class to chat. I remembered—vaguely—that as we exchanged pleasantries, he said he'd wanted to be a fighter pilot but he went to law school instead—Harvard Law School—so I tried not to act impressed. I didn't think much of his I-wanted-to-join-the-military schtick at the time. That's the type of thing people say to get credit for being virtuous without actually having to sacrifice anything. Like at church when people talk about how their strange metabolism prohibits them from fasting or when people forget about sponsoring the child in Africa after the late-night television commercial flickers out of consciousness. They mean to, but...

The man I met that day was an attorney. (I used that term instead of "lawyer" because he'd never ask if you or anyone in your family was

the victim of a fraudulent weight loss pill.) We were ma
months, moved to Manhattan on a whim, and got a Gram
apartment with a view of the Empire State Building...if you
out the window and used your imagination.

But he changed careers over the course of his professional life. I
taught at Cornell Law School in Ithaca, New York, and even practiced
energy law in his hometown of Lexington, Kentucky. Gradually, he
became adept at a certain type of law—constitutional law. This meant
he protected the First Amendment and all that makes America free,
but couldn't do the basics.

"I don't even have a will myself," he'd joke when someone would
ask him if he could assist in this rather practical task. "But if the government oppresses you, I've got you covered."

Unfortunately, oppressed minority groups rarely had the money to
hire good legal representation, and the other partners rightfully objected
to his ever-growing list of pro bono cases. And so we moved and my husband became the president of a nonprofit free speech organization.

From our little enclave in Philadelphia, David protected the Constitution right next to the Pennsylvania State House, where it was
originally written. My daughter's school was so close to the Liberty
Bell that it was evacuated every time a tourist accidentally left behind
something that might resemble a bomb.

And life was good.

We lived in a renovated hotel with one of the grandest ballrooms
in the city. Invariably, we'd run out for ice cream, only to emerge from
the elevator and be surrounded by men in tuxedos and women in ball
gowns, drinking champagne. The ballroom was booked every weekend for years in advance with weddings—once even a presidential
debate—and we couldn't help but to slow down to observe the cele-
brations. The photographers arranged the ever-changing brides and
grooms around a fountain in the middle of the marble expanse. Their
faces were sometimes splotched with anxiety, but always glowed with
the luminescence of high and unrealistic expectations. We admired
the bridal gowns, critiqued the bridesmaids' dresses, and hoped no
one fell into the fountain—with such a hyperemotional event, you
never know. Brides across Philadelphia will look back at their albums

underdressed people walking through the back-
ographs, holding ice cream, carrying mail.

cause of our downtown Philly surroundings.
urity guard, an overweight guy with tattooed
s on a thick chain, and drew him pictures of
hang on his refrigerator. They secretly nick-
attendant Chuckles, because he looked one
_om strapping on explosives and ending it all. Plus, gro-
cery delivery was free and the deliverymen wouldn't accept tips, even
though they carried the food in temperature-controlled containers up
the freight elevator and straight to our kitchen.

That's where I stood that day.

All of these brushstrokes—the building, the groceries, the door-
man—helped complete my picture of the ideal family life. Life
would've been perfect if we'd had a dog, a picket fence, and a valet
that didn't look homicidal. But for city living, we had it pretty good.

Until that moment.

"I read an article in the *New York Times* about a guy who was
wounded in Iraq," David said, "and then at the end of the article, it
mentioned that he had two kids and a wife back home."

I began to cry.

"And it dawned on me that there's no difference between him and
me. He doesn't love his kids less than I love my kids. He doesn't love
his wife less than I love you."

I loosened my grip on the barstool, pulled it from the table, and
eased into it.

"The only difference is that he's doing his duty for his country and
I'm not."

The Army was facing a recruitment shortfall and David had
lamented more than once that America was losing its resolve to finish
what we started.

"And then I realized that America hadn't lost its resolve. I'd lost
mine."

When I finally found my voice—which was hiding behind "Expectations" and "Perfect Family Vision" in my mind—I offered half-
throated objections.

"But you're a lawyer."

"Good lawyers could've prevented Abu Ghraib."

"But you're...old."

"Yesterday, they raised the maximum age limit because of the recruitment shortfalls."

This meaningless conversation went on for a few minutes. Like a car salesman and a buyer, both of us knew the real negotiations would happen after a little back-and-forth.

I didn't say it, but I'll confess to thinking it. Why would anyone with a Harvard Law degree voluntarily do something so dangerous when no one asked them? Not even President Bush had asked for that kind of sacrifice. After the 9/11 attacks, he could've stood in front of the American people and asked young men and women to enlist in the military. The nation sat in front of televisions waiting for someone to make sense of the still-smoking hole in New York City. We were waiting for a call to action, anything that would take away the empty, throbbing sense of powerlessness. But instead, he told us to go shopping.

Which was honestly just fine with me. Throughout history, Americans have participated in the "war effort," and I would be no different. If they planted Victory Gardens, canned food, and saved scrap metal, the least I could do was run down to the Apple Store to buy the new iMac. Anything for the troops.

At the time, I didn't recognize the impotence of the president's suggestion, or the fact that he missed an opportunity to rally us collectively into something significant. People were certainly willing—they gave blood, stuck "God Bless America" magnets on their minivans, and hung flags in windows and from front porches. But it wasn't enough, and we all felt it.

By the time I was sitting at the kitchen table that afternoon, months had passed, even years, since we all wanted to wear American flag lapel pins. The national support toward the war effort was evaporating before my very eyes and I couldn't even conjure the image of Republicans and Democrats singing "My Country 'Tis of Thee" on the steps of the Capitol. Even worse, a backlash erupted against what some people called mindless "jingoism." At my daughter's school, someone donated a flag that had flown in Iraq, and parents protested, saying the stars and stripes were too controversial and could make students of other nationalities feel uncomfortable.

In other words, it wasn't the right time to join the war effort, like booking a *Titanic* cruise after the iceberg. Plus, we lived in Center City Philadelphia—not a hotbed of support for the war effort. What would our friends think?

Earlier that day, I was with my friend after we picked our kids up from school and took them to the park surrounding the Liberty Bell and Independence Hall. This is yet another place packed with people taking photographs, and we frequently received annoyed glances from the tourists irritated that the kids sometimes ran through their photos. That day we had an enormous blue ball that bounced against the stone statues erected to honor historical figures.

"Who are these men?" asked Austin, merely four at the time.

"That man is George Washington," I said, pointing to the large carved letters and the smaller identifiers below. "It says he was a 'planter,' 'lawyer,' 'soldier,' 'general,' and 'President.'"

"Guess he couldn't keep a job," my friend quipped, undermining my effort to take advantage of what experts call the "teachable moment." We all laughed.

"Who's that?" Austin asked, pointing to a different statue.

"John Barry," I said. "It says 'farmer,' a 'soldier,' and the 'creator of the modern Navy.'"

Austin looked up at me with wide eyes.

"Why would they make a statue for a farmer?"

"Well, people do a lot of things before they do the thing people remember them for."

"But who *were* they?"

I knew my son. He was wondering what he needed to do to get his own statue, and was already hoping his monument would fit next to his bunk bed.

"Well," I began, trying to figure out the overarching theme, "I guess they were all patriots."

"What's a *patriot*?" He struggled over the word.

"Someone who loves America so much that he does something about it."

"Are we patriots?"

The question struck me to the core. Other people were standing around, mildly bemused, clearly waiting to hear my response. Even there in Independence Hall, some tour guides talked more about our founding fathers owning slaves than bravely creating a nation that eventually would offer unprecedented freedoms. Cynicism was the lingua franca of my social circle, largely comprised of my fellow newspaper columnists, pundits, and mothers-in-the-know. Something about the simple question unnerved me.

"Yes, I guess we are," I said. And when I said that rather ineloquent sentence, I almost wept. I didn't know why, but it seemed momentous. A few of the other mothers chuckled knowingly, the way they might after hearing another mom reassure their kid that yes, Virginia, there is a Santa Claus.

Not two hours later, I was sitting there in the kitchen trying to find a way out of this conversation with David.

"But," I wailed, almost unable to form the words, "you don't even have a will."

"The Army helps you write one," he reassured me. "But I'll be fine. They don't send lawyers to the front line. I'll be in the Green Zone somewhere doing boring office work probably."

"You'd go to Iraq!" Up to now, I hadn't connected all the dots and had a hard time even imagining my thirty-seven-year-old, out-of-shape husband in a uniform.

"We are at a time of war," he said gently with a soft voice that wrapped around me like an embrace. "It's kind of the point."

I could tell he'd been thinking of this for a long time and had waited to bring it up. His answers were all prepared and flowed out with exactly the right amount of sincerity. "But aren't you afraid?"

"There's an old Stonewall Jackson quote, which goes something like this: 'My religious belief teaches me to feel as safe in battle as in bed. God has fixed the time for my death. I do not concern myself about that, but to be always ready.'" I knew if he was quoting Confederate generals that this decision was all but made. He continued, "'That is the way all men should live, and then all would be equally brave.'"

"Didn't Stonewall Jackson die on the battlefield?" I said.

He moved closer to me and we wrapped our arms around each other tightly. We'd been married almost ten years, but I never felt I needed him more than I did at that moment—the second I realized he could go away.

"I've done a lot of things in my life," he said. "I've been a lawyer, a professor, and now I want to be a soldier." I thought of the statues in the park. "I know it's the right thing to do," he said.

"But I love you," I sobbed, although it came out with as much eloquence as a walrus reciting the alphabet.

"I've always loved America. Why else would I practice constitutional law?" he asked, but I could tell he didn't expect an answer. "Do you realize that when you take the military oath of office, you don't vow to protect the country? You promise to protect the..." He cleared his voice. "The Constitution, from its enemies from without and from within."

Like a sponge absorbing water, I was becoming heavier with each drop of incontrovertible evidence. David loved the Constitution and had spent his career defending it.

"It just feels like a natural culmination of my life's work," he said. "Even though I've done all kinds of jobs, I mostly feel like..." He paused.

"Go on," I prompted, desperately wanting to end this conversation but afraid our lives would never be the same afterwards.

"It just sounds so silly, but I've always felt the theme of my life was that I was a patriot."

And with those words, I knew David was going to join the Army. We both agreed he should do it—and I knew God Himself had prepared my heart to receive the news.

That's what it took.

After our tearful conversation, I got into bed and pulled the covers up to my chin. I vowed not to tell anyone of our decision just yet, because I knew if I said the words "David's joining the Army and I support him," people would see straight through me.

My life had just unfolded and I suddenly felt ghostly, frail, and way too inadequate for the task.

2

LEARNING TO FIGHT

David

I LOOKED LIKE A Q-TIP with a marble in the middle. I'd always been skinny, and the completely sedentary lawyer's life I'd been leading hadn't really changed that—except for my gut. If you looked at a picture of twenty-five-year-old me next to thirty-seven-year-old me, you'd see the same overly thin arms, the same slender legs, a lot less hair, and a big bulging middle. For a man, it might be the least attractive look imaginable.

But there I was, gut hanging out, standing nearly naked with fifty guys who looked like they'd just stepped out of high school football practice. In fact, on the bus on the way over, many were wearing their high school jerseys—show-offs—while I tried to pretend that I fit in with the muscled, tattooed kids talking about their "airborne" futures. They were very polite to me—even called me "sir"—but they looked at me as if I was the poor old guy at the Y. *What's he doing here? Is he going to live through this?*

I was in Fort Dix, New Jersey, the time was about 0630 hours (I was learning military time), and I was getting my Army physical.

Before I'd normally had my first cup of coffee and read the first page of the *New York Times*, I'd flunked.

Beads of sweat were standing out on my head as I found out my blood pressure was simply too high.

I couldn't quite believe it. All the angst, all the soul-searching, and now this? Get up at four in the morning, drive to Fort Dix, stand in line with the male cast of *High School Musical*, flunk a blood pressure test, and go home?

"Could you please take it again?" I tried to control my voice. "I've never had high blood pressure before."

"We'll take it as many times as you'd like." The nurse smiled. "But you'll have to pass the test or this is the end of your military career."

I tried to think calming thoughts, to think about peaceful surroundings and conjure some sort of serenity. Would that Lamaze breathing we learned when Nancy was pregnant work? I was desperate to try anything, a desperation that unfortunately didn't help matters. The nurse sat me down in the chair, strapped on the blood pressure monitor, and frowned as she finished counting.

"Better, but not good enough."

She sent me through the other stations...which meant stripping down, "crab walking" across the floor, and doing all kinds of humiliating exercises. The nurse glanced at my middle-aged paunch and said, "Sir, do you think you could do the minimum number of push-ups?"

"No problem," I lied.

"I don't believe you, but that's not part of the test...today."

That exchange made me nervous, so when it was time to take the blood pressure test again, I failed miserably...again.

"Grab that chair from the corner, close your eyes, and just try to relax. In a few minutes, I'm going to give you one more chance. You can do it."

I walked into a corner of the waiting room, sat back in the chair, and tried to push ever-encroaching thoughts from my head. I'd never felt this old before. Had I really let myself go? Should thirty-seven-year-olds really be this frail? Or was I just comparing myself to the jocks who had gathered around my chair?

"You got this, sir!" said one of the nineteen-year-olds. I'd become their special project...Must've been Encourage the Elderly Day at Fort Dix.

I tried to relax as much as I could without lapsing into a coma. The nurse came over, pumped the little balloon, and looked at the dial. I couldn't make out anything from her expressionless face, until she looked at me, looked at the dial, then smiled.

"Well?"

"Congratulations, soldier, you're at 121 over 79."

The room exploded in applause. I'd passed my physical. I was one step closer to my goal. I picked up the phone and called Nancy, who sounded less enthused than the strangers in the room.

But I didn't let it dampen my mood. The nurse had called me "soldier."

Joining the Army meant making some changes.

For starters, we couldn't stay in Philadelphia. After all, it wouldn't be fair to a small nonprofit if its president (and chief fundraiser) was out of the office for weeks—or months—at a time. Plus, we were hundreds of miles from our families, and the thought of Nancy and the kids staying in Pennsylvania—so far from our southern roots—while I left for training or deployment was intolerable.

So I left the Foundation for Individual Rights in Education (the board was extremely supportive), said goodbye to the City of Brotherly Love, and moved to Nancy's home state of Tennessee, to my mother's hometown of Columbia, and to a house in the country only a mile from our new church home.

Joining the Army also meant paperwork. Lots and lots of paperwork. I literally spent weeks assembling my application packet comprised of references, certifications, and fingerprints. I had to chronicle the course of my entire professional life for the security clearance documents—including listing the name of the manager of the Big Lots I worked for in high school—and had to be interviewed by a JAG officer. Far from being a "come one, come all!" branch of the service, the standards are high, and the scrutiny can be a bit uncomfortable.

At the beginning of April 2006, however, it happened. I became an officer in the United States Army . . . in the most anticlimactic way possible.

I got a letter in the mail that informed me—in the driest bureaucratic language possible—that I'd been accepted in the JAG Corps. The only thing I needed to do was to acknowledge my commission as a first lieutenant. (JAG officers start as first lieutenants and then become captains shortly after completing their initial training.) How? By attending a swearing-in ceremony? Shouldn't my family be here when this happened? Shouldn't I have, like, a uniform or something?

Apparently not.

I looked at the letter for a while, gathering my thoughts, and called out to Nancy. "Hey! They accepted my application! Once I take the oath of office, I'm an officer!"

She popped her head in from another room. "What? How do you do that?"

"Apparently you just sign this paper in front of a notary."

"Hmmm. That's it? No ceremony?"

I shook my head. "Nope. Seems strange, doesn't it? So I just walk up to a notary, sign this paper in front of her, and bam! I'm an officer in the United States Army." The whole thing seemed so strange that the moment was drained of all drama.

"Well, are you going to go do it?"

"I suppose so."

"Where?"

"I guess I'll go to the bank right now. They have notaries there."

"While you're there, can you deposit a check for me?" Nancy handed me a check or two from her freelance writing work, and I drove to the bank, walked in, and put the deposit slip on the counter—along with my oath.

"Making a deposit?" The teller smiled sweetly. We'd only been back in Tennessee a few weeks, but she knew us by name already.

"Um, yeah. And can someone swear me into the military?"

"Excuse me?"

"I need someone to notarize my oath of office. I'm joining the Reserves." I showed her the piece of paper.

"Ooookaaayy." I could tell that she'd never sworn in a soldier before. She grabbed her notary seal. "Do you want to just sign it?"

"No, do you mind reading it out loud while I hold my hand up? You know, like a real oath?" It seemed like the right thing to do.

"Sure, honey."

So there I stood, in a local bank, wearing my business casual clothes, with my hand in the air, and recited the oath:

> I, David French, do solemnly swear that I will sup-
> port and defend the Constitution of the United
> States against all enemies, foreign and domestic;
> that I will bear true faith and allegiance to the
> same; that I take this obligation freely, without any
> mental reservation or purpose of evasion; and that I
> will well and faithfully discharge the duties of the
> office on which I am about to enter. So help me
> God.

Then I leaned down and signed the paper. She notarized it. I became Lieutenant David French on April 11, 2006.

As anticlimactic as taking my oath was, next to the jar of suckers they
give to kids at the bank, basic training was just plain miserable. On
June 20, roughly nine weeks after my anticlimactic day at the bank, I
was at Fort Lee, Virginia, enduring day twenty-two of my Officer Basic Course. I was hot (it was a humid ninety-five degrees), exhausted
(no sleep for almost forty-eight hours), and—worst of all—covered in
poison ivy. It was between my fingers, on my scalp, on my beltline,
on my neckline, on my stomach, and on my ankles.

To make matters worse, I was also dead. I had just been "killed"
by one of my fellow classmates, a former Ranger turned lawyer who'd
single-handedly snuck behind a line of seventy JAG officers and
mowed most of us down before we could even figure out where the
gunfire was coming from.

The drill sergeant stood beside my "dead," itching body and
laughed.

And laughed.

And laughed.

Then he turned serious. "That was pathetic. What have I told you
about 360-degree security? What have I told you about discipline?
Don't think for one second if you go downrange that you'll just be
sitting at a desk while the 'real soldiers' fight! Some of you guys are
going outside the wire! Some of you guys are going to see some things
that you won't believe, and—yes—some of the people in this class are

going to be shot at! And if you're shot at, what will you do? I'll tell you what you'll do. You'll remember the day you died in training, and you'll keep your eyes looking where they're supposed to look!"

It was all quite simple. There were two guys out in the woods, both former Rangers, and they were tasked with infiltrating our "base"—guarded by seventy JAG officers. Two against seventy. We were supposed to be guarding every avenue of approach to the base, eyes fixed on our areas. But—suddenly—we heard the unmistakable sound of an M16 firing three-round burst after three-round burst, somewhere to my right. I turned my head to look, straining to see something, anything. In fact, seventy heads turned as one. There was some wild firing from our defense line, then more firing, then still more. Someone tapped me on my shoulder.

"You're dead, sir."

Lesson learned. One of many. Only three weeks into my basic course and already the "lessons learned" included:

- It's silly to rename the obstacle course a "confidence course" if your confidence-building exercise includes falling flat on your face from fifteen feet in the air;
- I had no clue how to put on the black Army beret without looking like a French painter;
- Four months of workouts before my basic course couldn't prevent me from puking on the football field during my second predawn workout;
- The mere fact that you grew up in the South doesn't make you a natural marksman with the M16, but it makes others believe you will be; and
- I had a long way to go before I really knew what it meant to be a soldier.

The day our field exercise ended, I staggered into the aid station, got a steroid shot to heal my poison ivy, and nursed my wounded pride. There's nothing quite like having your heroic ideal collide with the reality created by your own human frailty.

A week later, Nancy came to pick me up. I'd finished my introductory "soldier skills" training and was ready for the military legal education. Law work. *That* I could handle.

As we drove across Virginia and into Tennessee to be reunited with the kids, whom I hadn't seen in more than a month, I talked so much I could barely breathe. I told her about military life, about other soldiers' war stories, about new friends I'd met that she'd likely never know, and about my (small) triumphs and embarrassing failures. She listened politely, laughed on occasion, shook her head sympathetically when it was appropriate, but she was mostly quiet. Mostly.

After a few hours on the road, she took advantage of one of the few moments of silence to look me up and down and then remark quietly, "You look stronger."

"I do?"

"Yep. And more confident."

I smiled. It turns out that basic training isn't just good for eighteen-year-olds.

After basic training, I started the one weekend a month, two weeks out of the year life that marked the prewar lifestyle for the typical reservist. Yes, I wore the uniform, but I was still a civilian at heart, still the office worker I'd become after almost fourteen years of white-collar life. But I wanted more. I hadn't joined the Army for the weekend service or for the two weeks of annual training in the woods and on the firing range. And so, in the midst of that annual training, when a full-bird colonel, a brigade commander for one of America's most storied combat units, looked at me and asked, "Will you go downrange with us?" I was ready with the answer.

"Yes, sir!" A brigade from the 101st Airborne was training with us (or, I should say, we were there with *them*), and they needed a lawyer. They were going back to Iraq ("downrange") in the fall, and the brigade commander wanted more legal help.

The fact that I said yes didn't really hit me until I got home a few days later and saw Nancy. I hadn't had the heart to tell her over the phone, so I waited. I waited until I got home, until I spent time with the kids, until we had dinner, and until they were fast asleep. Then I asked Nancy to sit down.

"What's up?"

"A colonel with the 101st Airborne asked me if I'd deploy with them."

"What did you say?"

The question was rhetorical. She knew I wouldn't say no. Deployment was the entire purpose for me joining. But still, as I kept learning, reality is different than you ever think it'll be.

"I said yes."

Nancy paused for a long moment. "We'll be okay. We'll get through it," she said. Then she started to cry.

But I didn't go. It turned out that while the brigade commander wanted to add a lawyer to his roster, the Army didn't want him to have one, so his request to bring me was rejected. I found out just as I was planning to leave for a month of training with the brigade at Fort Polk, Louisiana, and I was crushed. I'd been preparing my mind and heart to leave, and now... nothing. I was back to being a husband, father, and lawyer in limbo—with no immediate plans to deploy but with no intention of staying home. In my heart, I *knew* it was my turn to go.

Limbo lasted a month. First, the Army asked me to volunteer to spend a year in Fort Dix, New Jersey. I said no. Then they offered a year at Fort Drum. No again. Finally, Human Resources Command called with a different opportunity: The 3d Armored Cavalry Regiment, America's longest-serving combat regiment, needed two judge advocates for a year. Destination: Iraq.

I said yes.

And this time there was no turning back. Once again, I went to Nancy and told her that I'd answered the call. Once again, she told me that they'd get through it. Again, she cried. This time I did too.

All that was left was to tell the kids.

3

THE DAY HE LEFT

Nancy

NOTHING SOUNDS GOOD at three o'clock in the morning, with the possible exception of "It's snowing and they called off school."

No matter how late David stayed up, gaming the night away on the computer or watching television, he jolted me awake from my deep slumber to wish me goodnight. No amount of glaring, stuffing my head under the pillow, or unintelligible profanity stopped him from the barbaric practice of smiling and whispering sweet nothings.

I think he envisioned himself an actor in a perpetual Hallmark commercial, a world in which well-dressed, perfectly coiffed parents kiss the heads of peacefully sleeping babies before easing off to a night of romance and wine. Our "real life," for whatever reason, never yanked him from this fantasy.

Not the fact that our kids—when they finally fell asleep—were so sensitive to noise that I never seemed to enjoy a truly peaceful night.

I saw his disrespect for sleep as a personal assault. When I first had kids, I'd struggle to get my newborns to sleep, gingerly put them in the crib, and tiptoe out of the room like I was avoiding land mines.

As soon as I put them down, thankful to have at least a moment's rest, David would smile and say, "Let's just go look at them"—but I always knew that phrase meant much more. After all, he could've "looked at them" from the safe distance of the hallway. When he used that phrase, he meant he wanted to walk in the room, pat their diapered bottoms, and kiss the wisps of hair on the back of their heads.

If they woke up, they woke up—he was going to have those late-night moments regardless of my protests.

"Just leave them alone," I'd beg, and he'd pretend to acquiesce. "Please."

I admit—the kids were adorable during the twenty minutes per night they slept. Eventually, though, I'd look up and see David sheepishly slipping out of the nursery, holding a crying baby who'd been admired out of her slumber.

"I don't know what happened," he'd say before handing her back to me.

By the time David was deployed, the kids were eight and six years old. Even though they'd been robbed of countless hours of good sleep over the course of their few years on earth, they were certain of a few facts about life: Vegetables were evil, Sunday morning sermons were long, and Daddy loved them enough to snuggle them late at night.

That's why they looked at us in horror when we broke the news to them.

"You know how those buildings in New York fell because the bad guys flew the airplane into them?" David asked on the way to Toys "R" Us.

It was his idea to tell them this way. Like maybe they wouldn't notice their dad was going off to war because they could buy a trinket. I know it probably should've been obvious that crass materialism is rarely the answer in times of crisis, but the children were so young we honestly thought it might soften the blow.

I'll never forget the moment. They were snugly in their car seats and had been excitedly chatting about their anticipated purchases. Camille was getting some sort of accessory for the tiny doll she clutched in her hand—a plastic brunette about three inches tall she named "London" and carried around all the time. Austin was going to shop around, considering perhaps a *Star Wars* building set. A mound of clothes waiting to be dropped off at the dry cleaners sat between them. These are the things you remember. I flipped down the mirror and pretended to look at my makeup.

"So Daddy has to help catch the bad guys," he continued. "In Iraq."

I saw the reflection of their little faces. In all my years of tending to scraped knees, visiting emergency rooms, mending broken hearts, and soothing away nightmares...I'd never seen their countenances reshaped by sheer devastation.

Inexplicably, the promise of new Legos didn't soften the blow. We weren't sure they'd "get it," but they definitely understood.

At the dry cleaners, I crawled into the backseat and held them as they sobbed uncontrollably. People in the parking lot stared at us in the way that strangers do when they're wondering if they should call the authorities.

Afterwards, the toy store was a haze of emotion, and we went through the motions of "things people do when they're happy," hoping that toys and pizza would magically lift the dread and make everything okay. When we got back into the car, full of soda and apprehension, we were eager to call it a day. But as Camille climbed into the backseat, she raised her soft, empty hands and exclaimed, "London!"

The tiny plastic doll for whom she'd just bought a new wardrobe was nowhere to be seen.

"Have you seen a little plastic doll?" I frantically asked the people the host had seated at the table we'd just left. I held up my fingers to suggest its impossible size and tried to hold back the tears: "It's just this big." I imagined after I darted to the waitress station, the busboy's apron, and the parking lot, that the people shrugged at what I appeared to be—a mother who seemed a bit undone. I certainly would've rolled my eyes over a mom apparently on the verge of a panic attack over a doll.

Of course, the object itself was of no real significance, but—in that moment—that tiny plastic doll came to symbolize all that seemed lost...in the same way that worn slippers, Dixie Cups next to the sink, or a favorite blanket can represent all the comforts of home. Sadly—to end a terribly awful day—we never found it.

The weeks that preceded his departure were filled with these hyper-emotional incidents, ordinary moments that took on extraordinary meaning. Every time friends came over for dinner, every grandparent visit, every second was imbued with the kind of sobriety that's hard to maintain on a day-in/day-out basis.

The first and last question everyone asked when they saw us—at church, parties, or Wal-Mart—was, "When does David leave?" In other words, the pall of his departure hung over us at all times, so we were intrigued when the Army gave him the option of leaving earlier.

"Going sooner means getting home faster," I said tentatively.

David nodded his head. "Yeah. Plus, I want to start counting down the days till I get home instead of the days till I leave."

"Right."

What both of us knew but neither of us said was that a change of departure meant a change of mission. We both sat silently in the discomfort and ambiguity of fate.

"If I leave early and something happens to me," he said very quietly, "you can't second-guess the change of plans."

I assured him I wouldn't, although I knew I would.

We decided to take the new option and he left in October instead of after Christmas. The autumn night before he left, we did our normal "night-night routine" with the kids, a ritual we've done for years with slight variations to the general drill of the oldest known hymn, "Gloria Patri," the singsong books of the New Testament, a recitation of John 3:16 and Acts 17:28, the Apostles' Creed, and prayer. We kept adding elements, to the point where the kids lamented that they expected us to pass the collection plate at the end.

"In Him, we live, and move, and have our being," the kids recited before climbing into their bunk beds. We'd planned this as the farewell "tuck-in." David had rented a car and was leaving for Fort Benning at five the next morning.

The kids fell asleep pretty easily, exhausted from the previous months of endless goodbye parties and unusually emotional adults. But my sleep was listless at best.

The next morning when the alarm went off, David climbed out of bed in the dark, put on his uniform, and went through the checklist one last time. I was still not used to seeing him in his Army Combat Uniform (he called it his "ACU"). A suit and tie? Sure. Shorts and a T-shirt that reads "Chicks Dig My Ride" next to a picture of a *Star Wars* TIE fighter? Definitely. But amid the half-finished puzzle on the kitchen table and the toys on the floor, the uniform just didn't seem to fit into the picture of our lives.

I felt I barely knew him, his bags in his hands and ready to walk out of my life for a year. He kissed me goodbye before running up to the kids' room "just to look at them."

Of course, he meant something more. I wanted last night to be the "goodbye scene," for Saturday to be a new day—the first we'd check off a calendar that hung on the kitchen wall, and the beginning of our new, yearlong life without Dad. But I didn't have the heart to stop him. The next time he'd see the kids, they'd be a year older, have fewer baby teeth, and wear different clothing sizes. Maybe—just maybe—because it was so early in the morning, he wouldn't awaken them.

Just this once.

We crept up the stairs and I paused at the door as he walked into the dark room. He put his hand silently on Camille's hair. Groggily, she sat up in the bed and immediately draped herself over his uniformed chest.

Austin didn't stir.

About three hours later—after David was much closer to Fort Benning and I'd managed to drift off to sleep—I heard the rhythmic pitter-pat of someone running down the stairs.

"Daddy?" I heard him yelling. "Daddy?!"

"He's gone," I reminded the little boy in the red flannel pajamas. "Remember, he's gone to Iraq?"

His eyes were barely open from the exhaustion of the past few weeks.

"He forgot to say goodbye to me," he said. Apparently, Camille had told him that David said goodbye to her, and Austin felt he'd slipped his dad's mind.

As I wiped away his tears and cradled him in my arms—not easy with a big six-year-old boy—I thought of all the times David insisted on sneaking into their rooms and foiling my best-laid parental plans.

And I was thankful for every single one of them.

4

EVERYTHING CHANGED

Nancy

LIFE, I WAS SHOCKED TO DISCOVER, went on.

A few weeks later, I felt people's eyes on me as I entered the sanctuary of two-hundred-year-old Zion Presbyterian Church for the first time without David. The kids and I ambled down the aisle during the opening hymn and slid into our pew. Without a word, the man behind us passed us a hymnal already opened to the song selection, "A Mighty Fortress Is Our God."

"And though this world, with devils filled," the congregation sang along with the pipe organ, *"should threaten to undo us."*

As typical, we'd already missed the first two verses, the opening prayer, and the bells that announce the "call to worship." Married for almost twelve years, David and I had developed unspoken but elaborate rules about being late: three to five minutes early for business meetings, "on time" sufficient for friends, fifteen to thirty minutes late to parties (to avoid the awkwardness among the first arrivals), seven minutes late to school (after that, the kids miss actual work), and five minutes late for church (eliminating the uncomfortable head nods to friends with whom we can't possibly chat until after the sermon anyway). In other words, David was my coconspirator in tardiness, a rebel without a clock, an ally in flouting the deacon-approved time schedule for services.

But without him there, I just seemed late—especially since I had to put on a robe and climb into the choir loft.

"We will not fear, for God hath willed," I tried to join in before noticing Austin's unkempt hair, *"His truth to triumph through us."*

My kids have never looked like they just stepped out of a Gap ad. One bitter cold January Sunday, I was in the choir loft preparing to sing when I noticed my family entering through the back doors. After I'd left home early for choir, David had dressed Austin in backwards jeans and Camille in a sundress. While other children wear smocked dresses and patent leather shoes or khaki pants and a tie, we're satisfied if the clothes fit reasonably well and don't have evidence of yesterday's lunch. Long ago, we decided that anything requiring getting up a few minutes earlier is simply not going to happen in the French household—after all, Sundays *are* made for rest. This made our lack of attention to appearance seem like a bold, countercultural stance against the tyranny of extravagant accessories like hair bows and...belts.

But without David there, we just looked like we'd crawled out from under the nearest overpass.

In churches, it's easy to get labeled. Just as there are jocks, geeks, rebels, and weirdos in high schools all over America, there are similar distinctions in churches. Most congregations, for example, have the Spiritual One, the emotional lady who nods during sermons as if she *really* gets it...compared to everyone else, who's mentally planning lunch. Her mirror image is Here's My Business Card Guy—a real estate agent who sits near the back on Sunday mornings but never brings anything to potluck. Guy Whose Radiator Blew Out lives thirty minutes from the church building and always needs a ride. Man Who Curses is either an old codger who forgot where his "damn glasses" were in Sunday school or a goatee-wearing Bono fan whose profanity is an affectation to prove he never voted for Pat Robertson. Always Has a Dry-Cleaned Shirt On pulls out a Mont Blanc to give you directions to his McMansion, but everyone wonders if he tithes. Proverbs 31 Lady knows Goodwill has half-price day on Saturdays and, when complimented, promptly announces she bought her whole ensemble for thirty-nine cents. Her opposite is Girl Who Dresses Like a Hooker, invited to church by a congregant checking out at her McDonald's cash register who upsized the fries and shared the gospel. She's a source of pride (look how we reach out to the poor!) until caught taking money *out* of the collection plate, using the nursery for free child care, and smoking a joint in the parking lot.

Congregations usually have a Neither in the World Nor of It Lady, who pretends not to know about the latest movie so she can casually announce she sees only rated-G movies. Over the years, I developed a two-word comeback to this line of reasoning—*"Schindler's List"*—since updated to a five-word knockout—*"The Passion of the Christ."* If you let these films dangle in the conversation, Neither in It Nor of It always reluctantly agrees there are *some* rated-R movies worth watching. (Of course, I've never seen *Schindler's List*, but it's the loophole I use to justify *Talladega Nights*.)

Everyone fits into some category. And if you don't know your category, you might be Person Others Wish to Avoid but Can't in Case They're Entertaining Angels Unawares.

Me? I forged a new category: the Person People Look at with Sympathy.

Suddenly, people with furrowed brows spoke to me in a soft tone. Instead of joking and laughing at the news of the day, everyone now wanted to discuss the intricacies of the war. They'd put a hand on my shoulder and demand I tell them—*really*, they emphasized—how things were going…all within earshot of my children.

"Is David in a really dangerous place?"

The kids' little ears perked up, unbeknownst to the well-meaning person dredging up personal details of a mission that haunted my children's dreams. "How long's he gonna be there?" followed promptly by, "A year!" My questioner never noticed the kids burrowing into my legs, listening to every syllable.

"Well, I just don't know how you're going to survive that."

I've been going to church three times a week since birth, so I know that in-depth, meaningful conversations don't happen on Sunday mornings unless something's seriously wrong. Other than Wednesday night prayer requests, church conversation is expected to be no deeper than the lyrics of a typical Mariah Carey ballad. Heck, even Earnest Guy Who Hands Out Bulletins knows the unspoken, rigidly enforced rule that "How are you?" means "I'm acknowledging you're here but let's not get so carried away that the Baptists beat us to the lunch buffet."

This conversational arrangement suited me just fine until David left—at which point my social skills deteriorated faster than Michael Jackson's nose. Even the perfunctory greetings left me speechless, and I began to stumble over the automatic responses that should've easily fallen from my mouth. Everyone knows "How are you?" is a quarter in the Presbyterian Vending Machine and "Fine" is the conversational candy, all dusty and stale...whether the dog died, the rent check bounced, or the in-laws stayed an extra week.

Consequently, the question "How are you?" led to deception either way...the answer was a false but reassuring "Fine," because the person wanted to hear it or because the kids needed to hear it. I often wonder if the dishonesty quotient at churches is statistically higher than the rest of society because of the liberal use of "How are you?" when "Hello" would suffice.

To avoid the whole scene, I skipped church...just as I did in 1998 when I was pregnant and one too many people asked, "Are you sure you aren't having twins?" However, as soon as people realized I wasn't there, I started getting texts from the pews.

"u ok?"

They expected me to be standing on the edge of a bridge about to jump. And since I lived so close to the church building, people could drive by my house and see my red car stubbornly sitting in the driveway.

Several years ago, I used to work with the youth at a Pentecostal church in Kentucky. We were a bit, ahem, *enthusiastic* about our evangelism. The church had what we called the "Soul Repo Van"—a dilapidated vehicle the kids would pile in if they knew their friends were ditching church. We'd show up on the doorsteps of their apartments and trailers and drag their hides to church, whether their hides wanted saving or not. If someone wasn't at church, a real sense of urgency prompted us to get in the van—their very souls seemed to be at stake, and we weren't going to let Satan keep someone away from God's healing power.

But Presbyterians don't operate that way. If a Presbyterian skips church, it has less to do with the workings of Satan and more to do with the golf schedule at the country club or whether an elderly congregant's "trick knee" is acting up. Nevertheless, I knew I couldn't miss two weeks in a row without raising eyebrows. They knew David was gone, and had vowed to keep an eye on us in his absence. Just as Molly Ringwald, Judd Nelson, and Ally Sheedy were forced together by detention in *The Breakfast Club*, the various and sundry characters that populate Zion are forced together by none less than being a "family of God." In other words, I wasn't going to get away from them unless I went to Iraq myself.

When the next Sunday rolled around, I had to convince them I was coping quite fine. I woke the children up early, dressed them in immaculate, seasonally appropriate clothing, and stroked mascara over my lashes, taking care to cover each one. After applying the perfect shade of lipstick and even straightening my hair, I took a final glance in the mirror and steeled my nerves.

If David could survive military service, I could survive the 9:30 service.

Everything began quite well, actually. I even made it through my first "How ya doing?" without breaking any of the Commandments.

"Awful," I said.

"Stands to reason," the man said, before smiling kindly and leaving me alone.

I smiled at my newfound emotional stability and smoothed out my ivory robe. I caught the eyes of my kids and winked at them from the choir loft. They sat in the pews to my right, holding a hymn book upside down between them.

When the associate pastor Don walked up to the pulpit in his black robes, I instinctively reached for my purse to get my phone so I could send him a text message (a running joke between us). But this time, my hand paused when I picked up the bulletin and realized it was a holiday.

Veterans Day.

Suddenly, I realized this was not going to go well. David had been away for only a couple weeks, and Austin and Camille weren't taking it well. From the outside, everything looked fine. But Austin had been getting upset when he saw patriotic displays. In class, his teacher asked each student what they felt when they looked at an American flag. The other kids had predictable answers—"happy," "free," "proud"—but Austin didn't write down an answer.

"Every time I see a flag," he told me with tears in his eyes as he got into the car at pickup time, "it just makes me miss Daddy."

"What did you write down?" I asked.

"I said it made me feel fine."

From that point on, Austin pointed out flags in people's yards as we drove down the street, his voice barely audible, so I knew he wasn't prepared for the patriotic hymns, flag ceremony, and acknowledgment of all the veterans in the church.

About thirty feet separated me from them, and I regretted every inch. Our choir loft sits at the front of the church, a few feet behind the pulpit and several feet away from the nearest pew. Normally, I'd leave home early and David would sit with the kids during the church service. Zion isn't one of those "seeker-friendly" operations, with children's church offering balloons and fudge-striped cookies as they chant, "Jesus is my best friend!" It's more like a time capsule, perfectly preserving the routine established in early 1950 that dictated that children should learn to listen to the sermon and sit still with their families as the pastor waxed eloquent for forty-five minutes about the Westminster Catechism. You never know when a kid might need to know these things.

From the loft, I looked at the two kids sitting in the pew with a conspicuously vacant space beside them. The empty area testified to how much their little lives had changed, and I regretted that they were navigating the ups and downs of the church service without an adult beside them. When the Old Testament reading happened, Austin didn't stand, and I felt powerless to correct him from several feet away in front of the church. However, a kind, no-nonsense lady reached over and gently pulled him up, just as David would've done had he been there.

Something about her simple motion weakened my composure, which grew weaker when Don explained to the children in the "mini-sermon" about the flag.

"We don't worship it, but it represents values that enable us to worship God," he explained simply. The children's sermon is the one concession the church gives the kids during the sanctuary time, when they sit in a circle at the front of the church and hear the word of God in ways they understand.

"Does anyone know what a veteran is?" Don asked the kids. Austin, who had managed to get out of the pew at the right time and sit on the floor near the associate pastor, held his hand up.

"My daddy?"

I gasped, never having really thought of being married to a veteran—after all, David had just left, and I wondered how long you had to serve to be considered one. It's a question that hadn't come up in the years of law firm life.

"He sure is," Don kindly said.

The lady beside me put her hand on my shoulder.

All of this sincerity was too much for me to take. I'd wanted to come into the church and continue on with normal life. But, even as I entered the church, passing the Revolutionary War soldiers' graves on the way in, I could tell something had changed deep within me. I'd always been patriotic—I'm the one who tears up at the Pledge of Allegiance—but something in my spirit quickened at the graves of young soldiers who'd fought the British, the Yankees, the Germans, and the North Vietnamese, and I realized our family's small inconvenience connected us with a long line of American history. As the service went on, I noticed the tired eyes of the World War II veterans who sat in the pews and struggled to stand when the pastor acknowledged them.

When the choir sang "Fairest Lord Jesus," my lips began to quiver. I tried with every syllable to steady my voice. But when we got to a certain lyric, it just simply obliterated my resolve.

"He makes the woeful heart to sing."

I began to cry, not in the elegant way a leading lady might as she dabs her delicate tears with a starched linen handkerchief, but in the mildly disturbing way Tammy Faye might've had someone stolen her makeup. I worried that the kids would notice and be terribly upset, that people would wonder if I could handle the deployment, or that

I was distracting the visitors who had no idea why the choir was so emotional. But I was stuck—in the middle of a cramped choir loft with absolutely no way out. And so I stood there, in all of my vulnerability, and cried.

Soon, many congregants were crying too, the first sign of emotion in our liturgical church since a visitor said "amen" in the summer of '97...1897.

After church that Veterans Day, I said hello to Don in the parking lot, embarrassed at my incredibly dramatic breakdown. His eyes were full of understanding and compassion and I sadly realized that—like everyone else—he was worried about me.

"I didn't realize it was Veterans Day," I said, "or I would've skipped."

But as the year progressed, I developed a deep gratitude for the church—for the busybodies who called when I missed the sermons, for the man who pulled my son's tooth for me when I became squeamish, for my jogging buddy who wouldn't let me cancel our workout ("It's only sprinkling!"), for my Small Group Leader who fixed my garage door, for the deacons who promised David they'd bug the daylights out of me until he returned...I mean, to prayerfully watch out for me in his absence.

In one of my brief conversations with David, I complained that church friends wouldn't let me wallow in my sadness. "Christians are the worst people in the world," he said, as both a good Presbyterian and a fan of Winston Churchill. "Except for everyone else."

And he's right. In the media, churchgoers are frequently portrayed as hypocritical, self-righteous rubes. And you know what? We are. At other times, however, we're kind, generous, and amazingly thoughtful. I've seen Dresses Like a Hooker change miraculously into Mom Extraordinaire. I've seen Guy Whose Radiator Blew Out get a good job and end up offering other people a helping hand. Many of us have fit into one category or the other, depending on the time of life. In fact, the underlying power of the gospel is that we don't have to be what we've always been...that we can change, improve our lot in life, and have joy in spite of circumstance.

Over the next few weeks, I'd begin to adjust to David being

gone, the kids would celebrate their birthdays without him, and we'd send nightly letters detailing the day's complaints and joys. And, yes, we'd go to church. Why? Because it's one of the only places left on earth where—when you're feeling down—some no-nonsense lady just might reach over and gently pull you up.

And that's something you simply don't want to miss.

5

MY NEW DESERT HOME

David

"CAPTAIN FRENCH, WE'VE BEEN LOOKING for you. Get your gear together. Full battle rattle. Basic combat load."

It was a Monday night when I heard these words. I was sitting in Camp Buehring, Kuwait, my home for three weeks where the five thousand members of the 3d Armored Cavalry Regiment were in the midst of their final "train-up" before we headed north, to Iraq, to the real war.

"Bag drop at 2330. Wheels up at 0615."

Translation: Get your duffel bags, put on your helmet and body armor, equip yourself with 210 rounds of M4 ammunition and forty-five rounds of M9 ammunition, meet in ninety minutes to get ready for a flight that leaves at 6:15 in the morning. Or, to put it more simply...

Hurry up and wait.

I ran back to my tent, packed away my clothes, towels, and bedding as tightly as I could, put on the body armor, grabbed my ammo, and struggled to carry all 175 pounds of gear the quarter mile back to the Tactical Operations Center (known as a "TOC"). Across the camp, a total of fifty-six other soldiers came out of their tents loaded with gear for the morning flight.

My mind was racing, but one thought dominated. *I want Nancy to know. I want Nancy to know.* Usually when I travel by air, I text her before the stewardess tells us to turn off all electronic devices. But of course, here there was no friendly stewardess handing out pretzels in shiny bags. Basic operational security dictated we *not* call our loved ones to say, "Hey Dear, just want you to know...catchin' a flight in six hours, landing in Iraq two hours later!" She could only know I was in Iraq after I got there, after my travels were over. This was the first—but hardly the last—time that I "went dark."

At 2315 we were all assembled (fifteen minutes early is "on time" by Army standards), and the master sergeant briefed us on the flight. He ended with a rousing send-off (quoted as best as I remember it—and with copious edits to remove profanity).

"You're going to war! I've been there, done that, and I can tell you the first day you start counting down is the day you get blown up. Don't be doing this countdown crap. Count down, and your mind's not on the mission. Then you're screwed. You're not leaving. Just look at it that way. You're there, and you're always going to be there. Brave Rifles!"

The 3d Armored Cavalry Regiment is called the "Brave Rifles." When a 3d ACR soldier salutes a superior officer, he says, "Brave Rifles!" When a group command is given, the officer or NCO shouts, "Brave Rifles!" You can't be a member of the regiment without hearing someone, somewhere shout, "Brave Rifles!"

No matter what the meaning or context, the response is always the same: the old Sioux Indian war cry, "Ai-ee-yah!" So when the master sergeant ended his speech with "Brave Rifles!" we all shouted—at the top of our lungs—"Ai-ee-yah!"

He turned to an officer behind him. "Chaplain, your turn."

The chaplain—a former Baptist minister—stepped forward. "Men, while I won't use the same language as the master sergeant, I want to say the same thing. Stay focused on the day. Saw the wood in front of you. If any of you need to talk or need prayer, I'll be wandering around with you until you leave. But before I pray, I want to tell you that the Lord has plans for you—plans for good and not for evil, to give you life and a hope. Let's pray."

I immediately felt the presence of God as the chaplain prayed, and I had this strange and surprising sense of thankfulness to be fighting for a country that honored God with its Chaplain Corps. When the chaplain said, "Amen," we again shouted, "Ai-ee-yah!" and turned to face the buses that would take us to the air base.

But we didn't get on the buses.

Not for an hour longer.

By the time we boarded, it was well after midnight. We pulled out of the gates of our camp and started our hourlong journey to the flight line. Several of the soldiers had already started to nod off. When we arrived at the air base, at least half of the bus was sound asleep, but I couldn't relax. My eyes were wide open, and my heart was racing at the thought of our flight into Iraq.

We stopped at the front of the base, stepped off the bus, and cleared our weapons to make sure none were loaded (we kept our ammunition on our body armor—not in the weapons), got back on the bus, and waited.

For one hour.

Then two.

Then three.

At 4:30 in the morning, the master sergeant boarded the bus and yelled, "I have great news!"

We all looked at him.

"There's no plane!"

We were so tired that we couldn't even muster up a "Brave Rifles" or an "Ai-ee-yah" in response. We just silently stared as we shuffled off the bus under 175 pounds of weight and back to our tents as dawn broke over Kuwait. Afterwards, we trudged over to the dining facility to eat breakfast and start our day—yet another day—under the hot desert sun.

That night we found ourselves at TOC again, bags piled up again, wearing our body armor again, and listening once more to the master sergeant's profanity-laced tirade about focus and to the chaplain's prayer. As we boarded the buses, the master sergeant yelled out, "We know there's a plane tonight! You're going north!"

This time we actually got out of the bus and waited in a tent for our plane to load and fuel. By 5:15 in the morning, the Air Force was ready for us. We lined up behind a C-130 cargo plane, and all of us—loaded down with body armor, weapons, and ammunition—

started to board. As I looked into the back of the plane, I immediately thought there was no way all of us (and our duffel bags) were fitting in the back of that airplane. But I was wrong. We jammed in shoulder to shoulder. Then another line came in—facing us. We were so close to the group in front of us that we actually sat with our legs interlocking. We were so close to the men beside us that we literally could not lean to the left or right. We were frozen in place, sitting straight up and staring right at the person across from us.

Just when I thought we couldn't get any closer, they jammed a pallet full of our gear onto the plane. It came up the back ramp and bumped into the last soldier in our line. Rather than readjusting the load, the Air Force loaders just pushed harder. We went from sitting shoulder to shoulder to being *squeezed* shoulder to shoulder. I could barely breathe.

The very instant the back door closed, the plane started to move. As we took off, I could catch a glimpse of sunlight from a small portal at the top of the plane. Aside from that portal, we were completely sealed off in a loud, vibrating metal cylinder.

The acceleration of takeoff actually compounded our discomfort. As the plane moved down the runway, the entire line of men leaned to the right—throwing their weight on those of us closest to the duffel bags. And that's the way we stayed the entire flight, in a slight lean to the right. None of us had he strength to straighten the line, so we leaned—in misery.

After five minutes of flight, my butt started to burn. After all, I was sitting on a hard canvas seat, completely unable to move, while I wore more than sixty pounds of body armor, ammunition, and weapons. After ten minutes, the pain was unbearable. After fifteen minutes, I felt like I was sitting on a stove with my rear end literally frying. We all felt it, and none of us could shift our position to relieve the agony.

After two hours of misery that made me long for the absolute luxury of a coach class airline seat, the plane began to descend. "Descend" is too gentle a word. It conducted a so-called combat landing. A combat landing is designed to minimize the airplane's exposure to shoulder-fired anti-aircraft missiles, so it dispenses with the long, slow glide of the civilian airliner and replaces it with a terrifying, nearly vertical dive from eighteen thousand feet—followed by a corkscrew landing directly over the airfield itself.

Experienced within the metal bowels of the plane, with no outside view, the "combat landing" consists of the following: (1) a sudden weightless feeling as the plane begins its dive; (2) a dramatic, collective change in our group lean from right to left as the plane's nose tips; (3) a series of collective leans forward and back as the plane performs its radical turns; and (4) a landing that feels more like a collision with the ground, a collision so violent it actually—through searing pain—reminded me that the tissue in my posterior had not died during the flight.

We'd arrived in Iraq.

Well, it was not really "Iraq" as the public understands it. We were in the strange parallel universe known as Balad—a gigantic, completely secure (except for the occasional rocket and mortar attacks) piece of America in Iraq. From the vegetation, temperature, and traffic, I wouldn't have been surprised if the sign in the terminal said, "Welcome to New Mexico."

We drove through morning rush-hour traffic (yes, Balad has a morning rush hour) to a series of tents that would house us until our evening helicopter flight to the "real Iraq"—Forward Operating Base Caldwell.

By this time, I was operating on almost thirty-six hours without real sleep. Yet we still had to unload our bags from the pallet, eat lunch, clean our weapons, receive briefings, and repack our bags for the helicopter flight. By 6:15 that evening, we were back in formation in time (in plenty of time) for the midnight "wheels up" deadline. Our next bus ride took us to "Camp Catfish," a corner of Balad with a small convenience store, a "Green Beans" coffee shop, and an enormous helicopter landing pad. From 7:30 until almost midnight, we lay down on our packs under the stars watching Black Hawk and Apache helicopters fly over our heads.

At 11:40, I heard a different kind of noise. This time the *thwup thwup* of the rotors was much louder and deeper. Our heads turned, and out of the blackness emerged two giant Chinook helicopters. They hovered over us as we put plugs in our ears, and then they landed. With their twin interlocking rotors still turning and engines blasting, I saw the back ramps lower. In the blackness, I could barely make out the door gunners tending their weapons. This was the real thing.

It was time.

As we stood, I threw my rucksack on my back (fifty pounds), my duffel bag over my left shoulder (fifty pounds), my weapon over my right shoulder (seven pounds), grabbed my backpack in my right hand (fifteen pounds), and staggered toward the chopper in my full body armor (fifty pounds with ammunition).

We sat in two rows, facing each other once again, with our backs to the sides of the helicopter. We were supposed to stack our luggage in the center, but the stack soon reached the ceiling. So they piled it on our laps.

And piled.

And piled.

By midnight, the men in my chopper were almost entirely hidden under (and crushed by) a gigantic pile of duffel bags, backpacks, boxes, and assault packs. Looking to my right, I could see the left-side door gunner as he loaded his weapon. All of my exhaustion was gone. I felt energized and alive. This was the first helicopter flight of my life—and it was a combat flight. As I heard the engines cycle up, I thought of Psalm 91, the "soldier's Psalm." It begins:

> *He who dwells in the secret place of the Most High shall abide under the shelter of the Almighty.*
> *I will say of the Lord, "He is my refuge and my fortress; My God, in Him I will trust."*

The engines were so loud my ears throbbed through the plugs. I felt my stomach drop to my toes as the helicopter lurched upward. We were airborne. The helicopter shook violently as we moved forward. The door gunner settled in behind his weapon.

Then, suddenly, the chopper started to descend. Within seconds, we were back on the ground, the ramp in the back of the helicopter lowered, and soldiers scrambled out.

What's wrong? Mechanical problems? A fire?

For the first (and only) time in my life, I was imbued with superhuman strength. All of our eyes were wide as saucers as we tossed off the heavy packs as if they were full of air. I literally jumped, body armor and all, over one pile of bags, scrambled over others, tripped at the edge of the ramp, and almost tumbled out of the helicopter.

Since I was one of the first ones on the chopper, I was one of the last ones off. I saw the rest of the guys jogging to get behind a concrete blast barrier, and I sprinted to catch up. Once safely behind the barrier, I grabbed a member of the flight crew to ask what happened.

"Topping off fuel," he responded with as much emotion as if we'd just pulled off I-65 at the BP station. Apparently we had to evacuate the chopper and run behind a blast barrier to get some gas.

With my heart rate down from the tossing-fifty-pound-bags-like-they-were-boxes-of-Kleenex rate to the more "normal" my-first-helicopter-flight-is-a-combat-flight-over-hostile-territory rate, we took off again.

Throughout the flight, I kept my eyes glued on the door gunner. Most of the time, he was crouched, motionless, over his weapon—scanning the horizon with his night vision goggles. Occasionally he leaned forward to scan a specific target. Off in the distance, fires burned. Every time he leaned, every time he turned his head, I felt my stomach churn. I was afraid.

I looked around the helicopter to see what my brothers in arms were thinking. Most of them were veterans of the regiment's previous deployment to Tal Afar, farther west. There they fought one of the largest urban battles of the war, a battle so vicious that it would have made world headlines had it not started right about the time that Hurricane Katrina made landfall at New Orleans. If they looked nervous and alert, then I should be nervous and alert.

Most of them were asleep. My fears eased. But only a little.

After thirty minutes, the helicopter started to descend. Through the gunner's window, I could see a dusty, poorly lit landing strip. The pilot eased down, we bumped to the ground, and the back ramp lowered. I grabbed my gear, walked off the chopper, looked up at my new surroundings, and saw the brightly lit minaret of a mosque.

I was in Iraq—the real Iraq—and it was my new home.

6

CONNECTING WITH HOME

David

WHEN I WAS A LAW FIRM LAWYER, I used to complain about my life. My hours were too long. I traveled too much. The cases sometimes stressed me out. The morning coffee was decent, but by the afternoon it was always bitter. Sometimes the catered lunches contained only pita wraps, vegetarian sandwiches, or other vile forms of "chick food." Worst of all, there were occasions when a mysterious member of the staff would actually *forget to flush the toilet* in our spotless mahogany and marble bathroom.

I even used to complain about the pay. It was never enough. If I made a pretty good salary as a first-year associate in Nashville in the early nineties, that was *just not quite enough* to buy the car I wanted while living in the apartment I liked. When I was in New York and making six figures as a second-year lawyer, it was *just not quite enough* to get us the apartment, the car, and the exotic vacations we dreamed about. We bought a house and wanted a bigger one. We bought a car and wanted a better one. We changed mobile phones, laptops, and other gadgets like some people change socks. But we always felt just a little bit deprived.

In spite of my naked materialism, I still considered myself an idealist. After all, I could still sacrifice. Rather than pursue a life of upper-class prosperity in the corporate legal world, later in my career I committed to something better—something far more virtuous— a life of "mere" upper-*middle*-class prosperity working for a public interest law firm. I made this drastic sacrifice (and occasionally felt quite good about myself) because I believed in a cause—some things were worth sacrificing for.

So we struggled through with a smaller house than we could've bought, flying coach instead of first class, Ruby Tuesday instead of Morton's, and a used Saab instead of a new Porsche. But we did make room in our budget for Macs instead of PCs. (We may have been easing financially closer to the masses, but we had to maintain *some* standards.)

But that was then. Now I was sitting at Forward Operating Base (FOB) Caldwell, in Diyala province, Iraq, laughing at my lifelong folly. FOB Caldwell is a marvel. While its actual origin has passed from human knowledge, the legends say that it was designed as an Army base by Eastern Bloc engineers (one day I heard it was the Bulgarians, the next it was the Romanians, but we finally all agreed that Caldwell was the brainchild of the Hungarians...or maybe the Yugoslavs) and built by Iraqis sometime during the Iran-Iraq War. In other words, the base represents the awful synergy of communist architecture and modern Iraqi craftsmanship.

The place is remarkably simple in its construction. The first thing I noticed when walking to my living quarters in the darkness was that there appeared to be no earth, no dirt. Fine dust blows from the neighboring desert, and the entire base seems to be built on a thick bed of gravel, with crumbling concrete sidewalks sitting directly on top.

As the buildings came into focus in the full moon of my first night, I was struck not just by their ugliness—they were tan three-story structures that looked like concrete shoeboxes—but by the wires draping all over the structures. I imagined that I was walking into the aftermath of a prolonged battle between Spider-Man and Venom, with the remnants of their webs covering everything.

I later learned the buildings had not only been built with insufficient internal wiring, but that their solid concrete construction made it virtually impossible to either repair the internal wiring that existed or to install new wiring as the facility matured. So the solution was to simply drape the wires all over the outside.

Aside from the wire-draped buildings, the FOB featured a dining facility, motor pool, large gym, a few tents, and a small "haji shop." At this point in the war, most large FOBs had at least one large PX (short for post exchange), a Wal-Mart-style department store where soldiers can buy everything from towels to DVDs to digital cameras. Because FOB Caldwell is not large, it had only a tiny haji shop.

Pardon me. I did not mean to use the term "haji." The word— derived from the Muslim practice of the Haj (the pilgrimage to Mecca)—has been deemed off-limits by the military as "derogatory." It is acceptable to say "Iraqi national." It is acceptable to call the en-emy "AIF" (short for anti-Iraq forces) or "AQI" when we're fighting al Qaeda (short for al Qaeda in Iraq). But we cannot, we must not, say "haji."

The "small shop owned and operated by an Iraqi national" was something to see. It's basically a long wood and canvas tent-shaped structure selling counterfeit candy bars, counterfeit soaps and sham-poos, pirated movies, and Korean electronics with unintentionally humorous packaging (I bought a small vacuum cleaner that billed itself as "good at cleaning any places" and "manufactured in Korea specification" but warned "do not suck the liquids").

The shop itself was called the Mountaineer Outpost. At least that's what I think the Iraqi owner intended to call it. He had painted a large sign that read, "Moun Tainer Oot Post."

While the Oot Post was the dominant commercial presence in the camp, it didn't capture the popular imagination quite as much as our beloved creek. The first morning at Caldwell, I walked out of my living quarters with my two new roommates, Leo Brodhead and J. Dave Robison, past the Oot Post, and toward our small dining facil-ity (DFAC). Thirty yards from the DFAC I was almost brought to my knees by one of the most foul, most overpowering stenches I'd ever smelled.

"What could that possibly be?" With our arms over our faces, the three of us staggered forward and came to a small creek (really a wide drainage ditch). We looked down.

Feces.

Lots of feces.

Floating feces.

Drifting feces.

Islands of feces.

And thus "Crap Creek" was named and became a permanent part of Caldwell geography. It wasn't really called that, but I couldn't bring myself to actually use its proper name. You can imagine what it was really called. In time, it became the central reference point for all Caldwell locations.

"Where's the dining facility?"

"Past the Oot Post, just on the other side of Crap Creek."

"Where's the aid station?"

"Just south of Crap Creek."

"Where's the Oot Post?"

"It's the small building right before Crap Creek."

But Crap Creek was only the beginning of the filth that plagued our lives. Only one of three bathrooms worked in my building, with the other two shut tight with handwritten signs ominously warning that anyone who drank the water on the FOB would suffer from the dreaded "double barrel" (Army slang for simultaneous vomiting and diarrhea). Of course the one bathroom that worked only worked for urination, not defecation. You see, the Iraqi toilets were not designed to handle, well, toilet paper.

And that brings us to an aside about the absolute idiocy of cultural relativism and the politically correct incompetence of our own government.

Just before I left the States, I read the State Department's Iraq "Smart Book" from cover to cover. The book describes Iraq's climate, briefly relates its history, and then spends page after page detailing its culture...all in the most glowing terms possible. One of the items I found most interesting was an extended discussion of Iraqi "cleanliness." Iraqis, according to the State Department, really do view cleanliness as next to godliness. Cleanliness is a command in the Koran, and since the Iraqis are allegedly a pious people, they are fastidious in their attention to cleaning their clothes and bodies.

I asked a three-time Operation Iraqi Freedom (OIF) veteran about this, and he laughed out loud. "You haven't smelled stink," he said, "until you've been in an Iraqi town and walked over the small streams of human excrement running in the streets." He paused for a moment. "Do you know why the left hand is considered unclean?"

"No. The State Department just says it is 'traditionally unclean,' and I should never offer my left hand to an Iraqi. I assume it's because of some kind of religious symbolism."

He laughed again. "Nope. It's because they wipe their ass with their bare left hand."

"What?"

"Yup. When you walk into an Iraqi bathroom, you'll often see some really nice tiles with a hole in the middle of the floor, no sinks, and a bucket of water by the door. You walk in, squat over the hole, wipe yourself with your hand, swish your hand in the bucket, then leave."

"Does everyone use the same bucket? Or is there a fresh bucket every wipe?"

"Same bucket all day—if you're lucky. Could be same bucket all week."

At that very moment, I realized why the State Department had suppressed this information. The politically correct bureaucrats at Foggy Bottom didn't want to destroy two generations of leftist efforts to convince us that our culture is in no way superior to any other. But if it became widespread knowledge that in some cultures it is just fine to wipe with your hand and share the same swish bucket, well then their entire ideological edifice would crumble in the face of a tidal wave of hygienic outrage.

I thought back to a panel discussion three years ago at the American Enterprise Institute, one of America's premier conservative think tanks. The topic was liberal bias in higher education, and one of my fellow panelists was Roger Bowen, then the general secretary of the American Association of University Professors. As a prominent defender of the leftist educational establishment, he was trying to argue that the relative lack of conservative professors was due to conservative choices, not to discrimination. In other words, because the academic disciplines themselves were liberal, it was natural that conservatives would choose not to pursue careers in those disciplines. He argued, for example, that conservatives wouldn't be interested in anthropology because it was dedicated to the study of the *"myth* of cultural or religious superiority."

Had I known then what I know now, I could have won the debate by simply declaring, "Iraqis wipe themselves with their bare hands and then share a swish bucket."

Myth indeed.

But the most upsetting thing about our living conditions wasn't the filth, the dilapidated buildings, or the lack of a PX, it was the almost total lack of a communications infrastructure.

The image of the American soldier in Iraq saying hi to his wife and kids on a webcam while putting on his body armor to go out on a mission is by now fully ingrained in the popular consciousness. In fact, it's fully ingrained in our troops. The first-time deployers all came over here willing to risk their lives, but they figured they'd do it while wired in with almost constant communication home. Internet access is arguably the single most important morale consideration in the unit.

Virtually everyone at the larger FOBs has Internet access of some kind, and they can instant message and email their families with their (sometimes slow) satellite Internet service. But not at FOB Caldwell. We had exactly eight telephones and fifteen public computers for almost a thousand people. These computers were so slow that most soldiers could surf perhaps three websites in their allotted twenty minutes of time, with entire ten- and fifteen-minute periods dedicated to watching screens load pixel by pixel. In the evenings (when it's morning in America) and in the early mornings (when it is late evening at home), there was a *minimum* two-hour wait for twenty minutes of phone or computer access.

For me, this is horrible. At home, I'm so connected to Nancy and the kids that I ask her to email me running updates on the day's events. I'll be sitting at my office desk—a mere twelve miles from home—and she'll shoot me short messages. "Kids and I are running to Wal-Mart, love you!" "Austin is playing with his new Army men. So sweet!" "You should see Camille dressing her new dolls." I felt like I *needed* them to get through the day. All too often in Iraq, however, I had no contact with home. While young enlisted soldiers have extra time to wait around when their shifts end, staff officers don't really have shifts. We're supposed to be available twenty-four hours a day, seven days a week. So taking two hours to make a single five-minute phone call was out of the question.

And when we could find the time to talk, conditions were...less than ideal. A civilian contractor had set up eight completely enclosed plywood booths, added a single cheap plastic phone and an old office chair, and called it a "telecommunications center." There were no lights in the booths.

At the end of your two-hour wait, you walked into the booth, sat in a chair as a cloud of dust kicked up around your body, picked up the invariably greasy phone receiver, and squinted to see the numbers as you dialed. To be fair, the phone reception was remarkably clear. But just when the conversation got going, you would hear a voice ring out, "Number eight, your time's up!"

It's always worse to hang up the phone when you *have* to go, rather than because you *choose* to. Someone in the family would always be crying when I had to hang up, and it was usually me. Sometimes it was all of us.

One day, soon after I arrived at the FOB, I was talking to Nancy and she put the kids on speakerphone. Moments later, I heard the dreaded words: "Your time is up!"

"I gotta go. Love you guys."

"Okay. We love you." I could hear Nancy's voice cracking.

"Don't cry." I started to tear up.

"I can't help it." I could hear little sniffles.

"Are the kids crying?" Now the tears were rolling down my cheeks.

"Well, they cry when I cry."

"Oh, great."

I heard the dread voice again. "Your time's up! Let's go!"

"Gotta go."

"Okay. Love you." I could tell Nancy was sobbing when I hung up the phone. I stayed in the booth for a few seconds to wipe my eyes, put my head down, and charged out the door—hoping I wouldn't see anyone. Of course I promptly ran into the squadron intelligence officer.

"French, are you okay? You look sunburned. You're beet red."

"I'm fine."

"You sure? What's wrong?"

"Nothing. Nothing at all." I kept walking—and silently resolved to *fix this problem*.

Fortunately, soldiers can be resourceful when we're under stress. A local border transition team, known as a "BiTT"—a small team of American soldiers who train Iraqi border guards, cousins to the "MiTTs," military transition teams—had purchased a satellite dish from Hughes Satellite Services and was placing it for sale as they redeployed home.

The BiTT guys had actually commandeered a military helicopter to have their dish delivered, but now they were desperate to unload it. They had paid $2,000 for the dish and were putting it up for auction. High bid got the dish and could assume the satellite Internet service (a mere $1,250 per month). The current top bid was $1,000.

After my embarrassing crying incident, I grabbed my friend and roommate Captain Leo Brodhead, our unit's liberal Mexican-American-Mormon-Catholic-Agnostic adjutant, and told him we *had to get that dish*.

"Let's bid $1,500. He'll take it for $1,500." He wanted it also, but was in more of a mood to negotiate.

"Nope," I replied. "We're getting that dish. I'm not leaving anything to chance."

We walked together over to the BiTT building and ran into the BiTT team leader just as he finished a webcam conversation with his family.

I got right down to business. "We want your dish."

"How much you willing to bid?" He grabbed a sheet of paper and a pen and looked up at me.

"Two grand."

"It's yours."

With that, I became the proud part owner of a satellite dish. There were two problems, however. We had to move it from the roof of his building to the roof of our building and configure the dish manually.

Oh yes, I almost forgot. This satellite dish was not exactly "authorized."

Thankfully, I was not the only motivated staff member. Two guys had new babies and wanted to see them on webcams. Two other guys had new wives, and one guy had, well, several girlfriends to maintain. When the word spread, the staff officers involved in "Operation Snakeyes" (the code name we used to clandestinely discuss the satellite project) came pouring out of the headquarters building.

I stood by our building with our fire support officer, a self-described redneck from Missouri.

"How are we going to get that dish on our roof?" I asked, looking up at the roof, which was more than fifty feet high and accessible only by a narrow metal ladder. The dish and its supporting assembly weighed perhaps five hundred pounds.

"I've already taken care of it."

As soon as the words left his mouth, I heard loud engine sounds, and a gigantic crane pulled around the corner of the building.

"I didn't know we had a crane," I said, shocked.

"Of course we do."

"Can we use it for this?"

"Well, we are using it for this, so the question is moot."

I nodded. "Fair enough."

The crane operator pulled up to a neighboring building and lowered the hook down toward the dish. Another soldier was already on the roof tying the dish to the hook. As the crane pulled the dish off the roof, the operator leaned out of his cab and yelled over the engine noise, "Where's the truck?"

"What truck?" I yelled back.

"I gotta put the dish in the back of a truck. I can't drive it over to your building with it swinging at the end of my crane. It's not safe."

"Sure it is!"

"No, not—"

I cut him off. "Sure it is. I'll hold it to keep from swinging."

He shrugged. "Your call, sir."

Ever so slowly, he pulled the crane off the roof and lowered it close to the ground. When it was about three feet above the rocks, Leo and I grabbed it to stop it swinging from side to side. We walked to our building, with the crane driving just at our heels.

Three of our team were already scampering up the metal ladder to the roof, ready to guide the dish home. Just as I congratulated myself for a well-executed plan, things began to unravel. Literally.

As we walked, I noticed out of the corner of my eye a series of wires hovering just a few feet over my head. I was used to wires draped over everything, but something bothered me about these wires . . .

Oh yes. There was a crane following us—with its boom extended in the air.

I turned and yelled at the driver at the top of my lungs, "Stop!"

Too late.

Snap.

The wires had been connected to our aid station, but the crane yanked them from the wall and sent them flying through the air. The crane operator looked like he'd just hit a dog.

"I hope the doc didn't need those wires."

Leo ran off to the aid station to check the damage, while I gestured for the driver to move on. This was no time to second-guess ourselves.

Just as we reached our building and began to lift the dish to the roof, the unit command sergeant major walked outside. He looked straight at me. My heart sank.

The command sergeant major is typically the most feared soldier on any base. The commander's right-hand man, he is almost always the most experienced (and ill-tempered) soldier in the unit. Although we technically outrank him, he works (and speaks) for the commander. Cross the sergeant major and you cross the colonel.

But staff officers plan things for a living. We don't leave anything to chance. Stationed right by the door was one of Operation Snakeyes's most valuable members, our chemical weapons officer. The "chemo" had a long and antagonistic history with the sergeant major. No one could take (or hold) the sergeant major's attention like the chemo.

"What is the crane doing?" Just as soon as the sergeant major said those words, the chemo grabbed his arm.

"Sergeant Major!"

"What do you want?"

"Come with me. I think we have a leak under the latrine trailer."

One of the chemo's projects was improving the base and making it more sanitary for the soldiers by taking care of spills or other possibly toxic health hazards. The sergeant major never passed up an opportunity to catch the chemo falling down on the job.

"A leak? Why haven't you told me about this before?"

As the chemo led the sergeant major off to the leak (which did exist but was tiny and insignificant), we realized we had a small window of opportunity and seized it. The crane raised the dish to the roof and lowered it in place. We unhooked the dish, thanked the driver, and urged him to return to the motor pool as soon as possible.

The crane had just rounded the corner and disappeared from sight when the sergeant major reappeared, looked at me as I stood by the corner of the building, gave me a quick nod of recognition, and went back inside. Just then, the squadron maintenance officer (my other roommate, Captain Jefferson David Robison, better known as J-Dave) peered over the edge of the roof and yelled down at me.

"Dave, could you get the power cord? We forgot it. It's down at the bottom of the ladder."

"No problem," I said nonchalantly, trying to hide the fact that I'm afraid of heights. Earlier in the deployment, I was passing through our recreation area while the 2005 remake of *King Kong* played on a twenty-five-inch TV in the corner. It was the climax of the movie, and Kong was on top of the Empire State Building. Seeing that height even on a small TV made me feel sick to my stomach (when I saw the movie on the big screen, I almost had to leave).

But I didn't hesitate. I climbed up the fifty-foot-tall rickety, rusted metal ladder with about twenty-five pounds of cable draped around my neck. After all, I was doing it for Internet access.

Mmmmmmmm. Internet access.

I moved quickly past the first floor, but made a mistake as I climbed past the second. I looked down and then looked up. It was about thirty feet to the bottom and twenty feet to the top—no-man's-land. My hands started to sweat.

I slowed down.

I gripped the bars as tightly as I could for a man with perspiring hands.

I looked up again, then down, and my stomach gurgled. Willing myself forward, I climbed one rung at a time until I made it to the ledge of the roof.

"Dude, what took you so long?"

"Couldn't find the cable," I lied.

I handed the cable to my friend, then I looked around at the view.

There is a memorable scene in J. R. R. Tolkien's *The Hobbit* where Bilbo Baggins, after spending many days in the dreary depths of dark and dense Mirkwood forest, climbs to the top of a tree to get his bearings. After days in claustrophobic darkness, the wind and sunshine are a revelation to him—lifting his heart and giving him the resolve to press forward. This may seem strange, but that's how I felt at that moment.

For weeks, I'd felt contained, trapped behind the tall barriers that ringed our base or in the dark steel cylinders of helicopters or cargo planes. Travel was at night, and there was no sense of space or place. But here it was. Iraq. Spread out before me. To my north was a sprawling Iraqi Army base, complete with a large mosque and its distinctive minaret. To my south was a seemingly endless desert, with huge smokestacks on the horizon. The sun was setting in the west, and a cool breeze was blowing on my face.

I'm really here, I thought. *I'm in Iraq*. The countryside was desolate, beautiful, and disturbing. I knew what awaited all of us...out there.

That very night, somewhere in that countryside, an IED went off and hurt three of Sabre Squadron's soldiers. No one was seriously injured, but as our artillery thundered a response, and I booted up my computer to reach out across continents to talk to my family, I wondered:

Will I meet the enemy?

No sooner had our last round of artillery shaken the foundations of our building than I watched with my heart racing as my family appeared on my computer monitor. First, I saw my beautiful wife, then two sweet little blond heads.

"Daddy!"

And for a moment, I didn't think about Iraq. I just felt blessed to be a dad.

7

HUMAN NATURE

David

THE PICTURE ON THE LARGE PROJECTOR screen was grainy, when it wasn't flickering or altogether fading to black. Sometimes the screen would be covered with electronic "snow." But you could make out what was happening.

Two men were digging in the middle of a dirt road.

At 2:00 a.m.

And they weren't digging at just any spot, but around a crater less than two weeks old—the spot where an IED blast killed a 101st Airborne soldier.

My commander, Lieutenant Colonel Paul T. Calvert, looked away from the screen and stared at me. "Lawyer, we're dropping on them. CAS [close air support] is inbound."

I knew I was about to watch men die. I was the only reservist with the unit, and an old guy at that. More of a civilian than anything else. *Soft.* Maybe. I had been called down from my office the moment the unmanned aerial vehicle spotted the late-night activity in the road. In this new kind of war, with complex rules of engagement, commanders often like to consult their JAG attorneys before launching attacks. But the squadron commander wasn't consulting me, he wanted to teach me—to show me how this war works. If you dig in a road at night—especially at a known ambush site—and we catch you doing it, you will die.

Colonel Calvert turned to the "battle captain" (the officer who orchestrates all the moving parts on the battlefield) and simply nodded.

"Roger that, sir." Using the same tone that one would use to order a pizza, the battle captain got on the radio with an orbiting F-16 and ordered an air strike.

"Falcon 1, Sabre X-Ray."

"Go ahead, Sabre X-Ray."

"Roger, Falcon 1, you are cleared to engage with JDAM hostiles located at grid square..." The battle captain delivered the precise location of the two men. With the series of numbers he gave the pilot, the pilot could deliver a 500- or 1,000-pound bomb almost directly on top of the target.

"Roger that. JDAM away in three, two, one...JDAM away. Twenty seconds to impact."

"Roger that." The air in the room immediately felt charged with electricity. A dozen pairs of eyes stared at the flickering screen.

"Five seconds to impact. Five, four, three, two, one...impact."

I waited for the boom. Instead I saw a puff. A huge puff of dust covered the screen, but through the infrared filters we could see a bomb sitting in the sand...unexploded. The two men (the "targets") seemed frozen in place, staring at the big black monstrosity that had just fallen from the sky. They wouldn't stay frozen for long.

"Falcon 1, Sabre X-Ray, negative impact. Repeat, negative impact. Drop again on same grid."

"Roger that. JDAM away in three, two, one..."

We repeated the exact process, but this time with soldiers yelling curses at the screen as the men started to run. Time seemed to slow down.

"Get them!"

"Get them!"

Just when I thought the men were clear of the impact area, the bomb exploded. Even though I was miles away, and no sound came from the screen, I still recoiled. The entire screen went black, then it was covered with smoke and dirt that seemed to take forever to clear. When it did, we saw the results of the bomb's work.

A huge crater "glowed" a slightly different shade of black as the heat from the explosion still radiated from the rocks. Beginning about thirty yards from the crater, there were other "glowing" spots...body parts.

The senior NCO punched the air with his fist.

"Good work." Colonel Calvert reached for the radio mic. "Falcon 1, Sabre 6."

"Go ahead, Sabre 6."

"Nice job, Falcon 1. You see anything else out there?"

"Negative, Sabre 6, I need to check out for fuel."

"Roger that, Sabre 6 out."

With that, the SCO put the mic down and without a word walked back to his office. I took that to mean I was dismissed. The battle captain smiled.

"Didn't do that in the law firm, did you?"

"Ha...definitely not."

I turned and walked up the one flight of stairs to my living quarters, processing what I'd just seen. What should I feel? Anything? All my life I'd read military history books and had thought about what war was like. Tonight, I saw it. I won't say that I "experienced it," because I was safe, watching it on a screen. I knew that I would truly experience life "out there," outside the wire, but for now I'd just seen it...and seen how deadly it could be.

As I mounted the steps and turned the corner, I glanced up and saw a completely naked body dash across a doorway. I heard muffled laughter. Below me on the stairs, Captain Brodhead was just getting back from the gym.

"Oh no." He laughed and shook his head.

"What?"

"Just wait."

We walked up to the third floor and turned down the hall. No one was there.

"Oh no." Leo put the key in our lock and opened the door...

And there we saw Captain John Smith (name changed to protect the guilty)—all of him. He was sitting in Leo's chair, completely naked, with his "junk" resting on the seat of the chair and his legs up in the air. The room exploded in laughter as the rest of the officers in the room emerged from hiding after the "surprise." The staff officers of Sabre Squadron, 3rd Armored Cavalry Regiment, had struck again. Four nights ago, Leo had walked in on a nude chorus line. Three nights ago, a nude officer on a Razor scooter had circled Leo in the hall. And tonight, his own chair was violated.

Captain "Smith," the Officer in Charge of "Operation Nudity," is part of the squadron's civil/military affairs efforts. Every single day, he donned full body armor, climbed into his up-armored Humvee, and visited the towns and villages in our area of operations. He attended city council meetings, he met villagers, he inspected water treatment plants. His single-minded focus was on improving the lives of Iraqis, and he risked his life every day to do it. By any meaning of the term, he's a hero.

But at night, no one could withstand his nude wrath.

Our battle captain's digital picture frame was hijacked so that snapshots of his beautiful wife were interspersed with a picture of more of Captain Smith than you'd ever want to see. Then the chief warrant officer who managed all helicopter traffic in and out of the FOB came in from a long day at the flight line to the spectacle of Captain Smith and Captain Jones (again, a fake name) lying completely nude on their beds with laptops on their stomachs.

"'Sup, Chief?" they said. "Wanna watch a movie?"

If I could describe the rhythm of my new life in one sequence, that would be it—from complete deadly seriousness to absurd farce in the span of seconds or the space of a walk down the hall. And how could it be any different? War is war and guys are guys.

But we forget that. At least I forgot. Because military service is so rare—with less than one out of every 150 Americans serving in uniform, and most of those who serve concentrated in large bases in the rural American South, well outside the major population centers—and because the war is so politically controversial, it seems that the media and many Americans just don't know how to think about soldiers, about us.

So we devolve into stereotypes. For many in the conservative community, we are heroes, with military service viewed almost reverently. We are the virtuous and brave few who dare to risk our lives to bring freedom and security. We are untouchable, with any political or cultural critique of our conduct or character off-limits. Our failures are the fault of others, and the only barrier to our victory is the left's failure of will.

For many in the liberal community, we're still heroes, but it's more like we're victim-heroes. We're the virtuous and brave few whose lives are being wasted on failed (Republican) foreign policy and misguided occupations. All too often forced by failed (Republican) economic policies into military service, we are poorer and less well-educated than the rest of the population. We can be criticized when we fail, but those who *really* deserve blame are the political masters who sent us to fight a war we didn't want with equipment that didn't work. Finally, unless there is massive state intervention, our postwar lives will slide into the oblivion of post-traumatic stress, poverty, and ignorance.

To still others on a vocal fringe, we're bloodthirsty mercenaries and hideous exploiters. Trigger-happy, we import a "Soldier of Fortune" mentality into ancient cultures, killing innocents and destroying social structures that existed perfectly well without us. *No wonder* there is an insurgency. *No wonder* the poor citizens of Iraq strap bombs to themselves to end the occupation. Wouldn't we do whatever it took to stop the American occupation? Wouldn't the Iraqi occupation end if there were no more mercenaries willing to kill to advance the interests of their political masters?

Obviously, I'm painting with a broad brush in describing these categories. Not even the most ardent conservative Republican believes soldiers are infallible. Not even the most partisan Democrat believes that all vets are victims. While some in academia come close to seeing all soldiers as killers, I would like to believe that even the most angry leftist heart can see some virtue in the service (or at least intent) of, say, medics and civil affairs teams. Yet the urge to categorize seems irresistible, in part because the categories are easy.

But all these agendas and all these preconceived notions run head-on against the reality of human nature. The Army is comprised of more than one million human beings, active and reserve, combat and support, male and female, from all racial groups, from all religious groups, and from all economic backgrounds. And they're just people—perhaps the most diverse and representative sample of real American life that exists in any American institution.

So that means you don't have to look very hard to find almost *anything* in the Army.

The morning after the air strike and the nude strike, a soldier came in to my office to tell me that he just *had* to leave Iraq. He just *had* to fly home right away. He seemed distraught.

Soldiers can sometimes be granted emergency leave in extreme circumstances, and one of my roles was to listen to their stories and make recommendations on their requests—to determine if a legal crisis, for example, really is a crisis, or to determine if the law can help them even while they stay in Iraq. It's a serious thing to keep a person in-theater when they are going through a personal crisis. Their mind is perhaps not as sharp. Their thoughts may not be on the mission. At the same time, it is a serious thing to send a soldier home. Someone else will have to take their place, and everyone else gets just that much more tired, that much more overworked, as they wait for their friend to come back.

I grabbed my notebook to take notes, and asked what was wrong.

"Somebody's trying to kill my kids, sir."

"Someone's trying to kill your kids," I repeated, seeing if the words coming out of my mouth made them more normal. "Who?"

"My girlfriend's husband."

In the Army you find the most, well, *creative* family relationships. Sometimes I had to ask soldiers to draw me a chart of all the children, stepchildren, ex-wives, ex-girlfriends, current girlfriends, and current wives. In this case, the soldier had a daughter with his girlfriend, they had a fight, she got married to someone else, and then the soldier and the girl "made up" (the soldier actually went AWOL to reconcile with her). About nine months after the "makeup" session, the girlfriend had a baby. According to the soldier, a DNA test had just proven that this other child was his also. The husband, for some unimaginable reason, was very upset.

"Why do you think your girlfriend's husband is trying to kill your kids?"

"Because he said if the test showed she cheated, he couldn't be responsible for what he did to the boy."

"You hear him say that?"

"That's what my girlfriend told me."

"Do you have the test results?"

"No."

"How do you know he's yours?"

"'Cause my girlfriend told me that's what the test said."

"Okay..." Now, this was a sticky situation. Since he didn't actually have the test results, and he didn't have firsthand knowledge of the threat, it would be hard for his testimony to initiate any kind of meaningful legal proceeding. At the same time, you simply can't take this kind of perceived threat lightly. *Something* had to be done.

So we called the police. From Iraq.

Of course, the police station was closed. The voice-mail recording admonished us to call 911 for emergencies. But 911 is not an option on a satellite phone in Diyala province. So I sat him down in front of the phone and told him to report the threat the instant the police station opened and ask the officer to investigate.

"Then, you *have* to contact your girlfriend to receive proof of paternity so that you can establish parental rights." These rights could allow him an order of protection against his girlfriend's husband.

In the early evening, I saw him on the FOB just as he was preparing to go on a mission, to risk his life for his country. He told me his kids were okay and away from the husband. He thanked me for my help and mounted his Humvee to drive outside the wire.

Is that soldier a hero? A victim? A good guy? A bad guy? In which category does *he* fit?

Later that same afternoon, a sergeant came into my office to ask a question about the rules of engagement (the rules that govern when— or if—we can use deadly force). Like the soldier before him, his face was etched with concern.

"Sir, I've got a question. Something happened last night."

Once again I grabbed my notebook. "Start from the beginning."

"We're driving down Route Brown at 2030 hours, and we notice two guys on the side of the road, and it looks like they're digging a hole. They're not on the road, or we'd know what to do, but they're kinda close to it. We watch for a while, and they just keep digging. We know this is an IED spot, and there's been some big IEDs there."

"What did you do?"

"Well, we sat there forever trying to decide whether we should engage or roll up on them and question them. Finally, we decided to roll up, and they were scared to death. Turns out they were farmers repairing an irrigation ditch. They were working at night 'cause it was too hot in the day. The whole thing kinda shook up some of the new guys."

IEDs, of course, are the most deadly weapons the insurgents have, and the soldiers risked their lives when they approached the farmers. Our guys risked death to *make sure* they were in the right before they pulled the trigger.

"What do you need to know?" I asked.

"If we hadn't done what we did . . . if we had *fired*, would we be in trouble?" He looked straight at me.

If last night didn't, encounters like this made me feel the weight of responsibility. Rules of engagement are not dry legal theories, but rules upon which human lives turn. I answered his question with the rules that applied in our area of operations and with suggestions for different approaches, but then ended with this statement:

"Look, you guys are making hard calls, and the last thing I want to happen is for a mom to lose their son or a son to lose a dad because a soldier is afraid somebody like me is looking over their shoulder. There are gray areas out there, you've been briefed on the rules, and if you're trying to do what's right, you don't have to worry about me."

"Roger, sir."

"It's a lot easier to answer questions from a lawyer than it is to learn to walk again."

"Roger that."

When the sergeant walked out of the room, I was struck by his determination to do what was right, by his compassion for the Iraqis who were so obviously terrified by our patrol, and by his concern for his men.

In that context, I'd call him a hero. But I don't know anything else about him. I'm pretty sure he has flaws.

By categorizing our soldiers, the public unintentionally separates itself from us. But really, we're not different. Some of us are venal. Some of us are heroic. Some of us are venal sometimes and heroic at others. All of us are flawed. But these flawed individuals do one thing few others do: They don body armor, grab a weapon, and climb into a vehicle not knowing if it will be the last ride of their life.

I don't think human nature changes all that much. I don't necessarily buy that the "Greatest Generation" was really greater than ours. They were an American generation that did great things. And they did terrible things. There were rapists and thieves in our armed forces. There were cowards and heroes.

There are other American generations that have done great things. Today, we can't even imagine the sacrifices of the Civil War generation, who endured losses that would stagger the imagination of even World War II–era Americans. But Abraham Lincoln never had any illusions of human greatness. David Frum, reviewing Shelby Foote's great Civil War trilogy, relates the story of Lincoln facing well-wishers during the late evening of his reelection victory in 1864. In his short address to the assembled crowd, Lincoln said:

> What has occurred in this case must ever recur in similar cases. Human nature will not change. In any future great national trial, compared with the men of this, we shall have as weak and as strong, as silly and as wise, as bad and as good. Let us therefore study the incidents of this as philosophy to learn wisdom from, and none of them as wrongs to be revenged.

And so it goes. When I boarded the Chinook helicopter on Thanksgiving eve, loaded with gear and ready to fly over hostile territory to our little FOB near Iran, I wasn't a hero. I wasn't a victim. I certainly wasn't a killer. I was just a regular guy. I was a husband and father, very far from home—a deeply flawed, frightened person trying hard to do the right thing.

8

GETTING MY LIFE TOGETHER—ONE PUPPY AT A TIME

Nancy

AS THE INITIAL SHOCK OF David's departure wore off and we got used to the "new normal," I knew that I had to do something to keep from simply marking days on a calendar, monitoring the kids' feelings, and praying (and worrying) for his safety. I needed a sense of purpose beyond "Let's just get through today." I married young—I was a sophomore in college and barely twenty-one when we tied the knot. I'd never really lived on my own, balanced a checkbook, or worried about things like getting repairs done (on the house or the car). I'd always had *someone*—first my dad, then my husband—to lean on when life got tough.

As the days stretched into weeks, I hit upon a very simple mission for me, while David was on his: I'd try to get my life together. Rather than just "hang in there" while he was gone, rather than simply try not to screw up the kids or the family, I'd try to make our lives better. I wanted David to return not just to an intact family, but to a *better* family. And since he wasn't able to be here, I had to figure out exactly what that better family would look like.

My first decision for family improvement was to get a dog. As soon as people found out that David was being deployed, they asked if I had a pet, presumably to help with loneliness. For months I resisted, because I'd gone down that route before... many years before. In fact, it was Valentine's Day, my junior year in high school, when two boys showed up at my house trying to win my heart. The first, a senior named Mike, handed me a green box with a gold foil seal on the top from the swanky gift shop in my hometown of Paris, Tennessee, Jack Jones Flowers and Gifts. It was a stuffed animal, but not the oh-so-overdone teddy bear with an annoying cursive plea written on a pink heart-shaped pillow, like "Be Mine," or "Friends Forever." No, the soft black-and-white dog had a pink leather tongue and a blue collar that simply melted my young heart. Just as I hugged it to my chest, a knock on the door interrupted the budding romance. The other would-be suitor, Jeff, stood at the door wearing a red fleece jacket that made him look pregnant with an overcaffeinated baby. Before Mike could properly excuse himself, Jeff unzipped his jacket and pulled out a tiny puppy, a black-and-white mutt, which he presented as if it were a tennis bracelet or diamond earrings. That's how, by the end of Valentine's Day, I had two dogs—but only one required regular feeding.

I called her "J.J.," the boy's initials, an unfortunate decision since J.J. was female. We always called her "him"—except my mom, who called him "pusillanimous pest." She was never much for dogs, but could tolerate one if he lived outside and performed some sort of function. According to her, there are two different types of people in this world—those with outside dogs and those with inside dogs. The former group consists of farmers who want to keep deer away from crops or squirrels off the porch. The latter group consists of unhygienic ignoramuses with mixed-up priorities about the world and man's place in it. (Cat owners, a morally weak bunch, did not deserve categorization.) My high school romance lasted just a couple of months, but J.J. stuck around for years—no matter what we did to him.

We never even bought him a doghouse. When my dad realized we had a pet, he went down in the basement, where the solutions to all life's problems could be found. Over his years of walking through the forests working for a paper company, he had found many things: blue bottles (mud bursting from their mouths), a Ruger target pistol, a gas mask from old Army maneuvers, an iron ore furnace, several wallets (promptly returned to careless hunters), dozens of deer antlers, and even a couple of two-thousand-pound rocks (which he gave my mom for Mother's Day). So when Daddy emerged from the basement, no one was surprised when he presented J.J. with a four-foot-tall metal tub that once had transported syrup for Coca-Cola. Daddy filled its bottom with sawdust, called it the "dog condo," and—after my mother rightly complained it was an eyesore—even spray-painted it with green and black splotches. Homemade camouflage, however, wasn't as chic as it sounds. Had we lived in a subdivision, the neighbors would've called an emergency community meeting and collected money for a proper doghouse. But because we lived on seven acres of forested land, the dog condo sat at the edge of the driveway, a monument to my dad's ingenuity and unwillingness to spend actual money on something like a dog.

And as an adult I didn't want to spend money on a dog either. In fact, I wasn't sure having a dog was a good idea at all, especially after researching various breeds and seeing how much they actually cost. I wanted a hobby, a friend, something to take the kids' minds off David's absence. But every time I thought of a dog, images of poor J.J. in his dog condo flashed through my mind. It wasn't that J.J. had a bad life—he had his run of the property and an unlimited supply of rabbits. But because we never bathed him, he became more a source of guilt than a part of the family—we couldn't even pet the poor thing without reeking of the dog condo and months of accumulated funk. The only real interaction we'd have with the dog was when my dad would pull swollen, blood-filled ticks off his back or when my mother would yell at him for gnawing on the porch swing.

So why even consider a dog?

Several years after I got J.J., David and I lived with our two kids in a cramped Philadelphia apartment, eight hundred miles and several years removed from the dog condo. We had an aquarium, a pale substitute for real pets consisting of a lot of work and not much enjoyment. With no room for a puppy, we stared into the cloudy waters of the tank and dreamed of the wide-open spaces people in the country enjoy. We'd comfort the kids with stories of things called "yards," which have green metallic creatures called june bugs, which provide endless fun by tying a thread to one of their legs and watching them fly in futile circles. Yards also have daddy longlegs, gangly-looking creatures with legs that easily popped off in the hands of curious children. And not to mention the magical lightning bugs collected in

Mason jars with pinpricked tin tops, little night-lights that flicker beside beds during May nights. Most of all, of course, yards have pets, the kind without fins.

We promised the kids we'd move south one day and have one of those glorious yards like the rest of America. "And we can even have a dog," we said, in the unthinking way people do when they believe the future is farther off than it is. After telling them that Daddy was going to war, how could we also deprive them of a pet?

That's how I ended up on the phone with the owner of a small home-based kennel nestled among the pines along a lake just north of New Orleans.

"Is your yard fenced?" the lady on the other end of the phone asked me. "I require my dog buyers to have a fenced-in yard." I knew immediately that my dog condo experience wouldn't impress this woman.

"And why do you think my dog is the right pet for your family? I've interviewed dozens of people who want to get a dog from this litter."

"Well—this is based solely on my research, mind you... I've never actually seen the breed, but I like that they don't shed." As soon as I finished, I feared my true identity as an Outside Dog Person had seeped out.

"Have you ever owned a dog before?"

"Oh yes," I assured her.

"What kind?"

I could tell by her website photos that this lady was serious about dogs. One photo was of her wearing a proud expression and a blue dress, holding a fluffy dog on her lap. She had the number 25 pinned to her sleeve, and the caption read, "Best of Show—2003 Nationals." I hesitated before I answered.

"Well, he, or she, really, was a Lab," I said. "Kind of. More of a Heinz 57, really. Her name was J.J."

She paused, as if taking the time to mark out my name with a thick permanent marker before proceeding. "You have kids?"

I heard something in her voice that made me want to minimize their significance. "Just two," I said, as if they were just decorations that I took out of the garage around Christmastime.

"How old are they and what are they like?" she asked.

Remain calm, I thought. I was just trying to get information about the strangely named breed of dog she was selling: the Löwchen. Although they've been documented as far back as the mid-fifteenth century, they were, according to the 1969 *Guinness Book of World Records*, the least common dog in the world, and I'd never even seen one. Why should I care if I didn't "make the cut"? "Löwchen" means, literally, "little lion," due to their fur's natural thickness around their heads, creating the illusion of little manes. Royal women, who had the dogs for companionship, trimmed the long silky coats on the back halves of their bodies and their back legs, leaving full "manes" at the front. In sixteenth- and seventeenth-century paintings, artists frequently depicted these dogs at the feet of knights in armor or beside ladies of nobility. The dogs had fringes of hair over their feet and a plume at the end of their tail. I always feel embarrassed for those whose bare butts are revealed to the world, like Paris Hilton's little dog, or Paris Hilton herself.

"They're eight and six," I said, as if it were a detriment. "Very conscientious and loving kids."

"Well, six is my cutoff," she said. "They need to be old enough to treat the dog right. Have they had pets before?"

I didn't mention Nemo and Marlin.

"Send me photos of the children, and we'll talk again next week."

At this point, I wanted nothing more than to get a dog from this woman. Although I'd called her simply for information, there was something about her toughness that made me want to impress her. "I don't sell my dogs to just anyone," she told me. Part of me wondered if she was Tom Sawyering me, but I still wanted nothing more but to whitewash that fence. That's why I spent an hour clicking through photos on my computer. One of them was of a bare-chested Austin, with the words "I AM A GIRL!" written on him in blue marker. He'd asked Camille to write "Superman," but—too young to read—proudly strutted around the house, as confused as poor J.J. I chose a different photo.

"Let me tell you about my puppies," the woman began during stage two of the interview process, which happened a couple of days later. Even though the dogs were only ten weeks old, she described their personalities with more details than I could've described my college roommate. Angus was affectionate and friendly, but the pack sometimes picked on him. Lola was a dominating bitch. (She used the word "bitch" like normal people would use the word "celery.")

She peppered me with information that I couldn't really process all at once. She told me the right way to housebreak a dog, about the evils of puppy mills, about walking dogs on leashes, and about "pack behavior." It was a tad overwhelming, and my carefully constructed persona of being a dog lover was threatening to collapse with every new fact. "And how do you plan on grooming the dog?" she asked.

I realized, with a tinge of sadness, that there was no way I could impress this woman. I didn't even possess enough dog knowledge to fake it. I barely go to the salon twice a year, so taking care of a dog's hair I'd never even seen was not one of the topics I could speak about confidently.

"Well, I doubt we'd trim it in that lion cut like you do," I began slowly. "In fact, I won't be showing him in any dog competitions, and I definitely won't be letting him wear those little sweaters that people think are cute around the holidays," I said. "I just want a dog that won't make me sneeze, basically. Plus, my husband's in the Army, and I need something fluffy to keep me company while the kids are at school."

Ironically, that's what moved me to the top of the list. Apparently, Löwchen Lady was keeping the best of the litter to show in dog competitions. Since all four of the puppies looked almost identical, she didn't want them competing against their siblings in the future. I think, after hours of interviewing me, she rightly concluded I'd never possess enough dog knowledge to enter into a competition. Plus, her husband was retired military, and she'd spent her life moving from one place to another. The dog was mine if I wanted it.

It was a little like being accepted into Harvard—an honor until you get the bill. I temporarily considered buying a midsized sedan instead of this dog, but that was before I got the photo. The dog was black and white, standing on a platform with his head being held up by a woman partially outside the frame.

He was colored the same as J.J., whom my children met once during a visit from Philly. They jumped up and down when they saw J.J. and immediately wanted to crawl into his magnificent condo. In fact, the kids told everyone in Philadelphia they had a dog, which lived temporarily with their Tennessee grandmother who generously had offered to give J.J. to them. As best I remember, my mother had tired of J.J. peeing on the porch and said, "Take that brilliant dog. You can have him." Immune to sarcasm, they were overjoyed at their new pet.

We didn't even tell them when J.J. died later that year. I figured they'd just forget about him completely and we'd never have to deal with the inevitable grief that comes with losing a "pet." Plus, I was always a little hesitant to ask about the circumstances surrounding the dog's death, since my dad had shot more than one of our dogs when they'd gotten sick. Honestly, I just wanted to forget about poor J.J. and hoped she was chasing rabbits in the great hayfields of the sky. By this time, I had no idea what had become of the real Jonathan Jeffrey, who'd given me the dog without realizing that one day my own children would be devastated at its loss. Of course, I still had the stuffed animal Mike gave me on that Valentine's Day, along with some photos of our Homecoming dance and the memory of running over a possum the night I drove his red Z24. Mike died in that car in a wreck his first year at college.

When I saw the photo of the little black-and-white dog, my heart felt heavy the way you feel when you've lost something and know you can't ever get it back: a friend, my kids' "pet," my chance to take care of J.J. and make her life a little more comfortable. Even my parents' basement, once covered in sawdust and full of junk, had been cleaned out by my unsentimental mother, who said, "If we don't do it now, you'll have to do it after we die." The dog condo, still on the edge of the driveway, was faded by the sun and looked less impressive now that the camouflage had worn off. Oddly, the little dog seemed to be a way for me to make things right...a way for the kids to have normal lives with yards, like the people who send Christmas cards with their families posed in front of fireplaces with dogs in Santa hats. At the very least, this dog would be a promise fulfilled.

And so I drove to the Kennesaw Kennel Club's Annual Dog Show in Marietta, Georgia. This is where the official handoff was going to occur—exactly halfway between Löwchen Lady's house and mine. It was apparently against Kennel Club rules to sell dogs at these dog shows, so I mailed a check in advance of our meeting. If asked, I could truthfully say she was keeping my dog for me, since the dog would be paid for, and therefore mine. It felt more like a drug deal than a pet sale.

The show was outdoors in an equestrian center. There were six rings under a metal roof, three on each side. In the middle, people stood anxiously with their dogs on leashes. One man's expression of utter sobriety seemed oddly juxtaposed with his constant squeaking of a rubber ducky to get his dog's attention. A woman in a purple business suit and tennis shoes was standing in the midst of everyone, her dog of a breed I could not discern.

"Excuse me," I asked her. "Do you know where the Löwchens are being shown?"

She looked at me as if I had insulted her mother. "Do you mean 'Luffshun'?" She spat the word.

"L-o-w-c-h-e-n?" I spelled it out.

"Luff. Shun," she said dismissively. "And why are you looking for them?" The people around me seemed to notice that I was without a dog, which was worse than being without clothes. They could probably tell I was an Outside Dog Person, and perhaps their dogs could still smell J.J.'s sorry stench on me after all these years.

"I'm meeting a woman," I said carefully, "who has my dog."

"*You* own a Luffshun?"

"Well, yes, I do," I said, feeling she could see through me. For all I knew, the dog on her leash was a Löwchen.

She pursed her lips and exchanged a glance with a man beside her. Then, suddenly, as if she'd just remembered she was late for her train, she ran past me into the dusty rink with her dog, past the judge, in large circles around the ring. The judge stared at her and the dog quite attentively, and I was both embarrassed for them and amazed at the way her dog stood proudly while his anus was checked out by a man holding a clipboard.

I couldn't help but feel partially responsible when the lady's dog didn't win. By that time, I saw the stands filled with people, cheering on the dogs and applauding when the judges announced the winners. In other words, I was in the wrong place—right in the middle of the floor of the competition, the dog show equivalent of walking into a Knicks game and asking the players on the bench for free-throw advice.

By then, however, I was addicted to the action on the floor. I saw tiny tables with dogs on them, their leashes lifting their heads, making them look snobbier than dogs on the Upper East Side. Their fur was being groomed with clippers, sprayed with hairspray, and their teeth brushed. Groomers with furrowed brows worked on their canine clients. Curling irons, hair dryers, and overhead lights were jammed into extension cords and reminded me of summer camp, when our cabins had three outlets for twelve teenage girls. But the girls at camp never looked as good as these dogs. I couldn't help but stare.

"What kind of breed is this?" I asked a bystander and motioned to the ring in front of us. I still hadn't seen anything that looked like a lion, and I was planning on scooting right out of there if the dog didn't look right. On paper, the Löwchen seemed like the perfect breed: hypoallergenic, small but not too small, and easily trainable. But as I stood there in Marietta, surrounded by all kinds of dogs (both beautiful and hideous), I began to feel that seeing a dog before purchasing it might've been helpful. Or at least any dog of the breed.

"Um, those are golden retrievers," she said, refraining from adding, "Duh."

"Of course," I said. From that point on, I decided to keep my mouth shut and just watch. I wondered how to gracefully make an exit if the Löwchen looked like some of the dogs before me...small, emaciated, and spoiled. On blind dates in movies, women have their friends call a few minutes into dinner—if the man shows promise, she won't answer it; if he's disastrous, she rushes out the door to tend to her "sick mother." I wished I hadn't shown Löwchen Lady a photo of me, so I could meander around, see the dog, and then decide if I wanted to reveal my identity. In the ring before me, I was amused when handlers ran through the course without their dogs to practice for the real competition coming up.

"After the humans run through obstacle courses, does the judge toss them treats?" I said to the woman beside me, who was not amused.

"Nancy?" Behind me, I heard a woman's voice call my name. When I turned, I saw a brunette in a nice suit approaching me. She was a little out of breath.

"We just won best in breed!"

I didn't quite know what that meant, as there were so many different categories, but congratulated her enthusiastically.

"It was your dog's aunt." Suddenly, and for the first time in my life, I felt canine pride swell within me. Even though I hadn't seen *my* dog yet, I knew he came from good stock. We chatted amicably while we walked past Winnebagos and vans decorated with bumper stickers that read "It's Hard to Be Humble When You Own a Bull Dog," and "Well Bred."

"Have you decided on a name?"

She'd asked me about this before, over the phone, but I was noncommital. The truth is, we'd picked the name six years prior to that day, when Camille was only two. We lived in the frozen tundra of Ithaca, New York. During the few days a year warm enough to go outside, we'd take long walks up and down the hills around the neighborhood. Camille was always snugly strapped in the baby jogger. When she'd see dogs from afar, she'd kick her legs in joy and horror, screaming her toddler equivalent of the word "dog": "Gawgo!"

Of course, we promptly dropped the word "dog" from our vocabulary, and even called frankfurters "hot gawgoes." We never even considered another name—although a lively debate raged in our household now that Camille was old enough to even discuss the appropriate spelling. We settled on G-o-g-g-o, because we could substitute the letters in the Bingo song—something we planned to sing to him once he was ours.

I know that normal people—especially people who take dogs seriously—might not appreciate the name Goggo. And I certainly wasn't going to tell her what we planned on naming our second dog. While we still lived in Ithaca, Camille later knocked her front teeth out and never quite said "th" correctly. She'd say "la" instead of "the" and everyone asked if we were teaching her French. Austin, years later, mirrored his sister's speech (even though he had teeth) and said "skanks" instead of "thanks"—something that sounded so profane that we never corrected him. We stifled a laugh every time a little old lady did a double take when he so politely said, "Skank you."

Of course, as time went on, Camille grew permanent teeth and countless adults took it upon themselves to correct Austin's "th" problem. Soon, they both sounded like everyone else, their funny verbal nuances lost in the pressure of conformity. Our plan was to get two dogs and call them Skanks and Goggo. That way, there'd never be a time when their mouths forgot the words of their youth. And there's something gratifying about inside family jokes.

"Goo-goo?" Löwchen Lady asked. "Like the Cluster?"

I stumbled over the explanation, about the dogs and the missing teeth, and even accidentally—against my better judgment—mentioned Skanks. This turned out to be a good thing, since the name Goggo seemed downright classy in comparison. We walked through the parking lot, a campground of canine lovers, until we got to a mobile home with an awning.

"I want you to meet my friends," she said. "But first, you might want to meet your dog."

She had a purposeful memory lapse, referring to him as "Go-Go," "Gow-gees," or "Goo-Goo," but I knew I'd passed the "first impression" test, since she still called him "your dog."

She opened the back of her vehicle, where two crates were nestled tightly, reached over, and unhitched a latch. "Quick, grab one!" she said. There were four tiny puppies who heard the sound of freedom, and I was horrified to realize the only thing standing between them and a parking lot of moving vehicles was my body. After I'd been moved to the top of the list, I'd tried my best to instill in Löwchen Lady a confidence that I could handle the responsibility of the dog. I'd asked questions, read books, and researched veterinarians. But the illusion of dog competency was ruined when I thrust my hands into the crate, horrified, and yelled, "I don't even know how to hold a dog!"

I grabbed a couple of the fluffs of fur—that's all they seemed to be—which squirmed determinedly in my arms. There was a chance I was holding the dog that, if treated well, could be a part of the family for the next ten to fifteen years. This, strangely, made me unable to even look at the thrashing puppies while I tried to keep them from harm's way. It was the opposite sensation of driving past a car wreck on the interstate—something so horrible you simply must look. The children had waited many years to have their first "real" pet—and honestly, the responsibility loomed heavily in my mind. I knew when I had a chance to really look at the dog, to hold him and gaze in his eyes, I'd be able to tell whether he'd be a blessing or a disappointment. And I put off that moment as long as I could.

Somehow, we managed to put all the puppies into a nearby pen, and I averted my eyes from the dogs as we met the people standing around the trailer.

"This is my new owner," Löwchen Lady said to them. Apparently, there's an entire dog culture that travels around America for these shows, like canine NASCAR, but with PETA bumper stickers on the vans instead of the number 3. These two men were her acquaintances from years of doing the circuit, and they stood holding sandwiches and looked me over. The older one had a single gold stud in his earlobe.

"I dated a man from Tennessee once," the younger man said. "Before I moved here." He and the older man exchanged furtive glances.

"Nancy's an author," LL said.

"What do you write?"

"Oh, nothing much," I said, horrified that LL would have brought this up.

"She's a Republican," LL said, "but the good kind."

I could tell that the men did not believe there was a "good kind," so I promptly tried to change the subject. I wanted nothing more than to escape from there, the little world where the dogs drank bottled water and the judges favored dogs whose owners gave sexual favors. I knew politics had more than its fair share of corruption, but at least those scandals concerned the leadership of the free world. As I stood under that awning and heard about dog competition corruption, I wanted someone to stop the world so I could get off.

Löwchen Lady turned to the pen and smiled. "But you haven't met the dog yet. Yours is the boy."

I know there are people who shamelessly look at canine genitalia, but I am not one of them. I stood on the edge of the pen as four identical dogs jumped for me, and pretended not to be able to get a good look. Eventually, I hemmed and hawed for much too long, and Löwchen Lady scooped up the puppy the others had been nipping. His white face was framed by floppy black ears and his legs hung loosely down as she held him to me. I fumbled in the handoff, and Löwchen Lady showed me the correct way to hold the small animal. I closed my eyes, buried my face into his neck, and breathed deeply. His fur was softer than cotton and smelled like fresh linens. The end of his tail was fluffy, and I noticed his "lion cut" had grown out a bit, per my instruction.

"You need to trim that dog," one of the men said. "I got some clippers right here, if you want me to do it."

"No, no," I said. "I wouldn't want to bother you."

"Nancy doesn't like the lion trim," LL explained to the men, who were sitting amid more hair products than I've owned in my entire lifetime. There was puppy spray, a perfume that made dogs smell better than my kids, hairspray, teeth whitener, and gels. The men owned several white poodle-looking dogs that yipped violently when anyone walked by the door to their trailer. Their dogs all had white Afros, perfectly coiffed.

"You're not going to show him?"

"Definitely not," I said, a bit too forcefully. "He's a pet."

"What's your feeding philosophy?" Löwchen Lady fed her dogs ground beef raw, with rice mixed in and occasional vegetables for good measure. Since we fed J.J. leftover SpaghettiO's and hoped he could catch enough rabbits to make up his dietary protein deficiency, I was hesitant to respond. I didn't know how I'd feed the dog, but I knew Löwchen Lady would give me enough food to make it through the week.

"Oh, I'm definitely pro-feeding," I said. Everyone snickered.

On the way home I drove very carefully, knowing Goggo was crated in the backseat. I didn't really look at him till I made it back to Tennessee, where two children hid behind their grandfather's legs, hesitant to catch a glimpse of their new, real pet. This dog would, over the course of several months, become a dear friend to us while David was away. He was gentle with the children and kind when he wasn't defecating in the bonus room. At night—the glorious nights—you could imagine that he was, in fact, a good dog. That's when he lay down next to me and demanded his own pillow. Which, of course, was okay because I still slept on my side of the bed even though David wasn't using his side. Goggo purred like a cat when the kids petted him, and I even did what I thought I'd never do. I bought the poor thing a cow Halloween costume. In other words, he became a part of our family, a bright spot during a difficult time.

Later, I got an email from an Asian friend. "Did you know that 'goggo' is a kid way of saying 'dog' in Chinese? It's like 'doggie.'" I knew from that point on, we'd have an out when people asked us what our dog's name was. "It's Chinese," I could say with an air of superiority. "What? Your dog is 'Max'? How clever."

9

MEET DAVE RAMSEY

Nancy

WITH A FLUFFY DOG IN MY ARMS, it was time to turn my attention to the next part of my family improvement plan. Believe it or not, I knew less about finances than I knew about dogs. I'd gotten the phone turned off at least twice in the course of my life—once in college, and the other during an ill-advised two-month period when David put me in charge of the checkbook. But there was nothing like getting a call from your church deacon telling you that your tithe check bounced to make you reevaluate your life.

Even though that was more than a decade ago, it was enough of a jolt to scare me away from learning about finances. At the age of thirty-three, I'd still never balanced my checkbook and couldn't tell you how compound interest works. I was what you might call a bystander to our financial lives, after embarrassing David enough that he started handling our money exclusively. Not only did it put more pressure on my husband, who already had a difficult job, but it sometimes made me come up a little short conversationally.

"Gas prices," a man lamented at a dinner party. "How much is the station near your house charging?"

These are the things adults keep track of and why I could never be the leader of the free world. In 1992, when the nation suffered righteous indignation that President Bush Sr. didn't know the price of a gallon of milk, I quietly put away all thoughts of political greatness and switched my major from political science to philosophy. After all, if you can't be president, why be employable? Milk, like fuel, is a necessity and you buy it whether or not it's overpriced.

"Too much," I said.

"And my heating costs have gone up too," a woman mentioned. "Have yours?"

If adults had superlatives, I'd be "Most Likely to Have Her Utilities Turned Off," so I tried to steer the conversation in a different direction.

"I'd have to look at my records," I said, feeling transparent as I said it. People don't consult their "records" on such topics. Heck, I don't even have records. Is our bill five hundred or fifty? I didn't know, and no—while we were at it—I didn't know our utility provider. I hadn't written out the checks in so long that I didn't realize that "writing out checks" was itself an anachronism. I hadn't debited or Quickened or autopaid anything, and I felt a little ashamed at myself for being "that kind of woman."

"Sure has been cold, though," I said.

"Your bill hasn't gone up?"

With one glance, the lady realized I knew more about Pam Anderson's fluctuating bra size than Wall Street's fluctuating markets. The look of pity and contempt expressed her view that I embodied all that was wrong with the women's movement. "You should know these things," she said, "and be more independent. You know, in case *something* happens."

Something happening is meant to induce fearful visions of the bank seizing my car because I couldn't figure out where to send our monthly check if David didn't come home. Like most, however, I felt invincible and full of life, not bothering to plan for the worst or, to be honest, even think of it. But before David left, we filled out some basic Army forms that ridded me of any of this false security. In case *something happened*, David made a box of important documents that would guide me through our finances. In case *something happened*, he created a will and taught me about our insurance policies. In case *something happened*, our friends in Boston agreed to travel with me out of the country, if necessary, and my neighbors agreed to watch the kids.

It sobered me. When David drove off that Saturday morning to begin his journey to Iraq, I feared for his safety, and he feared he'd return home to a house with a yellow ribbon on the porch and a foreclosed sign in the yard...an all too common occurrence. Soldiers give power of attorney to their parents or girlfriends and return to realize their "loved ones" have bought new satellite televisions, pickup trucks, and—in one case I heard of—plastic surgery. Wives, who already feel deserted, think they're entitled to live it up while their husband is gone, or—in my case—lack the know-how to keep things afloat.

One night, I was reading Clarence Thomas's autobiography, *My Grandfather's Son*, and came to a chapter that changed my outlook forever. There, in the discussion of his meteoric rise to the Supreme Court, was this jewel of a confession: When President Bush nominated him to the highest court in the land, he still had not paid off his law school debts from Yale. This struck me as even more embarrassing than the pubic-hair-on-the-Coke-can drama with Anita Hill, and I vowed to—finally—get control of our finances. If the president ever came calling for me to be on the Supreme Court, I'd be ready.

I felt like Scarlett O'Hara holding up a fistful of dirt. "As God is my witness, I'll never be hungry again." Of course, we weren't hungry—had never *actually* been hungry—but I identified with how, emboldened by Rhett's departure, she made a vow that depended solely on her ferocity. Plus, southern women all want to be in some way like Scarlett, and our eighteen-inch-waist similarity ended back when I was in kindergarten.

I had no idea how I'd pull it off, but I felt the figurative dirt in my fist and the fire in my belly. The answer came as I was driving in my car and came across Nashville financial guru Dave Ramsey's talk show.

"I give you the same advice your grandmother would've given you, except I keep my teeth in," he said, describing his old-fashioned money advice. It got my attention. To get started, he advised something called a debt snowball. This is when you list all your debts from the smallest to the largest and pay the little debts first. Theoretically, if you can get over the shock of seeing all your debts in a list, it'll give you immediate emotional gratification to get rid of one naggingly small debt at a time. Once the smallest debt is paid off, you take the money you would've paid on it the next month and pay on your second debt. By the time the final debts are reached, the extra amount of cash you have to pay them off will grow quickly, just as a snowball rolls downhill and gathers momentum.

It sounded good, its simplicity appealing and understandable. It reminded me of the time I joined Rosie O'Donnell's "Chub Club" back when she had her own talk show and pretended to be in love with Tom Cruise. My friends and I called ourselves "Jabba the Club," and followed her very simple advice: "Eat less, move more." Although our dedication to weight loss lasted only long enough to get the free T-shirts in the mail, my new motto would be "Spend less, work more." And this time, I thought, I'd stick to the plan until every last cent of debt was paid. Well, except the house, unless by some miracle I won the lottery without playing it. I was financially illiterate, but even I knew not to play the lottery.

One day, with Clarence Thomas's book on the table, I sat down and decided to look at our numbers for the first time. I felt like a child with a scraped knee, afraid to assess the damage.

"Complete Lists of Debts," I wrote on a page of a notebook I'd ambitiously titled "A New Leaf." I even drew a house in the woods with a tire swing on the cover, believing that all projects deserve to be housed in a properly decorated three-ring binder. David had given me carte blanche and power of attorney, realizing he couldn't monitor both al Qaeda and my checking account, so I decided to keep this whole adventure a secret. I wrote down each item of debt, which represented anywhere from just a few to several thousand dollars. Revealing the wound was painful, each item causing me to physically wince...Sallie Mae (David's Harvard loans); PLATO (I-didn't-even-get-a-degree loan); Land Rover (overpriced gas-guzzling loan); Saab (car that might or might not have a gearshift loan); American Express (new laptop); and Visa (too many dinners out).

To start the snowball rolling, Dave Ramsey suggested having a yard sale or selling something of value. In seeing it all laid bare like that, I got a lump in my throat, took a deep breath, and did what any red-blooded American girl accustomed to hard work would do. I went to Craigslist.com—a virtual yard sale where you can look for erotic companionship or a certain edition of a Nancy Drew book—and listed David's vehicle.

"Al Gore's Worst Nightmare," I titled the photo above his hunter green SUV. Since it was going to be sitting around for twelve months without a driver, there was no reason to pay the high monthly payments. Taking advantage of the fact that Tennessee's electoral votes went for George Bush in 2000 (even though Al Gore was our very own senator), I had some fun. "Enlarge your carbon footprint in style," I wrote before listing the vehicle's many attributes.

Many times along this journey, panic seized me. I wanted to surprise David with my new economic prowess, so I followed Dave Ramsey's baby steps to financial freedom and prayed I was doing the right thing. When people found out David was gone, they'd wrinkle their brows and earnestly ask, "Are you guys okay... *financially*?" It was a tricky question. Because David's employer, the Alliance Defense Fund, had been generous when they found out he was being deployed, our financial situation hadn't significantly changed. However, our status quo was not all that great. Like most normal Americans, we carried credit card debt, had high monthly car payments, and were paying off student loans at glacial speed. Suddenly, "normal" made me feel vulnerable and unsteady.

The Al Gore thing worked. The next night, I was standing in my driveway accepting payment in cash from some guys in Nashville who work at a Harley-Davidson store. When they drove away, they took my garage door opener, my Prince CD, and an enormous financial headache with them.

I hadn't thought this all through. David would eventually return and need a vehicle, but I planned on being filthy rich by that time. Now? I got out a Sharpie marker and wrote down the amount of my monthly Land Rover payment and designated it for next month's American Express. Our financial chart hung next to our calendar on which the kids would take turns marking each day off.

I didn't keep a visual record of how long it had been since I talked to David, so the kids wouldn't worry. But I knew in my mind that every morning when I woke up there should be at least a short email from him. Occasionally he'd miss a day, and I'd try not to imagine why. However, my newfound "hobby" of financial reform gave me a certain amount of power. I couldn't control our communication, but I could at least try to control our finances. And then, as if to emphasize the point, I suddenly stopped hearing from David. There were no phone calls, no morning emails, and no evening Internet chat. He was simply gone.

So I sold things on Craigslist, bought all of Dave Ramsey's books, and focused on getting rid of debt...a snowflake of an idea turning into a snowball of momentum. Whether it would roll or melt was yet to be seen. But there was something intoxicating about making something happen, rather than sitting around and fearing that somewhere, across the world in some sandy wasteland, something had.

10

RAIDER HARVEST

David

"GET READY FOR WHAT MAY be the biggest battle since Fallujah."

Now *that* will get your attention. All of us knew about Fallujah, America's largest urban battle since Vietnam, a place that had claimed more than a hundred American lives. Some of the men in the room had been there, and they never wanted to go back.

We had been at FOB Caldwell for exactly three weeks, and, for rookies like me, the war hadn't felt "real." After our first air strike, it seemed like the enemy pulled back for a bit. Our patrols went out, met with local leaders, and returned. Other patrols tried to establish a presence in the villages. There were no firefights, and only a couple small mines that hadn't caused serious injuries, only minor damage to vehicles.

As for me, I settled into an actual routine (or "battle rhythm" in Army lingo). I helped soldiers, worked on military justice issues as they arose, and generally handled all legal issues that crossed my desk. Twelve-hour shifts, every day, followed by a workout in the base gym and then a long instant message conversation with Nancy.

But then we got the word... "Operation Raider Harvest" was kicking off just after the New Year, and Sabre Squadron was going to provide a large chunk of the combat power. We were moving north, to Forward Operating Base Normandy, to participate in a major assault on a significant al Qaeda stronghold in the Diyala River valley.

And I was going.

I was leaving my nice little three-week-old FOB Caldwell life and going to…a battle? The lawyer?

It made sense, actually. We expected detainees, and I ran detainee operations for our squadron. We expected media coverage, and Lieutenant Colonel Calvert had just appointed me the squadron's "public affairs officer." We expected extensive enemy contact, which meant rules of engagement and targeting issues. As I joined in the preparations, my hours got a lot longer and my instant message conversations home grew shorter. I think Nancy knew something was going on, but I couldn't say. I couldn't even let on that anything had changed.

The preparations were nothing like I expected. I'm not sure what I expected, really. After all, at that point I still felt pretty much like a civilian in an Army uniform. *Everything* was new to me. But I know I expected more drama. In the movies (or TV classics like *The A-Team*), units prepare for combat via the martial "montage." Stirring music plays in the background while weapons are assembled, ammunition loaded, main guns test-fired, and helicopters fly overhead. Grim-faced soldiers (with bulging biceps) stare at map coordinates and point at the distant enemy.

All of that happens, of course (well, except for the music, the biceps, and the pointing), but I didn't see much of it. I'm a staff officer, and staff officers in high-tech armies prepare for battle with…

PowerPoint.

Lots and lots of PowerPoint.

Just as the Army does its best to drain the drama from any trip to a combat theater through endless waits and even worse discomfort, it does an even better job of draining the drama from a looming battle by subjecting staff officers to hundreds of slides full of "graphics," maps, flow charts, pie graphs, and photographs.

In the space of ten days, I attended, in order, a rehearsal of a course of action brief, a course of action brief, a rehearsal for the op order brief, the op order brief, a rehearsal for the op order frago brief, the op order frago brief, a rehearsal for the actual operation "rehearsal," and the "rehearsal" itself (which was not an actual rehearsal of the operation but a walk-through with a map laid out on a gym floor as we followed along with—yes—printed-out PowerPoint slides). Each of these briefs lasted no less than two hours and contained no less than seventy-five slides.

After this deployment, I vowed to *never* voluntarily give a Power-Point presentation.

But twenty hours of meetings and 750 slides do have a cumulative effect. I knew the plan, and I knew it cold. I knew what I was supposed to do. Heck, I even knew what the squadron maintenance officer was supposed to do. And I was bored out of my skull.

On New Year's Eve, I put on my body armor, said a silent but fervent prayer that God would protect me, climbed on a Black Hawk helicopter, and took off for FOB Normandy, the Diyala River valley, and the first real battle of my deployment.

It was anything but boring.

On the night of January 4, a massive armored force assembled at the edge of the battlefield. Roughly five hundred troopers from our squadron with almost fifty tanks, armored fighting vehicles, and Humvees readied for a road march from FOB Caldwell. The 2nd Brigade, 4th Infantry Division massed its Strykers in FOB Normandy, and the 82nd Airborne Division's Task Force Falcon boarded its Black Hawks for an air assault.

As for me, I stood in front of a bank of computer monitors at our new temporary command post at the corner of FOB Normandy. Sound waves from outgoing artillery fire shook the flaps of our tent as I watched footage from unmanned aerial vehicles. The tension was palpable as we all prepared to do our part.

In a few moments, I was going to link up with reporters from the *L.A. Times* and the American Forces Network and drive to meet our tanks on the road north. I had clarified the rules of engagement with our troop commanders, and our detention facilities were ready to receive any prisoners. I felt reasonably confident that I was ready to play my own (very small) part in the coming conflict.

Then we saw rain clouds approaching on radar, called our western bases, and found out it was sprinkling in Baghdad and the operation was postponed for seventy-two hours. (Or, in Army lingo, "The op was moved to the right for 72.")

That's right. Our mighty army—with equipment designed to engage the full might of the Red Army in the driving rain of a German spring or to drive back hundreds of thousands of North Koreans in a howling Korean snowstorm—ground to a halt.

All the plans were made, all the op orders briefed, all the equipment in position. So that left one thing to do: video games.

Within moments, each of the laptops in the command post became a miniature entertainment center. I fired up *Command and Conquer*. Our intelligence officer, Captain Steve Beckner, started his quest to dominate the world in *Civilization 4*. Our civil/military affairs officer, Captain Jon Norquist, went old school with the original *Final Fantasy*, while a group of soldiers huddled around Private Fields and his copy of *Booty Call* (an animated game that featured a "playa" named Jake's quest to "get some booty" in a variety of settings— sorority house, Vegas strip lounge, beachside bar, and the floor of the New York Stock Exchange). As we played for a couple of hours, the combat vets in the group started swapping stories. Then we moved outside the command post and huddled around a burning trash barrel as one of our staff sergeants told us about the "best day" of his first deployment.

"It was Eid [a Muslim holiday], right? And I was told that we had to buy some sheep, drive them into town, and hand them out to the locals. I knew that was a screwed-up idea, but—you know—orders. So we mount up and drive over to a farmer's place, buy his sheep— he was happy about the cash—put them into the back of the Bradley, and start driving off.

"So they can't stand in the back of the Bradley 'cause their hooves can't stand on the steel floor. They're all slidin' around goin' 'baaa' and crappin' on the floor while we ride into town. We were laughing our asses off.

"We get into town and open the ramp, and all them sheep fall down on each other trying to get out. I grab one of 'em and handed it to this guy, and he's all 'Allah akhbar' and going crazy he's so happy. So he pulls out his knife and cuts its throat right in front of us. The lamb goes 'baaaa,' and all its blood runs out on the road. We were like, 'Damn, dude.'

"This crowd gathers 'cause they saw us handing out them sheep, and then all of a sudden, blam! We got contact. Some jihadi is on a roof firin' down on my Bradley. So there's like this stampede as all these people try to get in my damn Bradley, and I open up on that dude and mess him up.

"Anyway, all that took like ten seconds. So there's still smoke comin' off the end of my barrel when we start handing out them sheep again. Dang, them people were so happy, all 'Allah' this and 'Allah' that.

"That was a good day."

I stood there just amazed by the stories of eight-hour firefights, of weeks spent sleeping on the hoods of Humvees. Some of my new friends described driving their tanks into the first floors of buildings, elevating their guns, and blowing up the entire second floor. Everyone had a story, but no one had a story quite like Sergeant Major Taylor, one of our most respected senior NCOs. He's been deployed multiple times, but his story had nothing to do with enemy action.

He was a young specialist working on an M1A1 Abrams when the tank turret suddenly traversed and the tank barrel slapped him in the side of his head.

"So it knocks me over, and I get to my feet, but something is strange. I'm seeing the sky and the ground *at the same time*. I put my hands to my face, and my right eyeball is hanging out of my head. I mean, it's just hanging there. So I passed out.

"When I came to, I was lying in the hospital with bandages over my eye. They told me that they put my eyeball back in and bore sighted it to align with my other eye."

Captain Beckner interjected, "Bore sighted? You mean like we bore sight the tank main gun?"

"Yup."

"So they took your eyeball and stuffed it right back in your head?"

"That's messed up."

With no one able to top a dangling eyeball, we left our trash fire and resumed our gaming.

I hadn't spoken to Nancy—by phone or email—in five days.

The operation finally kicked off during the late evening of January 7. For me, "kickoff" meant intently watching a series of blue rectangles and circles on a map. Our "Blue Force Tracker" (BFT) is a GPS-based system that allows us to monitor all units in the field from the safety and security of a rear command post.

The BFT maps were projected on two screens in our small command tent, with the cluster of blue in the lower right-hand side of the map representing the tanks, personnel carriers, and Humvees of Sabre Squadron and the cluster of blue on the upper left-hand side of the map representing the advance forces at FOB Normandy. The command post's radios crackled to life. As soon as the blue dots started moving, the mission was under way.

While for me the true start of Raider Harvest meant nervously watching a map, for almost four hundred of my fellow soldiers it meant jamming themselves and their gear into armored vehicles and beginning a slow and dangerous drive up almost forty miles of road that had not been cleared of IEDs, the improvised explosive devices that were the insurgents' best weapon. Typically planted in the dark hours of the night, these bombs, which could be mines, old artillery shells, or even buried barrels full of explosives, caused more casualties than any other weapon in al Qaeda's arsenal. Typically, you didn't know an IED was there until it blew up under your vehicle. Needless to say, I was nervous about the drive to the battle.

Our part of the plan involved two of our cavalry troops (Fox and Grim troops) "road marching" the forty miles to FOB Normandy, refueling at the FOB, and then attacking to establish our blocking positions to the north. As soon as the "block" was established, 2nd Brigade, 4th Infantry Division would sweep in from the east and (hopefully) drive al Qaeda into our waiting guns.

Fox and Grim troops began their road march at 1800 hours, the tactical refuel was to begin at 2100 hours, the attack would launch at 2300 hours, and everyone was to be in position by 0600. It was going to be a long night.

My job that first night was simple: link our embedded media with the troops and then be available to deal with any rules-of-engagement issues (those pesky "shoot, don't shoot" decisions) that arose. Media crews were waiting in a nearby tent—wearing their own body armor—ready to endure their own sleepless night in the field.

I'd already learned something about the media in Iraq. As a general rule, they report facts. As a general rule, they are both honest and courageous—exposing themselves to danger again and again to "get the story out." But as a general rule, they report the glass as half empty rather than half full.

The beginning of Raider Harvest represented the perfect example of "half-empty" reporting. As our guys marched north to FOB Normandy and the refueling point, there were no IEDs. As they turned into the refueling point and headed to the vulnerable refueling trucks, there was no small-arms fire and no RPGs, and as they headed to their blocking positions, not only was there no "contact," they didn't see a single person moving outside.

Other units made similar reports. Minimal contact with the enemy. No real problems. I went to bed at approximately 4:00 a.m., just as we established our block two hours ahead of schedule. I went to bed happy.

The next morning, al Qaeda woke up to find American troops moving through their safe haven and American tanks blocking their escape routes. I could hear the crackle of small-arms fire and the deafening boom of answering artillery. Helicopters, including Apache attack helicopters, flew overhead continuously.

After facing its first small-arms fire of the morning, Sabre Squadron discovered a substantial weapons cache and a stash of al Qaeda propaganda. We sent media to the site to "exploit" the find. While weapons caches are important to find and destroy, locating al Qaeda literature is important for a different reason: It defeats claims that the insurgency is nothing more than a "homegrown" response to an oppressive occupier; instead it is part and parcel of the larger war against jihadist terror.

As 2nd Brigade pushed through its own attack, it called in Hellfire missile strikes on insurgents holed up in houses and engaged in numerous smaller firefights. So far, so good. After only four days of operations, almost a dozen al Qaeda terrorists had been killed, several weapons caches discovered, and the operation was ahead of schedule.

The Diyala River valley was being cleared, but it was certainly no Fallujah.

So how did the *New York Times* report the events? By declaring that coalition efforts to maintain operational security had failed, and many insurgents had fled the area before the attack began.

This is undoubtedly true. The *Times* was not making anything up. There was minimal contact with the enemy because at least some—if not most—knew we were coming. Even if there were no "loose lips," it is incredibly difficult to hide the movement of thousands of men and hundreds of machines through the open desert. FOB Normandy was suddenly overwhelmed with a flood of soldiers. Helicopters were clattering overhead all hours of the day and night. Al Qaeda leaders had to know *something* was going on.

Yet escape (for some, or even for many) does not represent a victory for the enemy. We were long past the point of believing that any set-piece battle will be decisive in this war. Instead, we are in the middle of a long process known as "clear and hold." Success is not defined by the number of insurgents killed (though always nice) but by the number of cities, towns, and villages rendered steadily more secure, more "normal."

The surge hadn't succeeded just because we put more boots on the ground, it succeeded in large part because it coincided with more capable Iraqi security forces and the explosive growth of local "Sons of Iraq" citizen groups who provided their own security after al Qaeda was driven out.

Before the surge, before the improvement in the Iraqi Army and police, and before the emergence of the Sons of Iraq, it would constitute far more of a setback if significant numbers of insurgents escaped the net. Once we cleared, we didn't have enough forces to hold, our tactics wouldn't even permit us to stay in place, and insurgents were able to filter right back into the communities they had just left. Now, even if they escape, they have much more difficulty coming back—the vacuum is being filled by Iraqis.

Using the personal weapons they're allowed under Iraqi law and employed by sheikhs who receive American money, the Sons of Iraq typically offer their members a living wage and fill the vacuum left by departing al Qaeda militants. When al Qaeda tries to filter back into society, they often find themselves outnumbered by the councils, and (thanks to American and Iraqi deep pockets) the sheikhs can offer more money to wavering villagers than the insurgents could have. Since the money comes to the men from sheikhs instead of directly from American troops, we strengthen the authority and credibility of friendly local leaders. Within months, the Sons of Iraq were supposed to be absorbed into the Iraqi police—providing permanent employment with Iraqi (and not American) funding.

This is the essence of COIN, the acronym for the Army's counterinsurgency doctrine. We no longer merely sweep through, but we hold the ground for as long as it takes for competent local authorities to establish—and maintain—order. On the ground level, this means our guys spend day after day, week after week, and sometimes month after month living out of tiny combat outposts, sleeping in the backs of their vehicles, and walking the same dusty streets of the same dusty villages. It's not a good life, but the results are impressive. As my friend Captain Robison said, "COIN sucks, but it works."

At the end of the operation, the Diyala River valley would be cleared of al Qaeda. Iraqi forces would be in place to hold the area and secure the gains we'd made, and those insurgents who left would have one less safe haven. As al Qaeda's safe havens disappear and its supply lines grow more tenuous, it loses men. It's tough to recruit and train while on the run.

At Fallujah and elsewhere, al Qaeda and other insurgent groups felt strong enough to challenge us head-on. Now they slip away in dwindling numbers, hoping to inflict just a few casualties and live to fight another day.

All of this sounds deceptively simple, but the reality is hard, brutal, and frequently confused. Our squadron commander and his troop commanders orchestrate a complex and multifaceted fight that can feature tank main gun fire one moment and tea with a local sheikh the next. The challenge of defending a population *from* insurgents when those insurgents live *within* the population is immense.

Early on the afternoon of January 10, you could almost feel our guys breathe a sigh of relief. One night with no contact was one thing, but a full day, then night, then most of another day was quite another. We were moving from our blocking positions and clearing our own areas, moving from house to house. Three more major weapons caches were located and destroyed. Citizens were coming forward to volunteer to start Sons of Iraq groups in their own neighborhoods. Things were going well.

And then...

Less than two miles from our position, ten men from 2nd Brigade entered a house—just like they'd done dozens of times already that day and hoped to do dozens more times. But this one was booby-trapped with hundreds of pounds of explosives. The blast echoed all the way to the FOB.

Six men died. Four were catastrophically injured. Just like that, an entire squad was wiped out—the worst single-day loss for American soldiers in months.

Our squadron operations officer, Major Cam Cantlon, got the news first. After swearing at the top of his lungs and taking a moment to gather himself in his personnel carrier, he called us to huddle around him.

"Brigade just lost six men in a booby-trapped house. Four VSIs ['VSI' stands for 'very serious injury']. You know the drill. The whole FOB is on an information blackout while they notify next of kin. We can't shut down our satellite because it controls all our comms, so I'm giving each of you a direct order: No communication home. Not until I lift the ban. Are we clear?"

"Ai-ee-yah."

And with that, we went back to work.

That al Qaeda strike didn't slow down the clearing operation for anything more than an hour or two. It did not allow a single terrorist to escape, because our blocking positions were never threatened. It just killed men without accomplishing any greater tactical or strategic purpose.

So, at the end of this indescribably sad day, more of Iraq was freed from al Qaeda, more Iraqis volunteered to hold their own country, but six men will never see their families again. Is the glass half empty? Or is it half full? I suppose, from a purely military perspective, it is half full. More than half full.

But not for six American families. And I wouldn't blame the *New York Times* for leading with that story the next day. We'd choose another day to insist they report the good news.

Some days are just too sad to spin. And I couldn't talk to Nancy for consolation. It had now been eleven days since I'd last heard her voice.

And then I got news that I'd go outside the wire. FOB Normandy has two levels of security—an inner belt that surrounds the American forces, and an outer belt that surrounds a neighboring Iraqi Army base. Both the American FOB and the Iraqi FOB were considered "secure," so you weren't really outside the wire until outside the Iraqi FOB. Even though I acted like I wasn't nervous, the prospect scared me when—on day ten of Raider Harvest—our squadron operations officer, Major Cantlon, asked me to accompany him on a kerosene delivery mission to Mansuriyat al Jabal. The town had not quite been fully cleared of al Qaeda, but its people were poor, and the nights had grown quite cold. The temperature had plunged to twenty-five degrees, and the villagers' simple mud or stone homes often lacked any kind of glass or other covering for their windows. With no kerosene to heat their homes or cook their meals, the villagers were in desperate shape. So we decided to risk a fuel delivery.

Major Cantlon made a last-minute decision to include me in the mission, and I'm glad for that. All my life I've been an insomniac, and spending much of the night dwelling on the dangers of the next day's mission was not my idea of a good time. I much preferred learning I was going about ninety seconds before the convoy rolled out. That gave me just enough time to grab my weapon, throw on my body armor (I always acted like it was lighter than it was), and jump into the back left seat of the lead Humvee in the convoy.

Missions gave me the opportunity to see our troopers do their jobs. As JAG officers, we are often called upon to evaluate the legality of a soldier's actions at a checkpoint, or during humanitarian missions, or during convoys, but many Army lawyers have never really seen these things in a wartime environment. By seeing the reality, I better understood a soldier's choices.

It's one thing to hear a soldier say, "I was manning a checkpoint, and a vehicle came around the corner at a high rate of speed. He was 150 meters off and approaching fast," then evaluate the decision to shoot or not shoot from my comfortable office chair. It's quite another to hear that same account and know what 150 meters looks like *and feels like* in an actual combat environment. If I was to serve these guys effectively, I had to know about their real lives.

For me, rolling outside the wire was the most extraordinary of many extraordinary experiences in the war. It was a multistep process. The convoy was always no less than three vehicles, and each of the vehicles *had* to be armored. We weren't permitted to leave the FOB in an unarmored vehicle. My vehicle today was the infamous up-armored Humvee—a ridiculously cramped, slow, overloaded, and vulnerable method of transport.

Once the three-vehicle convoy was assembled, we conducted our radio checks and started the slow drive through the FOB to the exterior gate.

Just before we left the Iraqi FOB, we went "weapons red," which meant locking and loading both my M4 rifle and my M9 pistol. Both weapons were kept on "safe" (we didn't put the weapons on "fire" unless we actually intended to fire), but we were otherwise ready to respond to enemy contact at a moment's notice.

There wasn't much conversation in the Humvee as we rolled down the road. We were all too busy scrutinizing every mound of dirt, every bump in the road, and every pile of trash (and there was trash everywhere) for IEDs. If the truck's gunner was alert, he also moved his machine gun to face the most likely threats—a stand of trees here, a clump of houses there.

On this day, our trip was mercifully short. After only a few minutes, I saw the comforting view of an enormous M1A2 Main Battle Tank blocking the roadway. We had reached the kerosene fueling point. Soldiers from Sabre Squadron's Grim Troop had already cordoned the area, and now hundreds of villagers were streaming from the village to the kerosene fueler, which we had parked inside a stone courtyard.

Although it was impossible to provide airtight security, the Grim troopers did the best they could. With two interpreters shouting instructions, the villagers were lined up in a long (and thick) line just on the outside of the courtyard. The tankers scanned the crowd with their optical sights while the combat camera crew embedded with Grim Troop used the high-power lenses on their cameras to look at each of the hundreds of individuals in line. We knew al Qaeda was still in the town, and we thought there was a good chance that some were in line.

As I was anxiously scanning the crowd, trying to appear anything but anxious, a medic walked up behind me and said, "Yep, I'd be surprised if AQI doesn't try to blow up this line. It's just too good of a target."

He was right. There had been a sharp increase in suicide attacks over the last few weeks, and we knew that al Qaeda was attempting to intimidate the locals so that they wouldn't trust us or give us information. What better way to deter our interaction with the locals than to blow our kerosene fuel mission sky high.

There was another problem. We didn't have enough kerosene for eight hundred people. We could probably serve five hundred, but not eight hundred. So how do you determine who gets the kerosene and who doesn't? The line was too fluid to use as a fair measuring stick, with the young men pushing and elbowing their way to the front, sometimes shoving women, children, and the elderly farther and farther back. Tempers flared, and the line started swaying as hundreds of people fought to move up.

I turned to the medic. "I think I'd prefer a riot over a suicide bombing, but I don't really want either one."

Because the line was hopelessly scrambled, Captain Robert Green, Grim Troop's commander, took firm action. Ignoring the strong shoving past the weak, he made a simple declaration: women and children first.

It was shocking to me how many small children were there with no apparent adult supervision. Carrying empty kerosene jugs that were in some cases almost as large as the kids themselves, they waited toward the end of the line. Grim troopers walked up and gently tugged them to the front. The women came right behind them. Clad almost exclusively in black *hijab*s, they avoided eye contact with the soldiers as they moved to the front.

At first, the line moved quickly. Then one of the pumps broke. We could only serve three at a time.

"This is going to take a while." I was not pleased.

"All the more time they have to blow this mother sky high," replied the optimistic medic.

But everything went smoothly. After the small children filled their containers, troopers helped them carry their heavy burdens until their parents appeared from the village and took the fuel the rest of the way home. The women hoisted the huge loads on their shoulders and staggered home.

I helped one little boy who couldn't have been more than four years old. He was holding an empty twenty-gallon container, and I led him to the fueler. He stood quietly as we filled the container with a fuel load that easily weighed more than he did. I carried it back out of the courtyard for him, looking for his parents, when he suddenly burst into tears and started wailing. *Oh no*, I thought, *he thinks I'm stealing his fuel.*

At that moment, a black-robed woman stepped from the crowd and pulled down his pants. The boy peed.

And peed.

And peed.

"Guess he had to go," said our medic.

"Yup. When they got to go, they got to go." I handed the kerosene to his mother (without making eye contact), and they walked hand in hand back to the village.

Nothing happened that day. No. Wait. That's what the mainstream media would say. To them, something only happens in Iraq when there are explosions, firefights, and torn bodies. Actually, a lot happened that day. We met the immediate heating and cooking needs of five hundred desperately poor people. We entered into two contracts to employ the men of that same town in a school renovation project and a canal cleanup project. And maybe, just maybe, we built enough trust to allow one of those villagers to tell us where the last al Qaeda holdouts were—so we could free that town of their terror once and for all.

I was always in a *fabulous* mood when I got back in the wire. I was tense and alert the entire time I was out. I wouldn't say I was afraid, necessarily (at least not all the time), but was definitely tense. All that tension would leave as soon as I heard the words "We're clear; safe your weapons." I'd clear my rifle and pistol, put the magazines back in my pouches, and feel like a normal human being again.

When we rolled back into the gate, I turned to Major Cantlon. "Do you want to hear my dream scenario for the Super Bowl?"

He's a farm boy from Wisconsin, and he loves his Packers—even to the point of once wearing a cheesehead into Veterans Stadium in Philadelphia, home of the nastiest and most violent fans in the NFL.

"Let's hear it, David."

"Brett Favre throws the winning touchdown pass with no time on the clock and then announces his retirement to the crowd at the trophy awards ceremony. It would be one of the ultimate sports moments of our lifetimes. It would have it all—the scrappy underdog knocking off the evil sports superpower, the aging legend enjoying one last moment of greatness, and the perfect retirement, the retirement Jordan should have had in 1998."

"That would be nice, but I'll just take the win."

"Agreed."

It was eighteen days since I'd last heard Nancy's voice.

11

DETAINEES

David

ON JANUARY 24, my thirty-ninth birthday, an al Qaeda terrorist almost threw up on me.

For the first three weeks of Operation Raider Harvest, I did many things, but not the one thing I was brought there to do—work with detainees. The problem of detainees has bedeviled coalition forces almost since the beginning of the war. The abuse scandals (like at Abu Ghraib) are well known—and thankfully rare. Less well known is the simple legal nightmare created by the detention of tens of thousands of suspected insurgents during combat operations.

No one can be detained indefinitely without legal process—not even in Iraq. Yet our soldiers are not cops, and our officers are not detectives. So gathering the appropriate amount of evidence on each detainee is an enormous challenge. Soldiers on a raid don't necessarily want (or have time) to sit down, draw out sketches of the site, jot down at least the beginnings of a sworn statement, and take the multiple pictures required by Iraqi courts. Police work in the United States, even in the most dangerous areas, is not conducted under true "combat conditions," yet we often ask our troops to provide *more* information than police back home... while under threat of hostile fire.

The process works something like this. Each time the coalition detains a person, he's brought back to the FOB and a "packet" is compiled. The packet contains no less than two sworn statements, evidence documents, apprehension documents, medical documents, pictures of the detainee, and pictures and sketches of the site where the detainee was apprehended (including pictures of any weapons and contraband). If everything is not done in exactly the right way, Iraqi courts will tend to release the detainee, regardless of the overall strength of the evidence.

Since our soldiers rotate home every twelve to fifteen months (while the legal process can take much longer), the packet becomes the critical part of convicting and imprisoning terrorists. Live testimony of coalition soldiers can be difficult to obtain, so the statements and the pictures sometimes have to tell the entire tale. While our guys have been trained in writing sworn statements, taking the pictures, and compiling the packets, that training occurred months ago. Early legal review allows mistakes to be caught, and it can also allow early decisions on continued detention or release.

That's why they brought me. I helped the soldiers write the statements, and correct mistakes in paperwork, and gave a preliminary legal opinion of the lawfulness of the detention itself. However, few JAGs actually work at the battalion level, so legal review typically happens up to twenty-four hours after the packet has been put together, after mistakes have already been made—mistakes that are difficult to correct.

Acting on the guess that Raider Harvest might be "another Fallujah," it made perfect sense to bring me along. If we brought in dozens of detainees, it would be more than a full-time job working on intake and perfecting their packets.

When Sabre Squadron rolled out of FOB Caldwell, I was ready. I stayed up late into the night until all initial reports came in.

No detainees.

I finally went to sleep (but with strict instructions to wake me in case we captured any insurgents) and slept till early the next morning.

No detainees.

No detainees all day.

No detainees the next day.

Or the next.

Or that entire week.

Or the next week.

It quickly became apparent that Raider Harvest was more of a community-building operation than a major battle. We spent our days distributing rice, flour, and kerosene, contracting local work crews to improve the roads and schools, recruiting local citizens to join the Sons of Iraq, and building permanent bases for the Iraqi Army.

However, at the end of a miserable thirty-ninth birthday that featured a wet, drizzly day, marginal food, and no communication home, the call came. We had a detainee. And not just any detainee, but a terrorist multiple sources identified as an al Qaeda sniper. Sabre soldiers seized him easily enough—they stopped him at a checkpoint and checked his name against a list of known fugitives. According to the call on the radio, he had not resisted arrest and was "very scared."

I had our radio operator tell the guys I'd meet them at the FOB's entry control point (Army term for "gate") and ride with them into the detainee collection point (Army term for "jail"). I jumped up, made my way to the gate, and arrived just as the troopers pulled up in their Bradley Cavalry Fighting Vehicle. As it slowed to a stop, the turret commander jumped down.

"Good evening, sir. Do you want a ride to the DCP?"

"Sure thing. I'll jump in."

The back of a Cavalry Fighting Vehicle is incredibly cramped. Two people can sit on the primitive seats—and not comfortably. The seats are together on the left side of the vehicle, with gear typically stowed on the right. At the instant the ramp started to lower, I had a sudden thought. *The sniper is in there, with one of our guys guarding him. Where am I going to sit?*

When the ramp lowered, I took in the scene. There was the al Qaeda sniper, sitting on the seats to the left. Directly across from him was our trooper, squatting against the side of the Bradley. The sniper was wearing slippers, loose gray pants, a cardigan sweater (yes, a cardigan sweater), and a dirty white T-shirt. His head was down, and his hands were tied in front of him.

"Take a seat, Captain." The TC gestured at the sniper. "He'll scoot over."

I stepped in, and the sniper looked up at me. He looked terrified. As I got closer, I noticed that he was trembling. He also smelled like a man who'd never heard of "deodorant" or "showers." I sat down and pushed up against him, and he scooted over. We were sitting literally knee to knee.

"You good? I'm gonna close the ramp."

The ramp raised with a groan and closed with a clank, sealing us in as the Bradley lurched forward. The road was heavily rutted, and we were tossed around in the back of the vehicle. The sniper's eyes, I noticed, were rolling before they fixed on me.

He started talking, but I couldn't understand a word.

He tapped his own shoulder. I didn't understand what that meant.

Then he started moving his hands in front of his mouth.

"Do you need to eat?" I made a motion like I was putting food in my mouth. I've never been good at parlor games, yet here I was in a Bradley playing charades with an al Qaeda member.

He shook his head vigorously and started moving his hands away from his mouth.

"Vomit?"

"Do you need to..." I put both hands in front of my mouth, gestured like I was throwing up and made a loud noise like I was vomiting. "Do you need to...bleeaeaaaaahhhh!"

He nodded vigorously, and the trooper and I started frantically looking around the Bradley for a container, something—anything— that could catch his puke. I saw a Kevlar helmet but stopped myself before picking it up. Applying the Golden Rule, I wouldn't want someone to let al Qaeda puke in *my* helmet, so I wouldn't let al Qaeda puke in *their* helmet. But there was nothing else. I resigned myself to being right next to a terrorist as he ralphed all over the place.

"What do we do, sir?" The trooper with me didn't want to be tossed on either.

"I have no idea. Can we ask the driver to stop?"

The terrorist closed his eyes and started to moan softly.

"Oh crap...here we go."

At that moment, the Bradley lurched to a stop. The ramp started to groan again, and it lowered. The sniper started to look better, and I breathed a sigh of relief. The trooper and I jumped out as fast as we could, and the driver appeared with a blindfold.

"Let's cover his eyes and get him to the detainee collection point."

As the driver covered the sniper's eyes, I was struck by two things. First, during this process—and during the entire detention process that I witnessed—the detainee was treated with remarkable care. He was not handled roughly or even spoken to harshly. When he exited the vehicle, there was a hand on his head to make sure he didn't hurt himself—not a harsh grip like you see sometimes in the States when police shove suspects into squad cars. Rather, it was a gentle grip, like a person uses when they actually don't want someone hurt. They led him by the arm across rocky ground, almost in the same way someone might guide a blind family member across similar terrain.

Second, I was struck by my own feelings toward the man. Perhaps it was the very human act of getting nauseated in the Bradley, or perhaps it was his obvious fear (he kept shaking), or perhaps it was his obvious poverty (his clothes were threadbare and looked as if they hadn't been changed for days). Suddenly, I felt sad. I didn't feel like he should be released. I didn't suddenly hate the idea of capturing other human beings. (In other words, there was no stereotypical "movie moment" where I had a profound epiphany about the nature of man and the horror of war.) I just felt sad. He was, in all probability, a terrorist. Malicious and vicious, no doubt, and perhaps even deserving the death penalty. But he was also pathetic.

In the months that followed—as one detainee became fifty and fifty became a hundred and a hundred became two hundred—I would see with my own eyes the horrific "handiwork" of some of these terrorists and would no longer be saddened. If anything, I sometimes regretted that we detained them instead of killing them.

The next day, we received a bit of good news. His identity as a sniper was confirmed by multiple sources, and higher headquarters complimented our "packet." It looked like our sniper was going to stay behind bars or perhaps swing from the end of a rope.

Four days later, we captured a second detainee, but this guy was definitely *not* a sniper. Acting in response to a BOLO (a command to "be on the lookout") on a silver Honda van that belonged to a known al Qaeda terrorist, our guys stopped a middle-aged man driving a silver minivan.

When our guys searched the van, they noticed that he had multiple identification cards, and we made the call to bring him in for further questioning. This time, I was slightly delayed in departing and missed the indescribable pleasure of the backseat ride with the detainee. I arrived just as the Bradley pulled up, followed by a tank . . . and followed by a silver *Hyundai* (not Honda) minivan. Rather than leave his van on the side of the road—where it would surely be stripped by the locals—one of our troopers risked his life (minivans are not exactly well armored) to drive it back to the FOB.

The minivan was full of flour for his family, and—it turns out—we had stopped him just outside his home. As we led him out of the Bradley, he wasn't shaking with fear, nor was he resisting. He was completely calm.

The section sergeant walked up to me and said, in a low voice, "Sir, I don't think this guy is bad."

"Why not?"

"Well, he didn't have any weapons, his hands came up negative for any kind of explosive or gunpowder residue, he's not on our lists, he says he's never been detained, and was super nice to us when we questioned him—even said he doesn't blame us for doing our job. Then his family came out and started to plead his case. I feel kinda bad, but you know—the BOLO and the IDs . . ."

"Don't worry about it. You did the right thing. If there's nothing there, we'll release him."

When we walked into the DCP, the MPs put him in a cell, and we began to process his paperwork. His van wasn't a Honda, and the man we were looking for was twenty-five years old. Our detainee was forty-one (but his weather-beaten face looked fifty or older). The "multiple identifications" turned out to be a driver's license, an expired ID card, a current ID card, and a special pass for taxi drivers to leave and enter Kirkuk. Everything was in order.

The NCO on duty asked me what I thought. For me, it was an easy call. There was no reason to even hold him overnight for questioning. I thought of his family, no doubt terrified at home. The more I was around him, the more I could see that he was just maintaining a façade of composure. Occasionally he would turn his head and quietly weep.

"I'm going to recommend release. Let's send my recommendation up for approval."

"Roger that, sir. Might take a while. Better get some chow before the chow hall closes."

As I walked to chow, I said a silent prayer for the man—that we were making the right decision, and that if we were, he would not be embittered by his brief captivity.

The decision came quickly. Release him. The interpreter and I walked back to his cell after dinner, as the MPs gathered and inventoried his personal belongings.

"Tell him that he'll be released to his family tonight."

The interpreter gave him the news, and he began to cry.

"He says, thank you," said the interpreter. "He has a sick mother, and she is afraid for him."

I know now that I was naïve (I saw many hard-bitten terrorists summon tears when convenient), but his words and gratitude touched my heart. "Tell him that our soldiers have been doing free medical clinics, and that he should bring his mother to the clinic." I pulled a piece of paper from my folder. "Also tell him our soldiers had to drive his van over rough ground to get it here. If his van is damaged, we'll make it right."

As the interpreter spoke, the man put his hands out, refusing to take the card.

"He says that any damage was meant to be."

"Inshallah?" I said, using the Arabic term for "God's will."

"Yes, inshallah."

"Tell him that it is important to us that we make things right."

She explained the situation to him again, and this time he accepted the card, with thanks. We gave him his belt (detainees' belts are removed so they can't use them as nooses), catalogued his belongings, and gave him a brief medical exam. By the time we finished with all the paperwork and mandatory procedures, it was almost

11:00 p.m., well past the curfew. He was going to have to be es-corted home.

As I heard the roar of the approaching tank escort, I talked to him one last time.

"These tanks will escort you home. A soldier will drive your van until you are off the base, then you will get your van back. Until you get off the base, your hands will be tied and you'll be blindfolded. After you get off the base and start driving your van, stay very, very close to these tanks and don't leave them until you get home. They'll protect you. But if you leave them, they can't protect you and the po-lice might arrest you for staying out after curfew. Do you understand all this?"

He nodded as the troopers bound his hands once again. Within moments, the convoy of the three gigantic armored vehicles and one dusty Hyundai van rolled off into the darkness.

As we watched them roll off, the MP beside me said, "It sure would suck if he actually turned out to be bad and we let him go."

"Yep, and it would suck if he turned out to be good and we held him. But we're not God." I paused for a moment and then said, "That's why I love the law."

"What?"

"I can't look into his heart and know the truth, so we have to go by evidence. The evidence makes the decision for us. Was there enough evidence to hold him?"

"No, sir."

"Right. So the decision was made. The law exists because lawyers aren't perfect—even though many of them think they are. We can't trust any person's judgment completely—no matter how good their instincts or how good their intentions. So every time we follow the law, we're implicitly admitting we just don't know everything. We trust a process."

"Makes sense." The MP walked off—probably trying to escape my dime-store philosophizing—so I turned and walked back to our dusty command post alone.

I had not spoken to Nancy in twenty-nine days.

12

"MAJ"

David

EVEN AFTER BEING MOBILIZED for almost three months, I was still about 91.2 percent civilian. Routine events for my friends were remarkable to me. While they walked past Apache helicopters landing fifty feet away, I just stood there in slack-jawed awe. While they hardly glanced at the M1A2 Main Battle Tanks that surround our headquarters, I leapt at the chance to climb into one and look through the thermal sights. While they sat around and swapped combat stories from their first deployment ("Hey, remember when I was treating that wounded insurgent, and he tried to bite me while he was bleeding to death?" "You remember when they were shooting down on us from rooftops, and we were so close I shot them with my pistol?"), I look at even the most routine mission as a heart-pounding test of will.

As a consequence, one of my roles on staff was to be the resident "normal guy." I'd remind the guys that literally everything about this experience was extraordinary—including them. When everyone you know is a combat veteran, being a combat veteran doesn't seem like a big deal. I was the guy that gave them perspective.

One cold January day, I took a big step away from the civilian world by going on a "presence patrol" through Mansuriyat al Jabal, a town we just called "MAJ." In other words, I spent the day walking through a formerly (and perhaps currently) al Qaeda–infested village with Lieutenant Colonel Calvert, Major Cantlon, and eight soldiers from the squadron commander's personal security detail.

"There are some interesting political conversations out there," the squadron commander said as he prepared to wrap up some construction projects in the city. "You'll like it."

I put on my body armor, doubting the Iraqis would be that interested in Republican politics. As I performed a functions check on my M4, I had a soon-to-be-familiar thought: *If I live through this, then I'll be glad I did it.* So I sat in the back of a Bradley as we trundled off to the town—the same town we had delivered kerosene to just a few short days earlier.

There are two things that strike you about rural Iraqi towns. First, as I've noted before, they are mired in poverty. The houses are often little more than mud huts. Garbage is thrown in the streets, and small sewage canals cut through the back alleys (and sometimes the middle of streets and sidewalks), giving the entire place a quite distinctive stench. Electricity flickers on and off—mostly off—and the wealthier parts of town are marked by the constant hum of generators. The people themselves, however, are often well dressed, and on occasion you'll see the distinctly strange sight of a new-looking BMW or a nice minivan parked in front of a mud hut.

The second thing that strikes you—literally—is the amazing number of children running unsupervised in the streets. As soon as we stepped out of our vehicles and started to walk across the damaged bridge that linked the town to Grim Troop's combat outpost, the children came at us in waves. Almost immediately there were at least twenty, and they were followed by twenty more, and twenty more. Finally, I lost count.

By the time we got fifty yards into the town, at least a hundred kids surrounded our small patrol. I was relieved. From everything I've heard, the absence of kids can be a good indicator of a looming attack. If the kids are swarming you, everything is fine. If their parents shoo them inside, watch out.

The kids wanted soccer balls and pencils. They'd push past each other, yelling, "Mister! Mister! Football! Mister! Pencil! Mister!" Then they'd ask your name. "Mister, name? Mister, name?"

"David."

"Mister, Bandar."

"Hi, Bandar."

"Mister. Babies?"

"Do I have babies?" (I was asked this dozens of times.) "I have two babies."

"Mister David two babies!"

And so it went. The same boys would ask the same questions and get the same answers—again and again. Soon they started chanting at us. "Football! Football!" or "Pencil! Pencil!" Then they would chant whatever we said.

"Be quiet!"

"Quiet! Quiet!"

"Stop!"

"Stop! Stop!"

My friend Jon always enjoyed going back and forth with the kids, particularly when they laughed at his name...apparently "Jon" sounds funny to Iraqi ears. The typical exchange would go like this:

"Mister! Name?"

"Jon."

"Jone? Jone?" (Uproarious laughter follows.)

Jon is perhaps the single most outgoing person I've ever met in my life. Every situation is funny to him, and every situation is dramatic. He has virtually no ear for diplomacy (he one time told his interpreter to tell an Iraqi contractor that the quality of his work was "so bad that it makes me hate my life"). So Jon decided one day to trip them up a bit, and the exchange had a twist:

"Mister! Name?"

"Mohammed!"

The kid did such a double take that Jon laughed out loud. So he took a step farther and decided to broadcast his "name" far and wide. He lifted his arm and yelled, "I am Mohammed! I am Mohammed!"

As he stood before dozens of immediately silent Muslim children, with their Muslim parents now staring slack-jawed from doorways, Jon suddenly realized that perhaps they weren't getting his humor. Red-faced, he put his arms down, lowered his head, and walked as quickly (and humbly) as he could to his destination. Fortunately no one was harmed in the making of that "joke."

But that was a different day. This day, we didn't risk offending an entire town.

Accompanied by the swarm of kids, we approached a girls' school that we had hired a contractor to repair. We wanted to inspect his work before we made the final payment. The gate was closed and locked. A little boy walked up to us and said, "Ali Baba?" "Ali Baba" is apparently the universal Iraqi term for doing something, umm, unlawful, and he meant that he could climb the wall and open the gate from the inside. We used it as a verb.

"Yeah, Ali Baba that gate."

That was all the encouragement that the boy—and his hundred closest friends—needed. "Ali Baba! Ali Baba!" They were chanting and clapping as five or six boys scampered up and over the wall. The gate opened, and we walked into the courtyard, then into the school, leaving the swarm of children behind.

We were in the quiet, freshly painted school building for less than five minutes before the headmaster and his contractor arrived. As the contractor and our operations officer stepped aside to discuss final payment, the squadron commander made small talk with the headmaster. He called me over.

"This is our lawyer. He used to be a teacher also."

The headmaster looked at me with interest. Through the interpreter, he asked me what I taught.

"I taught law school."

"You taught lawyers?" He seemed puzzled. "At university?"

"Yes, but in America, people go to law school after university." I kept it short and sweet, figuring he didn't need to know that I taught at Cornell, in upstate New York, where my wife was perpetually cold.

He still seemed puzzled. "If you were a teacher, why did you become a soldier?"

I gave him the first answer that popped in my mind. "To help the people of Iraq." (Honestly, I was completely ashamed of the answer. I sounded ridiculous, like a politician throwing out a sound bite— "Why did you go into politics?" "Because I love children.")

But sometimes even sound bites have meaning. He dropped his head and said something quietly.

"What did he say?" I asked the interpreter.

He said, "Praise be to God, and may God bless you."

We left the school moments later and were swarmed by the children once again. The chanting was almost deafening. As we walked by the soccer field, a ball came rolling toward us. To the kids' infinite delight, the squadron commander stopped the ball with his boot, lined up, and kicked it in the general direction of the goal.

Laughing, we turned away and started to walk down a narrow street heading toward the newer area of town.

Then a rock the size of a softball whizzed by my head.

Instantly, we raised our weapons, looking for the source of the rock. The kids froze, and some scattered. Then another rock flew by. Then another missed the platoon sergeant's head by mere inches. Seeing the look of fury on his face, the rest of the kids scattered in every direction. Within seconds, the once lively streets were deserted. My heart was pounding.

"Did you see who threw that rock?" The squadron commander was angry.

"Yes, sir!" The platoon sergeant was staring straight at a teenage boy sprinting about fifty meters away. "That older kid in white."

"Well, let's take him to his father."

"Yes, sir!" Several troopers dashed forward to grab him, and I jogged along behind, scanning the rooftops for any sign of snipers. We passed a narrow alley, and I saw three military-aged men, wearing all black, glaring at me. The streets were still empty.

As we ran, the young boy stayed about fifty meters ahead. Every few moments, he'd look back, see us still following him, and run harder. A thought ran through my mind: *Baited ambush.* But it was no such thing. He was just a scared kid, and he ran straight back to his house. Seconds after he ran through the door of his small mud hut, the squadron commander was knocking on his door.

His father opened the door to the sight of a lieutenant colonel in the United States Army and his entire personal security detail standing at his doorstep. If I wasn't still fearing for my life and trying to catch my breath after my run/jog through town, I would've laughed.

The Iraqi's eyes were wide with surprise and fear, and his son (who looked to be thirteen or fourteen years old) was huddled behind him, almost as if he was trying to hide in the folds of his dishdasha.

"Sir, your son has disrespected me," said the squadron commander.

"Surely not." The man was panicked. The boy's mother appeared, glaring at us through the door.

"He threw a rock at my men. Do you believe that's acceptable?"

At that moment, the boy spoke up. He was speaking rapidly until his mother smacked him on the side of the head.

"It is not acceptable. I am sorry." The father glared at his son, and the mother smacked him on the side of the head again.

The squadron commander looked at the family for a moment. No one said anything. I was trying to monitor the conversation even as I kept scanning the streets. People were starting to come back out of their houses. I saw a child or two peek around the corner.

"Thank you for your apology. Is there anything we can do for you?"

I couldn't hear the response as I moved farther away from the door to get a better view of a nearby alley. But there was quite a stir in the house, and after a few moments the father appeared again, holding a little girl with deformed legs. His daughter.

The squadron commander signaled for the medic to come over. The medic carefully and gently touched her legs.

"Sir, I think it's a birth defect. I can't do anything. Can we send her to our doctor?"

The squadron commander scribbled on a piece of paper and handed it to the young father. "Sir, this is a note from me that will allow you to bring your daughter to our base to see one of our doctors. I don't think there's anything we can do, but you can get good medical care and good advice."

The man was extremely grateful. The tension was over, and the children were back. And then, almost as if on cue, the sick and the lame from the village came pouring out of their homes. Our medic was overwhelmed, as he was suddenly treating terrible burns, hacking coughs, and high fevers. The medic looked at each patient while the kids chanted and played and we pulled security.

After about thirty minutes, Lieutenant Colonel Calvert walked up to me and said, "Well, lawyer, should we head back?"

"If you'd like to, sir."

We retraced our steps, heading back to our vehicles. As we walked, the squadron commander stopped and talked to virtually every shop owner. I walked up to a dusty storefront that had some bread. I opened up my wallet and asked, "Can I buy bread with American dollars?"

The shopkeepers didn't understand what I said, but they did understand me gesturing at their goods with money in my hands. I paid (way too much) for a few pieces of Iraqi bread, and they gave me change in dinars. As soon as the money hit my hand, I thought of Austin. He loves "foreign money," and one of the things he asked me the night before I left was, "Daddy, can you bring me some Iraqi money?" Well, now I had some.

I walked back to our vehicles feeling faintly ridiculous holding an M4 with a plastic bag full of groceries wrapped around my wrist and a big smile on my face. As I looked around at the dusty Iraqi village, the chanting children, and our small patrol of heavily armed soldiers, I had one thought: *If Nancy could only see me now.*

Climbing into the vehicle, I was struck by the way the squadron commander handled the rock-throwing incident—in a way that firmly responded to improper action but still respected the dignity of the family by going through the boy's father. I was also struck by his immediate transition away from disciplining the boy to caring for the little girl.

I didn't know how many "hearts and minds" we'd win while we were there. In fact, most of the guys were deeply cynical about the prospect of truly winning over anyone. But I'm not sure that the squadron commander had "hearts and minds" foremost in his mind as he did what he did. I think he helped that little girl simply because it was the right thing to do. I was proud to serve with him.

When we got back inside the vehicle, and as the back ramp of the Bradley clanged shut, I let out a small sigh of relief. I felt safer there—even though we still had to drive back to the FOB—than I did on the streets. I sat in the back with two privates as we cleared our weapons and waited for the convoy to roll out.

We kept waiting.

For two hours.

It turns out that a political conversation happened after all. Just as he was getting into his Humvee, the squadron commander was stopped by a local sheikh who went on a tirade about the Iraqi central government and apparently asked my commander if he could appeal to "Premier Bush" to remove the Iraqi prime minister and replace him with someone competent.

In the meantime—while the squadron commander talked politics without me—the two privates in our vehicle were carrying on their own interesting conversation, about strippers.

"Hey, sir, you should come back to Fort Hood with us! There's some incredible strippers in Killeen."

"Really?"

"Yep, and the bartenders have lists of all the strippers that are hookers."

"Okay..."

"Oh yeah. We'll take you out when we get home...show you a good time."

"I don't think my wife would like that."

"Sir! She doesn't have to know!"

Finally we started to move, and the privates nodded off to sleep. Apparently, lawyers are boring conversationalists. I leaned back and closed my eyes as well, praying for the sleeping troopers next to me, for the little girl with birth defects, and for myself—thanking God for the experience of a day in Mansuriyat al Jabal.

I hadn't heard Nancy's voice in thirty-one days.

Finally, after thirty-five days, Raider Harvest was over. I'd had several missions outside the wire, spent night after cold night in a tent (I hadn't packed my warmest sleep gear, stupidly thinking, *I'm in Iraq. It's not cold in Iraq*), and lived day after long day in a tiny, cramped command post.

We road marched back to FOB Caldwell in a gigantic line of armored vehicles. I rode in Lieutenant Mike Medders's Bradley. Mike was (at that time) Grim Troop's executive officer and one of my favorite people in the squadron. A big guy—a former high school football star in northern Ohio—he had an easy smile, always seemed to be laughing, and just *loved* the fact that he was carrying "the lawyer" in his vehicle.

"Sir, if we get any contact on the way back, I'll just drop the ramp and you take care of it, okay?"

"You know it."

Mike was my tour guide on an almost two-hour trip across Diyala province. As I looked at the countryside through the Bradley's optics, he pointed out Sunni towns, Shiite towns, flags supporting the Shiite warlord Muqtada al Sadr, flags supporting Sunni political parties and leaders, old IED craters, and potential ambush points. And through it all—through the deadly serious business of a road march through hostile territory—he supplemented his commentary with wisecracks and a near-constant laugh. This was Mike's first deployment, but already, less than three months in, he knew what he was doing—and he was doing it with an indefatigable goodwill.

I have to confess, I wasn't as cheerful as Mike. My will could be defeated, and two hours of bouncing in the back of a Bradley made me grumpy and more than a little nauseated, but all that faded away when the distinctive ugly buildings and walls of Forward Operating Base Caldwell came into view.

Home.

After we cleared our weapons, I profusely thanked Mike for the safe ride, bounded out the back, and ran to my room as fast as seventy-five pounds of gear and a fifty-pound pack would allow. As I staggered up the stairs, Leo passed me on his way down—wearing a brand-new mustache—and greeted me by simply saying, "Dave, I blew up your Dustbuster."

I'd get upset about that later (that Dustbuster was a prized possession!), but for now all I could think of was three names: Nancy, Camille, and Austin.

I powered up my computer, connected to our precious satellite Internet, and signed on to instant messenger. Nancy was on (it was early morning in the States), and I clicked to video chat. By a miracle, it worked, and within seconds I saw her grainy picture, two little blond kids with bright smiles right behind her, and—most importantly—heard their cheerful voices.

"Hi, Sweety."

"Hi, Daddy!"

"Hey, guys!" I responded. "Kids, your daddy had quite a month!"

As I said those words, I felt different. I felt a little less like a rookie. Perhaps even like a veteran.

But I was wrong. I still had no idea what war was. I would soon learn.

13

A SAAB STORY

Nancy

THE FIRST FEW DAYS WHEN I didn't hear from David, I was beside myself with worry. Then, slowly, I realized he was probably safe. If he'd been hurt or killed, I'd know it very quickly—at least that's the way it happens on television. When I didn't hear anything, I knew that he had to be on a mission, perhaps a big one.

I watched the news very carefully, and, sure enough, I began to see stories of a new "offensive" in Diyala. I saw references to David's unit, and I knew he had to be somehow involved, though I secretly wondered why on earth they'd need their lawyer with them on these missions. So I prayed for his safety, kept sending my email messages, and kept working on my debt snowball.

One day, I noticed that he had logged onto iChat, and I almost cried with relief. I called the kids into the room, we turned on video chat, and were a family again—for a few moments. Soon—too soon— the picture flickered and faded away. We were left with text chat, and we did our best to catch up. I asked him about his month, and he was noncommittal. He asked me about mine, and I filled up the screen with stories of Austin's basketball league, Camille's Girl Scout adventures, and a few tidbits of church gossip. But while I filled the screen, I didn't tell him everything. It had been a month, after all, and I wasn't ready to tell him about my new financial endeavors. Part of Dave Ramsey's "baby steps to financial freedom" is to use what-ever money you have in savings to pay off the debts, and David would completely worry if he knew I'd used most of our "cushion" money in our savings account to pay off debts. In fact, I didn't tell him any of it. A newfound financial stability would be my gift to him upon return, and things were working out nicely. I used the money I got from selling his Land Rover to pay other debts. And I didn't want to tell him that I'd just paid off the car.

Oddly, I was managing to pull off the "big things" but couldn't muster enough energy for the details of life. I'd never get hair appointments soon enough, for example.

"I need to schedule appointments for Austin and Camille... Really? Not for two weeks?"

I knew Jocinda at Studio 16 was popular among her Columbia clientele from the first time my friend Kim suggested her.

"There's always a two-week wait," she said, her perfectly styled blonde hair waving in the breeze. "So just schedule your appointment as you leave."

The very idea of committing to a hair appointment every month just seems so limiting and unnecessarily binding. After all, who knows when you might need another trim? It's not like you can predict these things.

I didn't notice the kids' hair until the day I looked across the breakfast table and saw the blonde-haired, blue-eyed version of Crystal Gayle pass the milk to her brother, Cousin It. My friends noticed that the kids needed a haircut about three weeks before I did. Once, my friend Tabby picked up Austin for a playdate and almost took him to Fantastic Sams on the way back.

"The school *does* have a hair policy."

Boys at Zion Christian Academy must have their hair cut above their ears—no Zack and Cody mops allowed. Once, after neglecting to get him an appointment, I trimmed the hair above his ears to meet regulations, inadvertently giving him a mullet. Having learned from that experience, I now just waited—and waited—for an appointment.

But it wasn't just hair.

Every month, when I got unusually emotional, thought I was going to die, and almost admitted myself to the hospital, my friend Kim talked me off the ledge.

"It's just that time of the month for you."

"Already?"

"It catches you off guard every single time, doesn't it?" she asked.

"There's just no way to predict such things."

When something truly unexpected happened—say, the lightbulbs went out—I just counted on David to repair them next year when he returned. After all, the kids' hair looked better in the dark.

The deployment magnified my weaknesses and people like Kim and my friend Tabby felt the liberty to offer help in the areas I'd apparently let go. When I walked through the church doors, I was asked, "What can I do to help you while David's gone?"

I always demurred. After all, *some people* offer help to get credit for benevolent intentions while hoping I don't take their offer up. So I always had a quick smile and a polite decline. "I don't need my yard mowed, but thanks so much for offering." Strangely, they persisted. I'd have to provide a list of reasons why I didn't need my yard mowed or they'd haul the John Deere over.

"Really, I'll even babysit your kids if you need alone time," one lady said.

"I make great homemade bread," said another.

It became more work to refuse their help than to take it, which made me suspect there was much more going on than a simple desire to be helpful. Turns out, most people in my congregation and neighborhood didn't know anyone going through the separation of deployment. Participating in our lives, even if just by rolling dough or running errands, was a small way to show their support for the war effort. And really...who was I to deprive them of their patriotic duty?

One Sunday, after the kids and I had been sick for a week, I relented.

"Pastor Arch, can you come and get Goggo for me so I don't have to fool with him?"

"Travis, I need some prescriptions filled at the pharmacy—do you mind?"

"Terry, I saw the most amazing rugs on Craigslist...sure would hate it if they were sold before I (*cough cough*) felt better. Oh, and you'd need to run by an ATM and get cash."

At various times during the deployment, friends mowed my yard, moved furniture, fixed my garage door, changed lightbulbs—the ones you need ladders to reach—and set up the kids' new Wii. A professional landscaper approached me at church: "I drove by your house and wondered if you ever needed help trimming those unruly bushes." Since these were the very bushes I'd spent hours trimming the day before, I meekly accepted his help.

Gradually, in spite of myself, I started having the appearance of a well-maintained life. Although I didn't have a husband around, at least my garage door worked. Although Austin didn't have a dad to help build the pinewood derby car for Boy Scouts, at least my purse was full of gift cards from well-meaning friends. It might sound like cold comfort, but it was much more. Throughout history, Americans have supported the war effort by planting gardens, canning food, saving metal, conserving at home, and inventing new technology to help the troops. Now Americans have to flip to the second or third page of major newspapers before realizing a war is even going on. The battle rages somewhere across the globe, but—hey—can you believe that guy on *American Idol?* Our lives are almost completely uninterrupted, without inconvenience, without a real cost to average citizens. The only clues that we're a nation at war are the bumper stickers—the ones that lament the cost of the military when schools have to have bake sales, or the red, white, and blue "God Bless the Troops."

"Oriental chicken salad and two chicken fingers," I proudly ordered at Applebee's to go with one of so many gift cards. My wallet could barely contain them and had stretched out like tight pants on a cheap woman. The kids and I were getting food for a special treat, after a particularly difficult day. Not having any contact with David was wearing on me. The kids didn't know I hadn't heard from him, of course, but they sensed the anxiety. I handed the bags back to them, smiled, and headed home.

However, the car—which had a manual transmission—wouldn't go into reverse. Though I wasn't sure of the technical reasons for this malfunction, I was pretty sure it had something to do with the fact that I'd paid off the car. Why would a mother of two even drive a stickshift? you might be wondering. The number of cars with manual transmissions has plummeted every year. I'm not sure if David was trying to hold on to America's automotive past or trying to maintain a certain level of virility in our car purchases—after all, minivans don't come with a manual transmission. But since we got married, we always have had at least one stickshift.

I grabbed the black knob and tried to pull it down into reverse, but it seemed to hit something. Thankfully, I was parked on a slight incline and was able to roll gradually out of the parking space. It was dark and no one was around, so I didn't feel self-conscious that I was rolling backward at the speed of molasses in January. It didn't alarm me—I just chalked it up to a freak inability to do something rote, like randomly forgetting your phone number in midsentence. After all, I had more pressing issues to think about. The needle on the dashboard indicated a dangerous need to fill the tank.

"Okay, guys, we have to stop for gas," I told my famished kids. When the light turned green, I lamented that I hadn't been more careful now that David was gone, and tried not to think of sitting on the side of a dark rural road. "It won't take long." The aroma of the food wafted through the car.

I slid the gear into first and took off. Or at least, I'd hoped to. Apparently, the problem with my transmission wasn't limited to reverse, something I realized a moment too late. A car pulled up behind me. Panic rose in my chest, the way it does when you're on a hill and the car behind you gets too close to your bumper.

"Neutral, now first," I said aloud, trying to will the gear to move. With one forceful push, the gearshift did finally move. But I realized in my moment of triumph that the gearshift was up in the air, detached from the car, as wires and cords dangled in the air. I felt like a mob boss who'd just severed some uncooperative soul's limb.

I gasped and tried to shove the stick back onto the shaft. After a few unsuccessful tries, the stick jammed itself into place, more or less. The knob was lopsided and sideways, but still operable as I shoved it into third gear and slammed the gas pedal. The needle on the tachometer swung up like someone startling from a slumber—had it been a metal detector, you'd think I found a treasure chest. But the car? It scarcely moved. Slowly, barely, it rolled through the light—now yellow—leaving the car that had waited patiently to catch the next green. When I cleared the intersection, I realized I'd been holding my breath and exhaled so strongly that the kids were alarmed.

"What happened?" they asked.

"Just pray!" I said, trying to figure out what to do. "And don't speak."

Up ahead there was an accident, so I stopped and took the opportunity to completely pull the stick out again. I tried to straighten it, thinking I could make it work if it was in there properly. But by the time traffic moved, I had no choice but to gun it.

"Gun it" is something I've probably never said and definitely never done. But that night, I shoved the stick into what I think was third gear and slammed the gas pedal to the floor—and I didn't have the gas to spare.

At this point in movies, cars lurch forward and lose the cops in a haze of speed and power. However, we slugged forward and an overweight jogger on the side of the road passed us. I had visions of leaving the clutch somewhere down the road—not that I could pick a clutch out of a police lineup, but that's the kind of thing people say.

The car puttered along at around thirty-five miles per hour just fine, but I realized it would probably never start again—in third gear—if I ever stopped. This made getting gas impossible, although I'd procrastinated so long I feared I'd run out before getting home anyway. Should I knowingly get stuck at a gas station after ten o'clock at night with the kids or should I take a chance and maybe get stuck on the side of the road without gas with the kids?

I was calculating these things while David's words smarted in my mind.

"Driving a stickshift gives you ultimate control of the car," he said more than ten years ago in the car lot next to a black sports coupe that just happened to be a manual transmission. "You'll pick it up quickly." My skepticism caused the salesman to give us the car for the weekend, so I could try my hand at the stickshift and see if I'd like it.

"Okay, it's simple," David said later that night. "This is the clutch, this is the gas. All you do is..." It was a two-minute tutorial, after which he sent me around the block. I trusted him inherently, took off from my house, and was promptly pulled over by a police officer.

"License and registration," he said after I killed the engine on the side of the road. Of course, it wasn't my car and I didn't have my license and I had to convince him I hadn't stolen it. This was my introduction to driving a stickshift, followed by years of tossing juice boxes into the backseat since I never had a free hand to tend to the children.

And now this.

He was halfway around the globe possibly dodging bullets, but I couldn't help being infuriated. He had a lot of theories about life—like that it's happier with a few fun things, like Viva paper towels and manual transmissions. The good life, to me, would've been a car that could drive above or below thirty-five miles per hour. One that could both start *and* stop.

A normal person would've probably pulled over right there and simply called a tow truck. However, this night had been about doing something fun and unexpected—"restaurant food at night," the kids had exclaimed—and I didn't want it to end up like my other recent attempts to conjure happiness (or what might pass as happiness if strangers had been watching). For example, I'd taken the kids to a children's movie about the Loch Ness Monster and the main character's dad had gone to war and gotten killed. Austin was too young to realize that the kid's marking off the days of the calendar until his dad got back was futile, but Camille sat in her velour-covered movie seat and just wept. Then, to salvage the day, we thought it'd be fun to send care packages to Daddy, but the guy in the post office line noticed the Iraq address.

"I just got back from there," he said, before proceeding to tell the entire captive audience how he used to dodge land mines and how his friends hadn't been so lucky. "We lost a lot of good men," he said, as my horrified kids stood motionless listening to the gory details.

But not tonight, I thought. I was getting home and my kids were going to eat those chicken fingers if I had to push the car all the way home. After all, if I could stay between thirty-five and forty-five miles per hour, hit the red lights *just* right, have enough gas to travel the ten or so miles, and make a right-hand turn without slowing down, I'd be fine. The kids prayed, I prayed, and—a half hour later—we saw our house.

"Hold on!" I said to the kids as I took a wild right turn at thirty miles per hour into my driveway and turned off the car for what might've been the last time. The kids' heads bobbed forward as I pulled the key out of the ignition and realized I'd sweated through my shirt.

"Let's eat."

I set the kids up at the dinner table and googled "Saab" and "transmission" and came up with 1.5 million hits. One took me to an "Online Saab Forum" where car owners traded tips and hints about their cars with incredible passion. One guy posted a photo of his car with the caption "low flying aircraft." Even the most random questions had been answered. "Does anyone have main/rod bearing issues?" "Should I replace the oil pickup tube along with the timing belt?" "How do I disassemble my antenna assembly on the Saab 900?" These virtual communities allow you to totally customize your friendships—down to the type of car you drive. Do you drive a 900? Because the '93s have their own forum.

There are online communities for every imaginable type of person. Are you Christian? There's an online community waiting to discuss the ethics of taking a sympathy scoop of the casserole no one's touched yet in the potluck line. Are you a pagan? There's a virtual community waiting to share clever aphorisms—"Atheism: the ultimate non-prophet organization."

I glanced down the posted questions about my car type and briefly thought about posting my own question since I didn't see anything about what to do once the gearshift comes completely out while your Oriental salad gets cold in the backseat and you're getting angry at the guy who's defending your nation because of this car and Viva paper towels. But before I did, I remembered a couple at church and found a slip of paper with their number on it.

"If you ever need anything," Jeff and Lora had said. "Really."

I fingered the paper and glanced at the clock, which read 10:35, about to test that word, "really." *There's a certain indignity at being at the mercy of others*, I thought, as I steeled my nerves, cleared my voice, and dialed his number. Jeff had already fixed my leaking dishwasher and secured the knobs of my cabinets that kept falling off. And I didn't know him *that* well. Although I was in choir with his wife and him, they tended to keep to themselves and lead happy, peaceful lives. He didn't even like my books.

"I started reading your last one," he said honestly, "but I didn't like the parts about living in New York, so I just put it down."

Nevertheless, he's the kind of guy you'd want with you on a deserted island. He has hearing aids because he's worked near heavy machinery his whole life, and he has a key chain attached to his belt loop. This is the type of man who can get things done. One of a dwindling class of people, he'd be able to create a boat from coconuts, build a house from palms, and weave a hammock from the remnants...all before you had a chance to use sticks to spell out "HELP." In fact, our entire relationship consisted of me singing slightly off-key in his presence during choir and asking him to fix things. The phone rang and I prayed he wasn't asleep.

"Jeff's Auto Service," he answered. "You break it, I fix it." He was joking—he actually is the manager of an industrial plant and had to be at work at five in the morning. But apparently he saw my name pop up on caller ID and figured I needed something.

"Funny you should mention it..."

Within ten minutes, he stood in my driveway, toolbox in hand. His calm demeanor—and absolute astonishment at the fact that I'd ripped my gearshift completely out of my car—was like a hot cup of coffee on a cold morning...soothing, settling. Not only did he fix my car while I put the kids to bed, he babysat while I drove it around the block to make sure I felt comfortable with the way it handled. Then, approaching midnight, he drove my car to a nearby town to get gas so I'd have a full tank when I woke up.

David's deployment put me in the uncomfortable position of admitting I needed help. I'd often mocked Hillary Clinton's book title *It Takes a Village to Raise a Child*, but was beginning to see it might take my whole community to get my kids to school. But you know what? The next morning, my car turned on, the engine hummed, and the tank was full of gas as I drove my kids to school fifteen minutes late. A worker came out of school—even though her official "car line" duties had long stopped—and opened the door with a smile and a warm greeting.

"You okay?" she asked, like she did every morning.

Real communities—in my case, my neighborhood, school, and church—are so much better than virtual ones, and you don't have to opt in with a user name and a case-sensitive password (with at least one numeral) to join. You're in the neighborhood community because a real estate agent happened to show you a house with a cool kitchen island and a bonus room and it was cheaper than the one your spouse wanted. You're in the church community because your middle name is Calvin and your mom whispered the Apostles' Creed to you in the crib. You're stuck in these communities with dozens of others who may or may not share your interests, lumped together by theology and low-interest financing. But that's what makes these actual communities so much richer than their flimsy virtual counterparts. Since they aren't segregated into micro-niches (Saab owners, atheists, Nancy French fans) you encounter people like Jeff, who have awful taste in books but are very helpful to have around in a crisis.

While virtual communities allow you to present your best (airbrushed) face—how many Celine Dion fans fill out their Facebook profiles saying their favorite music is the Rolling Stones?—real communities know who does and does not pull their garbage from the street in a prompt manner. But that's the beauty of it. You don't have to be Emeril Lagasse to provide a meal for someone in need or Mary Poppins to babysit for a new mother. Basically you can be a contributing member of a community if you're alive, if you open your eyes on the way to the mailbox to see the need. What my neighbors and fellow congregants taught me over the past year is that when you're alone and afraid, and need someone to help in a pinch, all you need to have is someone there who's willing to show up at night and stick your gearshift back on.

But there was no way I'd tell David any of this during our first iChatting session... He was still on his mission, and I didn't want to tell him tales of transmissions dangling, friends rushing to help in the middle of the night, and death-defying trips to Applebee's.

"All is well, the kids are happy, and there's not much new to report," I typed.

The truth could come later.

14

OUR FIRST LOSS

David

THEY THOUGHT THEY WERE FIGHTING the Iraqi Army. That was the only explanation that made sense.

In the late evening hours of February 8, Fox Troop commander Torre (pronounced like "Tory") Mallard got a tip that a high-ranking al Qaeda leader was meeting with his men at a village not far from his FOB. Torre didn't hesitate. Within minutes, at least two full platoons were heading toward the village, driving without lights across the desert countryside.

Perhaps it was the darkness. Perhaps it was the al Qaeda militants' confidence after operating undisturbed from the village for months. Perhaps it was just inattention and stupidity. Whatever the reason, they didn't detect Fox Troop's approach.

As the Fox troopers neared the village, the approach got more dangerous. The ground was crisscrossed by deep irrigation canals, and a wrong turn could send a Bradley tumbling down into reeds and water below. The order was given: lights on.

The Bradleys' lights came on, bathing the desert—and the village in front of them—in a stark white light. Almost immediately men came running from a house ahead and piled into a truck.

That part made sense. Al Qaeda militants almost always made a break for their vehicles when cornered. The next part didn't make sense. Rather than running away, they unleashed a torrent of machine-gun fire at the approaching headlights—headlights that looked the same size and had close to the same spacing as the Iraqi Army Humvees that occasionally patrolled the area.

Fox Troop's response was instantaneous. Instead of the higher-pitched chatter of machine-gun fire, the insurgents heard the deeper, slower, and indescribably more ominous sound of cannon fire, the 25mm cannons mounted on the Bradleys' turrets. Almost instantly, the insurgents' truck exploded in flames. Some of the insurgents jumped from the truck and began running, firing when they could. The insurgents next to the truck ran too, desperate to escape.

It was a futile effort. With deadly accuracy, Fox Troop killed all but one of the enemy, shattering their bodies, blowing them into chunks that covered the countryside. The one who lived surrendered. He threw his hands into the air, and the disciplined Fox troopers immediately ceased fire and moved, in the middle of the fight, to detain and protect him.

When the smoke cleared, Torre discovered that his men had killed perhaps the most high-ranking al Qaeda leader in the region, a man wanted for murders, rapes, smuggling, and bombings. His brother (and his right-hand man) was in our custody, and al Qaeda had just suffered its first serious setback in eastern Diyala in a long, long time.

But victories were sometimes short-lived in Iraq.

Just two days later, I was sitting in my office one floor above our tactical operations center when a breathless trooper burst in the door. He was practically shouting.

"CPT French, the squadron commander needs you right away."

I grabbed a pad of paper and walked out of my office. The trooper was there, waiting for me. "Sir, there's been a KIA. In Grim Troop."

I felt like throwing up. KIA meant "killed in action." We'd lost someone. I immediately started thinking about all the guys I knew with Grim. Every time I'd been outside the wire, I'd been out with Grim. Could it have been Mike? Rob? "Doc" Allen? I hated to even ask.

"Who was it?"

"I don't know, sir."

When I arrived in the TOC, the place was eerily quiet. It was a beehive of activity, and the radios were still crackling, but everyone was speaking in a hushed voice. I eased into the squadron commander's office and stood beside Major Schmalz and Major Canrlon.

The squadron commander, or SCO, was facing the wall. Major Cantlon broke the silence. "Sir, the lawyer is here."

"All right." The SCO wheeled his chair around to face us. "We lost a soldier a few minutes ago to an IED. Sergeant Corey Spates." *Sergeant Spates. Do I know Sergeant Spates?* My mind raced to place him. I did know who he was...He was one of the soldiers who attended chapel. I could picture his face.

"I'm going to roll out in a minute to go bring him home. We need to get a hero flight here as soon as possible, we need to appoint an officer to collect his belongings, we need to appoint an investigative officer, and we've got to contact the rear. A blackout is in effect."

All the unclassified computer and phone lines had been disconnected. No one was able to call home or send email until after the Army notified his family of their loss.

The SCO continued. "The sergeant major and I are rolling out right now to bring him home. Is everyone clear on what they're doing?"

We answered at once. "Yes, sir."

As we walked out, I saw Sergeant Major Taylor, our operations sergeant major, putting on his body armor. A young soldier asked him why he was going out.

"One of my boys is out there," he said, "and I'm going to get him."

Within moments, the SCO and Sergeant Major Taylor were out the door, while the rest of us put into motion a process that had—as of that time—been repeated more than thirty-nine hundred times in Iraq since March 2003.

The instant we knew we lost a trooper, we imposed the communications blackout and Fort Hood started the family notification process. When the news finally reached his hometown of LaGrange, Georgia, his young wife was working on filing their taxes, his mom was at Wal-Mart looking for a hot plate to send to him, and his dad was repairing his house.

In the meantime, an officer was assigned to collect and box up the trooper's personal belongings for transport home while the aid station prepared to receive the trooper's body for the hero flight—the two-helicopter flight that begins the trooper's long journey to his final resting place.

We investigate every soldier's death in Iraq. An investigative officer interviews other soldiers, interviews the commander, and examines the vehicle. The investigation helps us to learn lessons, but also allows the family to know and understand what happened. Poorly done investigations can have horrific consequences—just ask Pat Tillman's family. Pat Tillman, NFL football player turned Army Ranger, died to friendly fire, but all the initial reports indicated that he was killed in a firefight with the Taliban. The horrible truth was covered up and concealed from the family, and when it was finally discovered, the news was devastating. When investigations are done correctly, they can help all sides achieve closure. It was my job to review all these investigations.

Sergeant Spates arrived back at FOB Caldwell two hours later. I walked to the aid station to talk to the investigating officer, dreading what I'd see. As I opened the door, a dozen weary and distraught faces turned to me. His platoon had accompanied him to the aid station and wouldn't leave his side even now. His body was behind a curtain, and a medic was guarding access.

I walked past Sergeant Major Taylor. His face was set. His uniform sleeves were covered in what looked like fine black ash. I'd heard he'd helped the troopers cut into the twisted hulk of burned metal that used to be a Humvee and had pulled out Sergeant Spates himself, holding the sergeant in his arms as they placed him into the body bag and brought him to the FOB.

A few moments later, when we were away from the rest of the troopers, I asked the sergeant major if he was okay. His response was typical of the man, a person I came to respect more than words can ever convey: "I just had to show that a leader always takes care of his soldiers."

The night seemed like it wouldn't end. At 2:00 a.m., most of Sabre assembled to escort Sergeant Spates to the landing field. At 2:30 a.m., they rolled out—a long line of Humvees and other vehicles. I stood at attention as the convoy rolled past me, stuck back at headquarters working on an unrelated legal emergency that required my immediate attention.

At 3:30 a.m., I heard the sound of the helicopters arriving.

At 4:00 a.m., I heard them take off and begin Sergeant Spates's journey home.

At 4:30 a.m., the officer in charge of assembling Sergeant Spates's personal effects walked into my office. He looked devastated. I asked him if he was okay. He paused for a moment, then spoke with a broken voice.

"I don't think I am. I mean, I didn't know him at all, but I'm going through his stuff, and I see the picture of his new wife, the stack of letters she wrote, and the stack of letters from church groups from all over. He's got a Bible, and this book about Psalm 91..."

He held up a book and I recognized it as one I owned as well.

"But the thing that really killed me was the letter he was writing to his wife. It was sitting on his bunk and looked only halfway finished. He was literally writing his wife when he left for the mission...I had to leave the room when I saw that. I mean, this was one of the good guys."

And he was. For the next five days, we all learned more about Sergeant Spates. He was the "golden child"—everyone's model soldier. He was chosen early for every promotion. He was intensely competitive, but everyone loved to play sports with him. He was an avid Georgia Bulldog fan—so much that his family would request that mourners wear black *and red* to his funeral. He was constantly smiling. He had unshakable faith and relied on his hometown church to help Iraqi children who had nothing—no soccer balls, no school supplies, nor anything to occupy them. Members at Western Heights Baptist Church collected more than a hundred pounds of crayons, paper, scissors, pencils, and other supplies that were sent to Iraq from LaGrange so Corey could hand them out. He and his wife had had their first wedding anniversary one week before.

And now he was gone.

Our firefight with al Qaeda on February 8 and Corey Spates's death on February 10 launched us into a new phase of the fight, with two opposing forces locked in a battle to the death. We were going to kill or capture the enemy, and they were trying hard to kill us, to limit our freedom of movement and to shatter our morale so that we stayed out of the villages, so that we left them to continue their reign of terror.

And so my days changed. The mornings and afternoons were somewhat "normal," dominated by the regular work of the military lawyer. I worked on investigations, handled military justice, managed claims, and even ran a free tax clinic.

The night was different. As the sun went down, Grim and Fox troops launched raids, our howitzer battery executed fire missions, and Rattler Troop rolled out again and again to recover damaged vehicles, deliver supplies, and bring back detainees. More IEDs went off, and troopers were hurt. But the enemy was hurting worse. The detainees came in an almost nightly stream. One here, two there. Three the next night. Slowly but surely, we were gaining the upper hand. Villages were being cleared and we were staying, building small outposts to maintain a presence. The city of Balad Ruz was friendly territory when we arrived, but the band of villages all around was dominated by al Qaeda. Now they were being pushed back.

I was never in bed before 2:00 a.m., and sometimes I was up with detainees until 4:00 or 5:00 in the morning. Even when there were no detainees, I found myself unable to sleep. So I stayed up anyway, chatting with Nancy on the Internet, telling her nothing about the mortal struggle that dominated all our lives, nothing about the steady drumbeat of IED blasts, medical evacuations, and enemy detainees.

Every day I worked with the troop commanders, Torre Mallard, Greg McLean, and Rob Green, to sort out detainee issues. When I rolled outside the wire, I'd roll with Mike Medders in Grim Troop or Tom Piernicky in Fox Troop. At night I blew off steam by arguing with Leo about politics and talking with J-Dave about Augustinian philosophy (not that I know much about it, but one can pretend). But every day—every single day—I'd talk to Nancy.

The ritual was the same. Each morning when I woke up, I'd see the email that she'd written the night before, right as she went to bed.

It described the day's events, described the kids' days, and gave me some insight into her feelings. She always encouraged me. She always expressed her love. And I wrote back, with messages far less detailed, but I encouraged her, told her that I loved her. At night, we would instant message each other, and that's when I got more of a real-time picture of events and her feelings.

These conversations were life itself to me, but I struggled to communicate. I just wanted to hear about home. I couldn't talk about our missions, about the vicious fight with al Qaeda, so I talked about the creature comforts, about the food, about the showers, about the hot and cramped tents that our troopers slept in. From Nancy's perspective, life in Iraq was a story of stinking port-o-pots, clogged drains, tiny Army towels, and grainy pirated DVDs sold by locals on the FOB.

And it was a story of death . . . the death of men—my friends—she would never know.

Five days after Corey was killed, we had a memorial service. All of Sabre Squadron turned out, as did all the other units on the FOB. The regimental commander flew in from Mosul; so did a general and two other colonels. It was a brilliantly sunny day. In the middle of a makeshift stage were a pair of boots, a rifle standing straight in the air, and a helmet resting on the rifle. On either side of the stage were two hulking M1 tanks.

A military memorial is a simple but profoundly moving event. A series of speakers, beginning with the squadron commander, delivered short remarks. The emphasis is not on oratory but remembrance, but the squadron commander moved us all—not by trying to either ease our pain or by trying to make any kind of statement about continuing the fight. Instead, he simply honored an extraordinary young man.

The squadron commander was followed by the troop commander, then one of Sergeant Spates's friends, and then by the chaplain. After the chaplain spoke, the troop first sergeant stood and called the roll.

"Platoon! Atten-shun!"

Sergeant Spates's platoon stood as one.

"Sergeant Gomez!"*

Sergeant Gomez's voice rang out loud and clear. "Here, First Sergeant!"

"Sergeant Morgan!"

"Here, First Sergeant!"

"Sergeant Moore!"

"Here, First Sergeant!"

"Sergeant Spates!"

Silence.

"Sergeant Corey Spates!"

Silence.

"Sergeant Corey E. Spates!"

Silence.

We were jolted by the rifle shots of the honor guard firing their salute. And then came the mournful sound of "Taps." I never really knew Sergeant Spates, but at that moment I felt his loss deeply. I also felt a powerful sense of pride and purpose. I felt pride in an institution that still understood honor—and that honor means paying tribute to heroes. I felt pride in a country that still produces men like Corey Spates, and I felt a sense of deep purpose in serving men like him. I would do anything for them, anything I could possibly do to serve them . . . and, when I got home, to honor their service.

Standing at attention eight thousand miles from home, I was exactly where I should be.

---

*The names of the other troopers in the roll call are used for dramatic purposes only and are fictional.

15

DOODILLY'S

Nancy

WHEN COREY SPATES DIED, something changed in David. Our nightly instant message chats became more one-sided. He told me less and less about his life and probed more and more for details at home. If he talked about his days at all, he'd tell a funny story or talk about his friends Leo and J-Dave. Sometimes I'd see them walking behind David if we video chatted, and I could only imagine what their personalities were like and what they knew of me. I wanted to know more about his life and friends, but I tried not to be too probing. With the unit's first loss, the danger was more palpable than ever, so I tried to keep conversation light. However, I wanted to help him in some way, to comfort him, to do something to make his life better. Though I sent care packages, there were only so many flavor packets for his water bottles, Skittles, and new DVDs that he could store.

So I just did the only thing I could do and stuck to my plan. Since I couldn't make David's life better in Iraq, I might as well try to make his life better at home. That meant working—and working hard.

And that work took me to some very strange places.

"American by Birth, Southern by the Grace of God," I read from the bumper on one of the many trucks lined outside DooDilly's. The gravel crunched under my high heels as I got out of my car—regrettably, the only vehicle without a gun rack—and I clutched my folder close to my thumping heart. Music wafted through the parking lot and the sky was pitch black. While I willed myself to walk through the door, I listened to the tune emanating from the building.

"I live back in the woods, you see, a woman and the kids, and the dogs and me-e-e..." I could see into the establishment, which was warmly lit, giving it a cozy appearance. A man with stringy gray hair strummed his guitar for the dozen or so people who sat around tables covered with half-filled bottles, watery rings of condensation, and plates with napkins wadded on them. I recognized the slightly butchered Hank Williams Jr. classic as he sang, *"I got a shotgun, rifle, and a four-wheel drive... and a country boy can survive."*

I can't do this, I thought. Easing back into the car, I shut the door softly, hoping no one inside had noticed me. The interior light of my car was dim, but I could still see page after page of empty lines. My stomach always felt like I'd gone on too many roller-coaster rides when I approached strangers to sign my petition, and this time was no different. It churned. I glanced at my empty sheets and reopened the door.

I don't think I've mentioned this before, but the events in this book happened during a presidential campaign cycle, and I worked for one of the candidates.

There.

Now you know.

The reason I hadn't mentioned it before is the same reason I got into my car and almost drove away from DooDilly's that night. No polite southerner brings up politics or religion, and for more than a year I did nothing but dive headfirst into both. You see, I didn't work for Rudy Giuliani, whom everyone admired for his leadership after 9/11. Nor did I work for fellow evangelical Christian candidate Mike Huckabee, who used every opportunity to talk about the Bible. And, no, I didn't work for Tennessee's own Senator Fred Thompson, who lived within a stone's throw of the bar I was walking into that very night.

With a forced nonchalance, I walked in and cased out the joint. Some local Republicans had told me lots of conservatives hang out at DooDilly's, which made it appealing for someone who needed to gather a thousand signatures. To my surprise, the place wasn't a bar at all. Rather, it was a convenience store, a deli, and apparently a showcase for our county's country musicians. Even though the place was full of music, clanking forks, and conversation, everyone turned and looked at me as I walked in. I looked all wrong. Had I been sitting in one of the chairs listening to Bocephus on a Tuesday night, I would've looked at me and thought, *Who does she think* she *is?* I was wearing a skirt, when overalls would've done. I was wearing tall black boots, they were wearing work boots. My jacket was Anthropologie, when Carhartt would've impressed.

"What else can I getcha?" the woman behind the counter asked me when I approached the counter with a Dr Pepper—a token of goodwill that I hoped made me look just like them, a thirsty person needing a drink and maybe some Patsy Cline.

"Well, nothing really," I said, dreading the fact that I'd agreed to be my candidate's statewide coordinator of delegates to the GOP convention to ensure he landed on our state ballot. How did a mother of two end up with this job? Anyone in this state with an ounce of political ambition had to work on behalf of our own senator. Since all of the main political activists were obligated to Fred, the campaign reached out to me as a personal favor.

They offered me the job, and I immediately heard my post-Rosie mantra—Spend Less, Work More. I've always been enamored of democracy, President Washington's refusal to be a king, and Benjamin Franklin's quote, "You've got a republic, if you can keep it." While politics is not everyone's thing, David and I had taken an intense interest in this election and had promoted our candidate since 2005—before he'd even decided to run. We blogged and attended conferences to work the straw polls, but this was my first paid campaign gig. It only lasted three months, so I planned to work hard to add the money to my Dave Ramsey debt snowball. I could do most of the work from home while the kids were at school, with the slight complication of needing signatures gathered from each of Tennessee's nine congressional districts. "Well, there's just this one thing." I held out my folder, as if she had X-ray eyes and would instantly understand. When I saw her blank look, I stammered, "Sorry, well, it's just a petition thing that I have to get people to sign to get my candidate's name on the ballot in Tennessee."

"You ain't working for Hillary, are ya?"

"No, ma'am, definitely not," I said.

"'Cause I'd vote for *Jesse Jackson* before voting for that woman." I could tell by her raised eyebrows that this meant a great deal.

"No, I work for Mitt Romney," I said.

"Matt who?"

"Romney. He's a governor and he cares about the things we care about."

"Well, I'm a tobacco-growing, tobacco-smoking, tobacco-loving Christian. That's what I care about," she said. By this time, the people who were pretending not to listen dropped the pretense. "Is he Christian?"

This was another reason I didn't want to bring it up. As you may know, Governor Romney was the most recent member of the Church of Jesus Christ of Latter-day Saints to run for president (his dad ran in '68). In other words, I had to convince Tennessee voters to sign their name on behalf of a Yankee governor from Massachusetts, whom they'd never heard of, and by the way, a Mormon. And to support Mitt, they'd essentially have to turn their backs on the drawling, pickup-truck-driving Tennessean who was running (strolling, really) for the same office—a man whose fans proudly slapped bumper stickers on their Ford F-150s declaring, "Proud to be a Fredneck."

"He definitely shares our values," I slowly said to the lady, knowing that the Mormon issue might get me kicked out on my skirt. I was walking a delicate line, since I was in a room full of people in the middle of a hotly contested presidential election, on behalf of one of the most talked-about front-runners. Although I'd spent the last year trying to explain that you can disagree with Governor Romney's theology while supporting his politics, I didn't want to plumb the depths of everyone's religious beliefs just to get some signatures. But certainly someone in this place would know that he's a Mormon and would bring it up?

"Yeah, the government is telling us we can't smoke in here no more. I've been coming here for thirty years and now they're trying to run them out of business," said a man standing in line with a package of beef jerky. "Growed adults and can't even smoke where we want to."

Great, I thought as I listened to the rapidly agitated conversation go straight to—where else—secession. You'd be surprised at how frequently people go there. When David taught at Cornell, dreadlocked students with hemp necklaces attended secession meetings while smoking cloves—opposite sides of the same coin, I guess. Nevertheless, I'd ignited a firestorm of conversation about whether the new anti-smoking regulations were enough to break from the Union.

"What does Matt think about us leaving the Union?" the cash register lady asked me.

"I doubt he knows you're considering it. He's . . . not from around here."

"He's not?"

"No, he was actually the governor of Massachusetts." If you ever want to rev up a secession conversation in rural Tennessee, take note. The cashier's eyebrow arched into a parenthesis of disapproval.

"Like the Kennedys?" the beef jerky man said, glancing at me like I had smallpox.

"No, not at all," I explained. "He's the opposite of Ted Kennedy. He tried to beat him in the Senate in 1994, actually, but he narrowly lost."

"I'm not voting for a Yankee," Beef Jerky Guy said.

And this is how I missed the entire religion conversation that night. I'd carefully honed my arguments about why Romney was the best choice for conservatives, especially compared to the other available options. I could give a pretty good speech about his economic prowess, his heroic stands for family values in hostile territory, and his ideas about foreign policy. But I had not prepared to spend the next ten minutes explaining why Christians could, morally, vote for a Yankee.

I didn't even need them to *vote* for him. Their signature just indicated that the person was a registered Tennessee voter who supported the idea of Mitt Romney having his name on our ballot. It was an archaic system that varied vastly from state to state, but it meant my signatures had to be retrieved from across the entire state. And ours is a dachshund of a state—flat but improbably long. If you lived in Mountain City, way up in Tennessee's northeastern corner, it'd take you longer to get to Memphis than to Pittsburgh. Overall, I had to get five thousand people to sign on the dotted line. And that meant talking to some of them about Joseph Smith, the popular HBO series *Big Love*, and polygamy. So that's what I did.

But that night in DooDilly's, I'd wanted to step into a room full of Republicans who knew the game, would sign my petition, and be on their way. Since I wasn't asking for their allegiance, their ideas, or even their support, it should've been an easy sale. However, I found people who hadn't paid attention to the game in quite some time, people with acute political leanings but no recent knowledge. (Was the Jesse Jackson comment a slam on Obama, or was he the last person they knew who ran for president?) I decided I didn't want to wait around to find out. I gathered up my papers and was about to apologize and get out of there when the guy with the beef jerky turned to me.

"What about the war?"

"He supports it," I said, which allowed me to stay on safe ground as I moved toward the door. Of all the issues they could've brought up, I thought this was a slam dunk in this crowd. But I'd misread the room.

"That's all I need to know, because we ain't got a bit of business over there," he said, getting a little red in the face.

"Here he goes. You can shove your beef jerky up your ass, because I don't serve communists, Buck," the cashier said. "My boy did two deployments there, and I don't want you bad-mouthing it."

"Those boys are being sent there to die," he shot back. "You're lucky he came home."

At this point, the argument spread over the entire room, which had previously been united on the important issues.

Pro: country boys, dogs, trotlines.

Anti: living in cities.

The man on the stool jumped off it and headed toward us as he told us his brother had lost a lot of friends in Iraq. As the conversation got more and more heated, my head swirled. Although I'd done an inordinate amount of work for Governor Romney on a volunteer basis, I took the paid position because I needed the money. To pull off my Dave Ramsey surprise, I needed to actually get paid. To get paid, I was standing in the middle of a potential brawl. The people around me kept talking about the severe costs of war—Beef Jerky Guy had begun explaining how our body armor was insufficient to deal with al Qaeda's explosives. I started feeling overwhelmed—about David's safety, about my naïve plan to get us out of debt, and about the fact that I was all alone. The scene was getting uncontrollably louder, and not even the babysitter knew where I was.

"You support the war, right?" the cashier yelled at me above the noise, before noticing a little lapel pin David had given me before I left. It had a star on it with the words "Army Spouse." "Well, bless your heart, honey. Is your husband there?"

I nodded, oddly getting a little choked up. Since David was in the Reserves, we didn't live on a military base surrounded by other military folks. Every single time I met someone whose family member had gone (and more importantly, come back), I got a catch in my throat. Amazingly, that slight little nod defused the situation. Suddenly, I was one of them. She came around the counter and put her arms around me. Even Beef Jerky Guy looked contrite.

"Okay, so you have to pray for your husband," the lady said. "And let me tell ya how I prayed my son home." For the next few minutes, she explained how she prayed—I can't remember it now, except that it was a combination of superstition and Christianity...she prayed every time a bell rang or every time she got hungry.

"Attention, everyone!" she said, after finishing her pep talk. Finding out David was in Iraq was enough to convince her. "This here lady needs you to sign her papers, and I don't want to hear a word about it."

I've worked on two presidential campaigns—the other was Lamar Alexander's unsuccessful attempt. (If you are a candidate, pass my name to your opponents for a guaranteed victory.) The point is, I've seen a great deal. I've interviewed candidates while CNN reporters leaned out the windows of their SUVs going seventy miles per hour trying to get footage of us inside the tour bus. I've seen my candidate on *Larry King Live* and called in during a commercial break to make sure the lint on his jacket was promptly removed. I've hosted debate-watching parties and attended galas. But, as the saying goes, all politics is local. I lived in Tennessee, and these petitions had to be done. Somehow, a guy running in Boston has to organize an effort in Tennessee, and somehow a guy running from Nashville has to organize it in Massachusetts.

I took my papers from one table to the next. As I watched them sign their names on the lines, I hoped they were registered voters. When I submitted my forms to the secretary of state, whose office checks every signature for legitimacy, address, and registration, these names might get tossed, so I made a mental note to make sure I had ample extra signatures. One man—and I'm not making this up—apologized briefly before signing his name with an X. "Some banks will take that," he said, looking embarrassed. In other words, the whole evening might have been a waste. Not only did I wonder about the signatures, it shook me a bit. The truth about politics—the reason I like it—is that it's not about the glitz or the glam of the campaigns. It's about America being the most vibrant democracy ever showcased on earth. Not only does our system eschew royalty, but voting gives us the ability to correct our political mistakes every four years when individual Americans go into a booth and vote their conscience.

But this night, with a husband in Iraq at the sole discretion of politicians we cavalierly love or hate, I realized that some "political mistakes" can't be undone. So as I stood there in DooDilly's seeing this wonderful democracy in action, smelling the unmistakable aroma of cheeseburgers ordered hours ago, and listening to Patsy Cline, I didn't know if I should be encouraged by our democratic process or horrified.

"The X is fine," I said, not wanting the man to feel embarrassed. "Matt won't mind."

16

FOX 6

David

ON FRIDAY AFTERNOON, MARCH 7, Fox Troop's commander, Torre Mallard, had some spare time, so he came to my office to do his taxes. Well, mostly he came to talk. But he didn't want to talk about the Army. Actually, he wanted to talk about anything but the Army.

So far Fox Troop had led a charmed life. Grim Troop had lost Corey Spates, and its vehicles were getting pounded by IEDs south of Balad Ruz. Fox had not lost anyone, had killed leading al Qaeda fighters, and was bringing in a steady stream of detainees. As Grim slogged through the south, bogged down in ever-lengthening operations, Fox seemed to have a freer hand, moving with lightning speed to disrupt smuggling and destroy terrorist cells.

But a successful fight is still a fight, and fights are hard. So Torre needed to blow off some steam, and he did it the way we all did it—by talking with friends, thinking about home, and dreaming about the future.

Since I was the old guy with the thirteen-year civilian career, everyone came to me to ask about jobs, college, and graduate school. They'd also ask whether they could "make it" outside the Army. Torre and I talked for more than two hours, about his wife, his kids, his career aspirations after the Army, and his frustrations. Finally, he asked me the question everyone seemed to ask.

"So how do you think I'd do out there?"

I laughed. Here was a decorated combat veteran, a leader of men, a graduate of West Point, one of the most impressive people I'd ever met...asking me how he'd do in the civilian world.

"Torre, you'll tear it up."

He laughed. "Why do you say that?"

"Are you serious? First, most men will be a little bit in awe of you. You've been tested in a way that they never will be. They're afraid that they couldn't measure up, and you know what? Most of them couldn't. You've really led guys, Torre. Do you know how few people can say that?"

"Maybe you're right."

"I'm definitely right."

At that moment, it was extremely easy to imagine Torre Mallard running a corporation, running for office, or doing something else that put him at the center of his community. He wasn't just one of the "good guys," he was one of the best.

And I had a personal soft spot for him. From the beginning, he'd been kind to me, treated me like an equal, and solicited my counsel. It took the other two troop commanders longer. Greg McLean, the senior commander of the three, looks like a clean-shaven, younger version of Chuck Norris. The first time I met him, I felt sure he was examining me with the same level of affection and detachment that he might conjure when examining a tick on a pet dog. Robert Green, Grim Troop's commander, simply ignored me. Both of those guys are among the best leaders I've seen and became dear friends. But at the beginning? I felt like I had something to prove. Understandably, they weren't ready to welcome the reservist lawyer into the fold—at least not yet. I never felt like that about Torre. He had no reason to trust from the start, but—inexplicably—he did.

During those two very brief hours on Friday afternoon, I was happy I could give something back to him, even if it was nothing more than a decent conversation and some simple reassurances.

Exactly two afternoons later, on March 9—my thirteenth wedding anniversary—a breathless trooper burst through my door. "CPT French, we need you in the TOC right away."

"What is it?"

"We got casualties."

"What?"

"Yeah, four guys. Fox Troop. It might be Fox 6."

Fox 6 was Torre's call sign.

"Roger."

I ran downstairs, and when I got to the TOC I could already see tear-streaked faces. I asked the battle captain for a quick situation report. No one had any hard information, but we knew that there was a big blast, we knew there were five VSIs (very serious injuries) and probably four fatalities.

The room, normally dominated by the loud crackle of radio communication, was again eerily quiet. The IED had gone off so far from the base that radio communications weren't always reliable. One of the strongest indications that Fox 6 was down was that we hadn't heard from Torre, the man who would take charge in the event of such a catastrophic hit on his men. Also, his vehicle had a radio.

The only way we could reliably communicate was through our Blue Force Tracker, the satellite system that allowed for short text messages.

We kept texting, asking for updates. No response. This was frustrating, but not surprising. No doubt the guys on the scene were scrambling to secure the site, care for the wounded, and search for the guys who may have detonated the bomb.

We talked to the medivac chopper and found out that he'd left with only one trooper. This was a bad sign. That meant four men were beyond help.

Then, finally, we heard from Lieutenant Thomas Piernicky. His voice sounded strained, even through broken radio transmissions. His vehicle had been in the lead, with Torre's right behind.

"We have four KIAs, but no battle rosters." We identified troopers by battle roster number, a combination of letters and numbers based on identifying information, in part so that the enemy couldn't hear names on the radio.

"Fox 6?" It was as much declaration as question.

"Roger."

It wasn't just Torre. It was also the American interpreter, Albert Haroutounian, and Specialist Donald Burkett and Sergeant Phillip

146   *Home and Away*

Anderson. Another trooper was terribly burned, but alive, and flying to Balad. Their Humvee had rolled over a truly massive IED. The blast was so powerful it flipped their vehicle. We still don't know how anyone survived, but the surviving trooper had somehow been able to open the heavy armored door and exit the vehicle as it burned.

Even worse, the IED was "command detonated." That meant someone at the very end of a long wire had watched the convoy roll by and detonated the bomb at just the right moment. That made it personal. The triggerman was out there, but Fox hadn't caught him. *He* had escaped and had just made himself our most important target.

Even now, years later, it's hard to describe or even process how I felt. Strangely enough, in my grief I remembered a movie review. I can't remember the name of the reviewer, but as he discussed his reaction to *Saving Private Ryan*, he talked about how it turned World War II movie conventions on their head. In the standard film, losses were real, but they were always somehow acceptable, understandable even. But in *Saving Private Ryan*, the losses were unacceptable. They were just too much to take. Yet somehow you fight anyway. It's right to fight anyway.

Well, March 9 was too much. It was unacceptable. It was shattering. Because we were a small unit on a small base, it seemed that each one of us had lost a friend. Across the FOB, men were weeping. My friends, my fellow captains, left the TOC and went to their personal spaces, desperately trying to pull themselves together. I felt numb with grief.

The squadron commander and sergeant major drove to the site to bring their boys home. That night we had another hero flight. We stood on the landing site as two helicopters landed. They turned off their engines out of respect as four bodies were loaded on board, escorted by the troop's first sergeant, who knew that you never leave a man behind.

Just a few days later, we had another memorial service. This time there were four sets of boots, not one. This time there were four eulogies, not just one. But there was one "Taps," one playing of "Amazing Grace," and one entire body of men standing at attention under a blazing sun.

We were full of grief, yes. It still dominated our hearts. But there was something else there as well . . . rage, a precisely focused white-hot rage. The men who did this would pay. Their comrades would pay, and they would be destroyed.

The hunt was on.

17

PAYBACK . . . AND OTHER THINGS

David

CAPTAIN TREY SMITH, a big, amiable guy, walked into an almost impossibly challenging position: the new commander of Fox Troop. Torre's replacement.

There are only a few ways to build credibility with battle-hardened troops, especially with men who've just lost friends and leaders they loved. But the best way, indisputably, is to get after the enemy, to pay back those who took your brothers' lives.

And that's exactly what Trey did. Not only did he vow payback, he launched something he called "Operation Payback." He and the rest of Fox Troop were going to crush al Qaeda in the northern area of our operation, or they were going to die trying.

Now, in our politically correct world, Trey made two mistakes. The first was naming the series of intelligence-driven raids Operation Payback, and the second was to tell the operation's name to a *Stars and Stripes* reporter who had just arrived to embed with Sabre Squadron. In our politically correct era, operational names aren't supposed to connote any particular bloodthirstiness, and at their best are supposed to be almost uplifting. "Operation Iraqi Freedom" and "Operation Enduring Freedom" are of course the classics of the genre. Even the Iraqis have gotten into the PC act, naming one of their operations (a sweep of villages in our area) "Operation Glad Tidings of Benevolence." On occasion you can be a *little* aggressive (Operation Fox Hunting, Operation Sabre Pursuit, Operation Sabre Tempest), just don't let things get out of hand. Operation Wolfhound—that's okay. Operation Feeding Wolf Puppies—better. Operation Payback—not good at all.

But no matter. Operation Payback kicked off in late March, regardless of the political conventions, and it yielded immediate results. Literally within days, we had captured one and perhaps two al Qaeda emirs, the brothers and uncles of the cell leader who had killed Torre (all of them insurgents themselves), and—in a thirty-six-hour firefight—demolished most of the combat power of the al Qaeda forces in our area.

The detainees came flooding in—instead of two and three at a time, it was five and six, then eight and nine, then fifteen or more, with equivalent numbers going to the Iraqi Army. I found myself in a frenzy of activity.

In early April, less than four weeks after Torre's death, Fox Troop was involved in yet another deadly firefight north of our base. This time, two insurgents were killed, and we had twenty-six Iraqi men in custody. I went to the site of the fight to help sort through the detainees, to determine who we were going to keep, who we'd give to the Iraqi Army, and who we'd release.

Even though my trips outside the wire were getting more frequent, there's no way I could compare to the line troops. "The lawyer" was hardly their constant companion, so when I did go, I tried not to look like a total idiot. I'd make sure my weapon was clean, my body armor and ammo load were ready, and all my gear squared away. But even then I was still a bit self-conscious when I walked up to a group of troopers—guys who went on missions constantly and sometimes lived in the field for weeks at a time. Their first comments were always something like, "Whoa, look at this! The lawyer's in battle rattle! You gonna sue somebody, sir?" I'd respond with my standard joke that no one is more "hard-core" than the "combat JAG," and then jump into the vehicle like I did it every day (no one was fooled).

On that day, I jumped into the Humvee still wearing my soft patrol cap. While we all belted in, I took off my soft cap and put on my Kevlar helmet. Well, I tried to put on my Kevlar. This may come as some surprise, but the up-armored Humvee is perhaps the most cramped vehicle in the history of vehicular travel. A Mini Cooper is a festival of leg- and headroom by comparison. I momentarily forgot the space was designed for a toddler and raised my arms to put on my helmet, moving too quickly and extending too far. My helmet hit the ceiling, bounced out of my hands, and hit me squarely on the bridge of my nose.

Breaking it.

Fortunately, no one saw what happened. I doubled over in silent agony while everyone performed their last gear checks. When I finally collected myself and put on my helmet and headset, I was a model of composure. In the meantime, a gigantic red knot grew on my nose and my eyes slowly blackened.

"Lawyer, what's wrong?" The driver had noticed my shining eyes, where I was blinking back tears of pain.

"Nothing, just dust."

"Roger."

And with that, we were off—driving down the same roads that Torre traveled the day he died, past the crater that marked the site of the fatal blast, to a small village in the middle of nowhere.

Just outside the town, a bullet-riddled sedan sat in a dusty field. My first task involved the sedan.

After a firefight, it's critical for troopers to do "SSE," or Sensitive Site Exploitation. That means to scour the area for evidence, photograph the deceased enemy fighters so that we can identify them against our own records, and collect weapons and bombs. For this particular incident, the pictures were my job.

So I walked up to the vehicle, after our explosive ordnance disposal team determined that the insurgents' remaining unexploded grenades were no longer a threat, and peered in to take my pictures. It was critical to get good shots of their faces, but there were no faces. Both men had been shot in the head by .50 caliber machine-gun rounds. The bullets had entered the top of the head and exited somewhere in the middle of the body. One man's brain appeared to have simply flown out of his head. It sat, almost intact, on the floorboard of the car. The other man's entire set of internal organs were lying outside of him, bunched up at his feet. Their faces were collapsed like Halloween masks, with their teeth sticking out at strange angles.

Quite simply, it was the most horrifying scene I had ever witnessed, and I felt nothing—nothing—but a small surge of joy that they were dead.

Perhaps it was the pain from my throbbing nose, or perhaps it was my overwhelming gratitude that they were dead and not some of our guys (one of the insurgents had thrown a grenade that landed just a few feet from the two Fox troopers who had approached to detain them), but I think I was mostly shocked at how little I was affected by the sight.

"Okay, well, I'm not sure these pictures will be very helpful. Let's head to town."

And so we moved on, to a small town where twenty-six men sat quietly in the shade with their hands zip-tied behind their backs. Twenty-five of the men were unremarkable, wearing their dishdashas and looking genuinely miserable. One of the men stood out, however. He was in a burqa, which is an outer garment worn by women in many Islamic regions to hide their entire bodies. This man's burqa was lavender at that.

"Sir, we don't have much intel on this guy, but we caught him trying to sneak out of the village with some of the women. A dude in a dress has got to have *something* to hide."

And with those words, three troopers broke out into a spontaneous chorus of Aerosmith's "Dude Looks Like a Lady." Several Iraqi Army soldiers broke into laughter and started walking toward the detainee. The Fox troopers shooed them away.

"Yeah, sir, we've got to keep the Iraqi Army away from him. They keep trying to pinch his cheeks and ass."

"Yes, I'd hate to see what they'd do with him," I said. "Let's take him with us."

With his fate determined, we worked on dealing with the rest. After checking lists, running detainees by informants, checking for gunpowder residue, and getting intel reports from our intelligence officers, we made our decisions. Six detainees came with us, six went with the Iraqi Army, and fourteen were released.

We loaded up the detainees and drove back the way we came, past the riddled sedan (where the Iraqi Army was collecting the bodies), past the "March 9 crater," down the road and onto the FOB...with my nose throbbing the entire ride.

Just another day in Operation Payback.

It's amazing how resilient people can be. A person can go through the most extreme conditions, the most extreme emotions, and yet after a day or two or three of shock, their personality quirks and their absurdities reemerge. The grief remains, like a dark companion, but it lives alongside the person you are and have been. And so it was with my squadron. If I had to describe the collection of eight hundred troopers with whom I lived and fought, I'd say that we were essentially a highly mobile, highly disciplined, courageous, violent fraternity—in both the "brotherhood" sense of the term and in the frat-house sense of "no action is too gross, no action is too crazy, and the primary goal in life is fun."

No one ever lives in truly all-male environments anymore. Men and women mix together in school (even in frat houses for that matter), in church, in businesses, and on athletic fields (if women aren't actually playing with the guys, they are certainly watching from the stands). But the combat arms branches of the Army are different, and my unit was a pure combat unit. That means there were eleven hundred men living together in a collection of buildings and tents. We live four to a room if we're lucky. Some guys are packed forty to fifty to a tent. And when you have that many men together in one place, it can mean only one thing.

Flatulence.

The air at FOB Caldwell was both toxic and flammable. Combine the food of our dining facility with zero social inhibitions caused by the total lack of a female presence, and we lived in the midst of a veritable symphony of farts.

In briefings: "Sir, on this slide you'll see the disposition of our forces as we approach—"

(Greasy sound escapes the posterior.)

"Nice one."

"Thank you, sir."

At dinner: "I'm going to grab a cup of coffee. Anyone want some?"

(Wind is broken.)

"I'll take that as a yes."

At night: "Hey, Leo, are you asleep?"

(Cheese is cut.)

"Dude, you really need to fix your diet."

A permanent cloud of methane hovered over our base. Combine the flatulence with the omnipresent snuff dipping and belching, and people with delicate sensibilities would suffer from post-traumatic stress syndrome.

We staff officers lived and worked in the same building. The Tactical Operations Center was one floor below the living quarters, and my legal office was on the same floor as our living quarters. Everything was remarkably cramped. Four guys lived in my room, and five or more lived in others. The late evenings often represented a peaceful refuge (except when there was outgoing artillery fire). Those staff officers on shift work, usually from 9:00 a.m. to 9:00 p.m., would have dinner, go to the gym, and watch a movie on their laptops to wind down. Those officers, like me, who don't have specific shifts still looked at the late evenings as a time of relative peace (unless, of course, we had raids in process or detainees inbound).

That peace was shattered by the constant sounds of the most atrocious garage band rock you can imagine...offbeat drums, warbling guitars, and the most screeching vocals you've ever heard. All this courtesy of the PlayStation 3 game *Rock Band*. The evil genius of the game is to give the players a microphone, two guitars (with buttons instead of strings), and a drum kit, and then allow them to play legendary rock songs by merely hitting the right buttons—or correct drum—as colored notes roll across the screen. If you hit the buttons (or drums) at the right time, the song plays beautifully. If not, well then...

The staff formed two groups, "Staff Infection" and "Pink Slips," and they regularly engaged in a "battle of the bands" (the vile game keeps score based on the quality of the play). Since it is oh so much more fun to play on maximum volume, the sound will sometimes reverberate through the entire building. Everyone could hear the sound. I recall a typical exchange with Major Cantlon:

Me: Sir, I have those strike packets you requested...
"YEEEEEEAAAAARRRRRRGGGGHHHHH!!!!!"
Major Cantlon: What was that?
Me: If I'm not mistaken, sir, that scream is from the
Who's "Won't Get Fooled Again."
Major Cantlon: I don't remember it sounding like that.
Me: Me neither, but...
"MEET THE NEW BOSS! SAME AS THE OLD BOSS!"
Me: Yep, that's "Won't Get Fooled Again."

But it wasn't all bad. One of the addictive features of the game is the ability to create your own character, right down to name, hairstyle, and even tattoos. This, of course, lent itself to endless mischief once you discovered the relevant passwords (to all those reading, passwords based on your hometown, your home state, or your children's names are a very bad idea). Just a week after the game arrived, my friend John logged on to see that his character, "Axle," was renamed "Dude Love" and had blazing pink hair and a huge tattoo across his chest that said "It's Raining Men."

Like I said, we were a rolling, deadly, disciplined...fraternity. But we kept losing brothers.

On March 19, a Humvee (how I was growing to hate those machines) rolled over on Sergeant Gregory Unruh, killing him instantly. In early April, an IED blast claimed the lives of Specialist Matthew Morris and Captain Ulises Burgos. In just about two months, that was eight men. Gone. And that didn't even count the terrible burns, the concussions, the broken bones, and the gunshot wounds that were taking so many others out of the fight.

Others faced ridiculously near misses. Trey walked by a house only to see bullet holes pop up all around as an insurgent fired through the walls at the troopers walking outside. Miraculously, none of the bullets so much as grazed his uniform. Two troopers were shot square in the chest by AK-47s, but escaped only with bruises because of their Kevlar vests.

By my count, between early February and early April, our small squadron suffered just about 20 percent of the total coalition casualties in Iraq. Every day brought news of a firefight, an IED blast, or a mortar attack. You lived with a permanent knot in your stomach, fearing for the lives of your friends. And every time I rolled outside the wire, I uttered a very simple prayer: "God, thank you for the life You've given me."

Nancy knew that this was a dark time. The frequent Internet blackouts, caused by deaths or serious injuries, told her all she needed to know. I was so much safer than the line troops, the guys who were out there every single day, but I was out enough to lose any sense of certainty that I would be okay, that I would live through the tour. Seeing death does that to you. It shatters your false sense of security, especially when you drive down the very roads, past the very craters that mark where your friends had been hurt and killed.

There was a song by Five for Fighting, a "group" really comprised of one man, singer-songwriter John Ondrasik. He wrote a beautiful song called "I Just Love You," about a conversation between a man and his wife who are far away from each other.

"I just love you." I loved that phrase—so simple and unconditional.

Over the first five-plus months of the deployment, the song had taken on huge meaning for both me and Nancy. It wasn't just the words, it was the simple sound and almost palpable separation and loneliness it conveyed. At home, Nancy would play it and cry. In Iraq, I would put on my headphones, play it... and try not to betray any hint of emotion in front of the guys.

But I vowed that if something happened to me in Iraq, those would be my last words to Nancy: "I just love you." And so I began a ritual. If I knew I was going outside the wire the next morning, my last signoff on our evening instant message chat would be, "I just love you." If I had to go on a mission unexpectedly, I would do everything I could to get to my office and at least type out a brief message... that always ended with "I just love you."

Because I didn't want to frighten her, or to broadcast across the Internet any of our movements, I never told her what that "code" meant, not until I got home. Had something happened, however, I believe it would have mattered. It would have mattered a lot.

18

IN CHRISTIAN LOVE, WALTER

Nancy

I'M NOT SURE WHEN IT HAPPENED, exactly, but at some point I realized that David and I were simply living separate lives. This might seem blindingly obvious, but it wasn't obvious to me until it happened. It was kind of like being on a train, falling asleep, and waking up somewhere very different than where you started, though you can't quite remember when you crossed over the border into unfamiliar territory. You see, I believed we would continue to be "a family" while he was gone. There was so much talk about how deployment affects the whole family, as one spouse keeps things going on the home front and the other on the front line. We're all in this together, everyone repeatedly emphasized. Somehow I didn't think the distance would really separate us, and that in fact we'd grow closer as we walked through this difficult journey together.

But one day, I woke up on the train alone, somewhere far far away from David. I couldn't imagine what he was going through. The men who died—his brothers in arms—were only names to me. That afternoon, against my better judgment, I googled the name of David's friend who'd died. I knew David had been completely shattered by his death, but that's pretty much all the information I had. Pretty soon, I was engrossed by the task of finding out all I could about this man, my heart beating fast, and I even came across a photo of him. I wondered if other wives were doing the same thing, desperately searching for information about someone they'd never know in an attempt to grow closer to their husbands. It felt voyeuristically macabre as I read postings of friends and mourning family members, wondering if I was getting more information than even David had. Information felt like power—inexplicably, it was as if reading about this fallen soldier meant our family was safe and protected. At least that's how I felt initially. Then, after an hour of reading and thinking about the death, I just felt scared, alone, and very vulnerable to whatever fate had in store.

And then there was this reality: No matter how I felt, my sadness couldn't compare to David's grief. He was living a life he couldn't even tell me about, much less accurately describe. And I was living a life that was merely inconvenient. I did all the things we did before—except alone. Yes, I had my new project—my secret debt paydown—but I still lived in the same house, spent time with the same two kiddos, and talked to the same friends. Since his life was so totally different, there were no built-in reminders of the life he left behind. Was he constantly reminded of me, or was I the sort of thing he thought about late at night when the chaos of the day subsided? For me, everything pointed back to David. When I lay down at night, for example, I slept on the left-hand side of the bed. And when I hosted Small Group at my house, everyone asked about David.

One of the biggest reminders of his absence, however, was the day-to-day ups and downs of the presidential campaign. We didn't intend to work side by side on the campaign, it just happened naturally as both of our interests aligned in Mitt Romney's conservative political values. In early 2006, I helped David organize an effort for a straw poll, which turned into a blog, which created a loyal readership and media interviews. Our success in a relatively few small things allowed us the chance to meet the Romneys, who were grateful for our efforts here in the Bible Belt. Eventually I ended up traveling through South Carolina on Mrs. Romney's bus tour and even—in an amazing opportunity—helping her write her memoirs.

In other words, the presidential campaign of 2008 grew to be an exciting element of our lives and marriage for a few years. On more than one occasion, David and I'd be in the middle of some event—at a swanky party in our nation's capital schmoozing with politicos or giving interviews with national media—where we'd look at each other and just laugh. Not only was it fun, but we really believed in our candidate. Absolutely nothing energizes your foreign policy beliefs more than having a husband being sent off to war.

When David left, following all the political goings-on here kept us close. He couldn't tell me the details of his missions and I couldn't tell him about the sadness of the kids, but we could always talk politics. In fact, we had so little time to communicate, people were amazed when I'd start a conversation with, "Well, David and I were talking about this new Hillary development and he thinks..."

"You mean to tell me—in your limited time—you choose to talk about Hillary Clinton?"

What they didn't understand was that politics bound us together in the way some couples play golf or watch movies. It gave us common themes and ideas, topics of conversation, and it dealt with the future of our nation, a subject understandably quite close to our hearts. During the campaign, I'd gotten to participate in a part of David's personality I'd never known—a quite attractive aspect, I might add. When anything happened on the news, he could easily explain it within the context of political history, and he had a way of cutting to the chase of complex geopolitical issues.

Once, he quoted a famous conservative British parliamentarian of the late eighteenth century when explaining that our real rights are rooted in both tradition and faith.

You speak Burkean? I thought, smiling like Gomez Addams when Morticia spoke French.

For years, the election allowed us to share the same joys and disappointments, the ups and downs of working toward a common goal. Since David and I were Presbyterians—and wrote about our home church quite frequently—we often got letters and emails from concerned Christians who lamented our support for Governor Romney. They sometimes were thoughtful, serious letters, detailing deep reservations about the theology of it all. Many, however, contained rude, insulting accusations—including such imaginative charges as the Romneys had bought us out, we were secretly Mormons, and that we had faked membership at our church. Thankfully, Zion Presbyterian gives two things to those who place membership—a commemorative plate and a plot in the church graveyard. When even my pastor got mail about this, he assured everyone we had our "plate and plot."

Ironically, the most disparaging, uncivil emails were signed with the automatic signature line they'd created for their friends. This made for amusing endings, with sentences like, "And I hope you don't die as a cult-loving sellout or you'll go straight to hell...which is what you deserve," followed by the automatic signature "In Christian Love, Walter."

What I learned was that some Christians will vote without hesitation for a skirt-chasing, alcohol-swilling, multiply-divorced candidate, as long as he says he loves God and isn't a Mormon. In response to the constant criticism and conversation, David and I discussed complex issues, such as how theology matters when it comes to politics.

"Of course it matters!" David would say over coffee. "If a candidate belonged to the 'Church of Killing Canadians,' for example, voters would rightly ask whether he planned on invading Canada and stealing their moose. Some theologies do lead to flawed political decisions. But Mormonism and evangelical Christianity have common moral and therefore political values."

This was what we'd talk about instead of who was going to take what kid to piano lessons.

"Plus we're already allied with them politically—their solid Republican voting is the reason we had President Bush rather than President Gore back in 2000. We should thank every Mormon we meet." We talked about it before he left, and we talked about it after he left. It's perhaps the one thing about our relationship that didn't change. We couldn't speak, we couldn't see each other, and we could barely communicate, but we could break down the Iowa caucuses in two hundred words or less.

Our "Evangelicals for Mitt" concept was a man-bites-dog story, and reporters from the *USA Today*, ABC News, *New York* magazine, and even the *New York Times* called to find out what evangelicals believe about this Latter-day Saint candidate. Once I was trying to explain to a reporter that his theology didn't bother me as far as the office of president was concerned. "I wouldn't want Governor Romney to teach my Sunday school class, but he's definitely the most qualified presidential candidate," I said.

Immediately, I started getting emails from distressed Mormons protesting that Governor Romney would be an excellent Sunday school teacher, ignoring the cold hard fact that our church thinks Mormons are flat-out wrong.

And you know what? The Mormon church thinks *we're* wrong too.

That's why they aren't Presbyterians and we aren't Mormons. I explained this on our blog one day, and tried to defend my Sunday school comment:

"After all, you LDS members wouldn't want me coming into your church to teach Sunday school. We believe different things. It's not offensive to admit this openly, while still being committed to the same highly qualified candidate."

We kept writing. Our readership climbed to eighty-five thousand readers per month, and (without compromising our view of scripture) we started getting fan mail from Mormons. Over the next couple of years, we were invited to hear the Mormon Tabernacle Choir, tour a new temple in Utah, take an exclusive tour of Salt Lake's Welfare Square, and see a Minerva Teichert art exhibit. (Don't know who that is? You probably aren't a Mormon.) Once, when David and I were in Utah with the other "evangelicals for Mitt" and friends, we even led a Monday night "Family Home Meeting" in the home of a Mormon friend.

I was certain Mitt Romney would win. In retrospect, that might sound weird to you, now that we know how the election turned out—with an audacious and hopeful leader who seemed coronated rather than merely elected. But at the time, I was knee deep in election minutiae—getting real-time updates on all the standings in the vital battlegrounds. I had so many people emailing me updates with various ways to look at the data that I'd convinced myself I'd eventually be at the inauguration with the ultimate accessory on my arm—a man in uniform.

That's why I said no.

The phone rang around ten in the morning—someone inviting me to go to CPAC, the largest annual gathering of conservative students, activists, and policymakers in America. After working in various ways to get him elected for two years, I'd gotten used to the acronyms, to straw polls held at conferences to draw the candidates' attention, and to the ebb and flow of the news cycle.

Everyone important to the conservative movement was going to be in Washington, D.C., dissecting the candidates' positions during this election year. Normally, David and I attended these large conferences and organized Romney voters for the inevitable straw polls that make headlines for a day or two. At the Southern Republican Leadership Conference in Memphis, I handed out T-shirts that read "Romney: Yankee Governor, Southern Values." At the Values Voters conference in D.C., I dressed head to toe in Romney paraphernalia and was yelled at in an elevator by Huckabee supporters who accused me—of all things—of being soft on the war. Even though David and I would've normally been in the thick of this action, I hung up the phone knowing there'd be other speeches at more convenient times.

When David left, my world got a great deal smaller. Since our home is located one mile from church, one mile from school, and within a mile of most of our friends, the Zion community is where I stayed...among mule-filled pastures and roads shared with sluggish hay-hauling tractors.

Although I could've left the kids with grandparents, that's the kind of thing we did when everything was stable, when life was constant. With David gone, however, I took a step away from the campaign work and decided to be at home every night to tuck the kids into bed. Plus, there was a great deal to do around the house. For example, I was learning how to garden and had accidentally planted impatiens that needed more liquid than Norm drank at Cheers. I could barely leave the house for lunch without returning to their withering petals begging for attention.

The next day, I was called again.

"Are you sure you can't come to CPAC?" my friend said. "I think it's going to be an important speech."

I sighed internally at my friend's passion and smugly realized how mature I'd gotten in David's absence. No longer was I glued to my computer screen, or rolling through emails on my iPhone. The deployment had given me an inner clarity about life. I knew even the most awful-sounding political crisis—over which I'd previously fretted—would climax as a joke on Jay Leno, in a punch line most people wouldn't remember by the time they got to the water cooler.

I calmly explained how I was needed at home. "Next time," I said, internally comforting myself at the thought of attending the inauguration.

A few days later, I was coming home from a PTA meeting—okay, so I made that up, I hadn't gone *that* far in my quest for domesticity. The point is, I was winding down a rural road listening to Rush Limbaugh's radio show, trying not to get frustrated at the tractor meandering in front of me blowing hay or at Rush's callers blowing smoke. I noted all the positive comments Rush said about Governor Romney and planned on blogging about them later in the afternoon. Even though blogging on our grassroots political site *Evangelicals for Mitt* wasn't the same without David, it was something I could do from my hometown. Sometimes what I'd write would get the attention of potential voters and media, and it was enough, I told myself.

Then I heard an announcement through Rush's golden microphone. "Word from CPAC is Romney dropped out of the presidential race moments ago. More to come, I gotta cut to commercial break."

It was literally that abrupt, that final—months and years of work, evaporated like water poured on yesterday's plants. I would've pulled over had I not been driving so slowly that I wouldn't have noticed the difference. From my driveway, I texted David, "WMR is out," pulled up the *Drudge Report* on my phone, and waited in the hot car for the program to come back on for details.

"In this time of war," Governor Romney's voice came through the radio, "I feel I have to stand aside for our party and our country...If this were only about me, I'd go on, but it's never been all about me."

Apparently he feared that delaying John McCain's nomination would weaken the Republicans' chances against the Democrats. And since we were at war, he bowed out gracefully.

The campaign had been such a big part of our lives, even during the deployment, that I suddenly felt incredibly bereft. One of the last things David did before he left our house that October morning was to sit down and write Governor and Mrs. Romney a thank-you note for a gift they'd sent—a gold compass with an engraved message on the back: "May your travels always lead you back home."

It was still dark outside when he grabbed a pen and scribbled out a quick note. "I hope when I return I won't shake your hand as a friend but will rather salute you as my Commander-in-Chief."

Usually, after twelve or so years of marriage, life settles into the predictable—car line at school, homework, bills, and taxes. But the election gave us deep and meaningful friendships, probing conversations, and some gut-wrenching late-night talks about the deepest of topics—faith, politics, and God's relationship to both. It brought us closer to each other in ways I only now can see.

But that moment in the car, our common goals, our lingua franca, and our multiyear pursuit suddenly dissipated, and David faced having a commander in chief he politically opposed. In the sweltering heat of the car, I thought of him in the desert and worried how he'd process this information.

My phone vibrated and I read a two-word response from David.

"I heard."

And with that cold international text, this chapter of our lives came to a close.

It left me a little adrift. Every morning for months, I'd had the same routine—I drank hazelnut coffee while reading David's morning email, followed by the *Drudge Report*, *National Review*, *Politico*, and *The Fix*. Afterwards, sure, there were polls to check, but I was as enthusiastic about John McCain as about holding a funeral for Austin's dead pet "Fishy." Because I couldn't conjure up enough concern to go ahead and bury the thing or flush it out of my life, I continued to blog and was a regular guest on National Public Radio's *Weekend America*. I just hoped no one would look too closely and notice how lifeless this election had become to me. At one point, the host of my radio show, sensing my unwillingness to enthuse about our GOP nominee, reminded me off the air, "Nancy, you're supposed to be the Republican in this show, remember?"

To make it worse, I'd alienated my friends with my constant campaigning and didn't want to see their smug faces. Once, an angry man at church accosted me during coffee hour. "Why do you have that bumper sticker that says 'Evangelicals for Mitt' on it? You can't speak for me!" I'd even mocked one of the elders at church for his unwillingness to support Governor Romney to the point that we'd frequently stand in the middle of church and bicker like teenagers. Now everyone was a political consultant. "Well, you should've done..." or "Demographically, he was behind the ball on..." Since they'd gotten most of their knowledge from the talking head on last night's *O'Reilly Factor*, I turned off my ringer, packed up the kids, took Goggo to a boarding place, and drove straight to the Hilton in Georgetown, Kentucky.

The owners of this hotel were my dear friends Chris and Rebecca, with whom I had passionately argued in their kitchen one abysmal afternoon. But being good friends, they called me the instant the campaign ended and offered the kids and me a week's worth of hiding out, five hours from where anyone knew I'd be. For five days, I read the back pages of newspapers, lounged while watching the kids splash in the pool, and ate food other people prepared. People from church left frantic voice mails: "Are you guys okay?" Others even offered to bring me meals, a common custom when people are going through a grieving process.

Weirdly, that's how it felt.

In a book about idioms, I read about a man who sat on his bed in his apartment after a long day. He pulled one shoe off and dropped it noisily on the floor before guiltily remembering that everyone in his building was probably trying to sleep. He quietly laid his other shoe by his bed. A few minutes later, as he was drifting off to sleep, a shout from the man in the apartment below awakened him.

"Drop the other one already! I can't sleep, waiting for you to drop the other shoe!"

In some ways, I was that man, unable to relax because I kept waiting for something else to happen.

It just didn't seem over.

Had I just gone to D.C., I thought, I could've heard his speech, seen my friends, and wiped away the tears as I blogged my last blog. It was kind of like falling asleep on the train—I'd missed the moment when we crossed the border into the awful territory of supporting John McCain. Although I may not have acknowledged it at the time, the "I'm going to tuck the kids in every night for a year" philosophy began to crack. Somewhere deep within me—buried between the unacknowledged truth that I wasn't going to lose ten pounds or cancel the premium cable channels after the free trial period—lurked an unspoken resentment about my less exciting life without David.

Looking back, it's obvious why Governor Romney's abrupt exit from the race depressed me so much. We were well into the deployment, and had settled into a routine. The kids were doing remarkably well. Austin still cried many nights, but both of them had learned to live without Daddy while not forgetting him. Camille would listen intently to any discussion of the news, while Austin always talked about being a soldier. It amazed me how much their pride in David's service helped carry them through the tough times. Plus, I poured everything I had into making certain their lives were tolerable. We took fun trips. We had their friends over for playdates. And—yes—I was always, always there to tuck them in at night.

But I was depressed. More depressed than I'd been since he'd left. And it was because our *joint* project—the thing we loved doing so much *together*—was over. Politics was "our thing." Electing Governor Romney was part of our shared purpose, and when that shared purpose ended, I worried that we would grow farther apart, that the gulf in our separate lives would simply grow wider.

Plus, I really liked Mitt and Ann.

A few weeks after the campaign ended, I got an invitation to an event in Salt Lake City. If I went, I'd have to leave the kids, to break my "always tuck them in" promise, but I wanted to go. I felt like I needed to go. At Salt Lake, I could see some friends from the campaign. Maybe I could get some closure.

David sensed my depression. "You need this," he said. "The kids will be fine, and they'll enjoy some grandparent time."

So I did it. I packed up the kids, sent them to Paris, Tennessee, to spend time with my parents, and off I went—to commiserate with my friends from the campaign.

This was my first time actually seeing Utah, though I'd imagined it in my head. I mentioned that I sometimes help write someone else's story, usually a celebrity or famous person who doesn't have the time to sit down and write the entire thing themselves. Although not widely known, it's common practice—up to 40 percent of the books being published today are written with the assistance of so-called ghostwriters. That's why I felt like I'd seen Utah.

After Mrs. Romney asked me to help write her memoirs, I'd spent hours listening to her stories and imagining her life—some of which took place right in that area. She attended college there and many years later her husband ran the 2002 Winter Olympics. The beauty of this career is that you get to inhabit someone else's world, literally writing words like, "My brother Rod and I used to climb an old tree in the backyard..." or "When I was First Lady of Massachusetts..." Although I'd written words about Utah and its glorious mountains, seeing them in person made me realize I simply wasn't a good enough writer to capture them. They wrap around the city like giant arms, simultaneously invigorating and soothing. They quietly remind you that there's something out there much bigger than whatever it is you're running to do in your taxi. They were familiar the way the White House is when you finally see it in person after looking at its image countless times. Ghostwriting does that to you; it makes things outside your experience realm faintly familiar.

Many times during the writing process, I felt like I'd developed an alter ego. At parties, people would mention going out on Jet Skis, and I'd have to fight the urge to tell them about the time I rescued some people from drowning on my Jet Ski after their boat had overturned on Lake Winnipesaukee. Of course, I've never been to New Hampshire, never ridden on a Jet Ski, and never saved anyone from anything, but I'd recently written the story of how Mitt and the boys had done so as if I'd been right there as the drama unfolded.

When I realized I was going to Utah, I emailed Ann's brother Rod and his wife, Cindy, to ask to finally meet in person. To my delight, they were going to be in town and agreed to meet at a local Salt Lake City restaurant. Mind you, I'd interviewed both of them over the phone several months prior. But a single phone conversation for each of them was many hours of listening, transcribing, writing, and deliberating for me. So when I walked up to them in the waiting area, I felt like I'd known them for years.

Rod was taller than I expected, a businessman. Cindy was blonde and fit. Had I not known better, I'd think she and Ann were siblings instead of related by marriage. This was what I was thinking as I walked straight up to them and embraced them. Only midway through the hug did I realize they hadn't spent months of their lives dwelling on *me*, listening to my voice, and were probably only now connecting the dots as to my actual identity. Regardless, Rod and Cindy were warm and hospitable to their new evangelical cousin from Tennessee, and arranged for us to take a tour of Welfare Square the next morning.

This amazing benevolence center was created by the LDS Church during the Great Depression to help the needy. When we arrived there, the sweet smell of bread wafted all the way through the building, as a gentleman called Elder Bates gave us a tour that included cheese and chocolate milk. The people there were kind and warm, and I felt obliged to match their earnestness with a serious yet soft expression on my face that emitted the right amount of holiness. After all, I couldn't be outdone.

But that's exactly what was happening. Apparently their church regularly sponsors food storage demonstrations, teaches young children to prepare seventy-two-hour "emergency kits," and operates canneries open to church members where they can their own food at no cost. Their benevolence was incredibly impressive. Before the '08 primaries, all I ever knew about Mormons came from television commercials—so I figured they all had kids with white teeth, played catch in Astroturf-green backyards, and blew bubbles in slow motion. Now I realized they could also make their own cheddar cheese. It was hard not to feel a little insecure.

"Are you going to hit the slopes before your flight?" Rod asked somewhere along the tour of the towering grain elevator, enormous food storehouse, cannery, milk processing operation, thrift store, employment center, and bakery.

I pointed at my wrist—out of habit, though I haven't worn a watch since I lost mine in college. "I can't—my flight leaves at four."

I admit now that the time of my flight was irrelevant. Just as I'd never get my nails done at an airport stand advertising "Get a Manicure While You Wait," I'd never ski on a business trip. Both should be done intentionally, not simply because you have a little extra time on your hands. There are considerations, after all. How can someone with questionably dry nails dig for an airline ticket, take off a belt, place the laptop in the gray bin, and jockey for a seat away from the lady with the baby? Likewise, as I'd scheduled the absolute shortest round-trip possible, I didn't have thick wool socks, a jacket, or those things you break that keep your hands warm. Skiing isn't a $3.95 game of bowling, after all, and people who casually rent gear and equipment when they have extra time are just made out of different stuff than I am.

"Oh, too bad. Utah snow is supposed to be the best in the world, you know," another man in our tour group added amiably. "They had the Winter Olympics here because of our good snow."

Of course I knew the 2002 Winter Olympics were held in Salt Lake. This was where Ann started riding horses, worked to overcome multiple sclerosis, and even ran a leg of the torch relay. "Yeah, I heard," was all I could say.

"Mitt Romney was in charge of the Games," someone else on the tour of the granary said. We all nodded.

"Are you a skier?" Rod followed up.

Even though I was standing in the LDS Church's benevolence mission and next to someone called "Elder," I lied.

"I love to ski."

The truth was, I went on a Baptist youth ski trip in seventh grade to a three-hundred-foot hill and a tug line in Paoli Peaks, Indiana—a state better known for its basketball and motor speedway. Later, David and I went to "Greek Peak," about twenty miles from our home in upstate New York. This, to me, counted as "real" skiing, since I wore a Fendi ski jacket I'd bought with my employee discount from a store in Manhattan that sold high-end sporting goods equipment to people who had more money than sense. In the South, when people ask if you ski, they mean, "Have you *ever* skied?" not, "Do you have a ski rack on your vehicle and lift tags hanging off your jacket?"

Plus, Ann—who is very athletic—was a great skier. So I'd *written* about skiing.

This didn't matter one way or the other. I was about to leave and get on with my post-campaign life, one filled with free time and without CNN. At any rate, I'd planned on spending the next few hours left in Salt Lake making a mental list of all my LDS friends. Though unwilling to give up caffeine, I at least wanted to know where to run in case of a dire emergency, such as a tornado or a flood. I kept some of my Evangelicals for Mitt business cards in the hope that some of my LDS friends will remember the work we did. Surely all that blogging is worth at least a few jugs of water and a couple of months' worth of spam.

Rod's phone rang somewhere between the cheesemaking factory and the chocolate milk–bottling demonstration, and he turned his back to our little group to answer it in a quiet voice. A few minutes later, with his cell pressed to his ear, he whispered, "Ann's jealous you're in town and we're all hanging out without her. She says hello."

I stifled the urge to grab the phone and start chatting. At one point, I traveled with Mrs. Romney quite a bit—stealing a few minutes on the road in her bus during her tour of South Carolina as film crews chased us down the interstate, riding with her on the way to fundraisers, chatting late at night as the excitement of the day gradually wore off. I hadn't spoken to her since Governor Romney dropped out of the race.

"She and Mitt are going to fly in Friday, and she wants to know if you can postpone your flight and stay for the weekend. You can stay at their house."

My heart dropped.

"What's that?" Rod said into the phone, before covering it with his hand and turning to me. "She wants to know if you can ski. If so, you can go on the slopes with them Saturday."

I realize now that God was giving me a chance to come clean, to have simply clarified my previous statement about being "good." As tantalizing as the idea sounded, unloading the kids for another several days so I could hang out with the Romneys would be the height of irresponsibility. There was simply no way I could do it.

"I'm actually a *great* skier," I said.

A pendulum, I always swing from one extreme to the other. For months, I turned down every opportunity, including inadvertently missing the final speech of the campaign at CPAC. Sick of missing everything, I added—in a remarkable show of restraint—"Of course, I'd have to check with my parents to see if they can keep the kids." Goggo was staying at his boarding place in Cool Springs, so I knew he'd be fine either way.

In retrospect, it seems weird that I didn't pause to consider the ramifications of this blatantly incorrect statement that would invariably result in my being found out. Right then, my intention was to make sure I ended up hanging out with the Romneys that weekend, not worrying about whether I remembered how to snowplow. Sleeping at their house and skiing in Deer Valley seemed like so much fun that there was no way it'd work out.

That night, when I got back to the hotel, I logged on to my computer, saw David was online, and asked him to call me.

"What should I do?"

"Stay," he urged. "Have fun, and the kids will be fine. You've already missed too much." David always encouraged me to live life to the fullest, and this didn't change when he was in Iraq. I'd put improbable restrictions on my life—to tuck the kids in every night for a year!—but he never did.

The next day, Rod was talking to Ann on the phone, and I acted like I was totally accustomed to extending trips and canceling flights and purchasing ski gear in a bind.

"No, she's got stuff you can borrow," Rod assured me the next day as he and Cindy drove me up into the mountains, past places I'd only read about, like Sundance, where we shopped at a gift store. My parents couldn't keep the kids, I'd discovered, so I had them unload Austin at his friend's house and Camille at hers. *Having fun takes a lot of work*, I thought as their car chugged valiantly up the nine-thousand-foot mountain. We stopped on the side of the road as moose drank from icy mountain streams. I definitely wasn't in Paoli Peaks anymore.

When Mitt and Ann came in late that evening, Rod, Cindy, and I were all curled up in blankets in their living room, lamenting the fact that Mitt was so cheap—sorry—economically wise, that he keeps the house cold enough to store raw meat. It was wonderful to see them again, to spend time with the people who had inspired so much work and effort over the years. During the campaign, there were always people milling around—aides, staffers, media vying for attention and competing against each other to sound the most clever and hard-hitting. Once, I ran into Governor Romney in Nashville at an event, and he greeted me on his way out the door.

"How's David?" he asked.

It was a difficult question. He'd only been gone a few months and his troop had suffered a great number of casualties. I can't exactly remember what I said, but it was something along the lines of, "So many of his friends are dying." It wasn't my best moment. I just didn't have my game face on and wasn't expecting him to ask about David. Governor Romney was being rushed out of the room to the airport, and I threw the verbal equivalent of a hand grenade. "His friends are dying," I said, like the person at a party who doesn't know how to act in public.

I was hoping that spending time with the Romneys would be more normal, less rushed, and a diversion from all the war talk.

And it certainly was.

"Do you ski?" Governor Romney asked me that morning as we tried to find clothes to wear, yet another chance to come clean about my skiing ability.

"I'm practically Jean-Claude Killy," I said, inexplicably. This kind of hyperbole would've worked in the South, with regular people who hang around other regular people. Only in hindsight did I remember that Governor Romney was actually a friend of Jean-Claude's, from his days running the Olympics. Nevertheless, I comforted myself in the knowledge that there must be some sort of scripture that invalidates the Ten Commandments' prohibition against lying if done so with a wink.

I had a plan, you see—to be obscure . . . to politely excuse myself while they headed off to the triple black diamonds. After all, the

Romneys would certainly go hang out with each other or some famous people and I'd catch up with them a couple hours later looking tired from all the fun I had skiing. In retrospect, I realize this may not have been a brilliant plan, but I'd watched enough *Three's Company* episodes to at least believe it was possible.

"Let me guess," Governor Romney said, looking at my feet. "Size eight?"

If you're doing a timeline of my demise, this was exactly when my plan started to go awry. He led me into a closet full of ski gear, but of course it wasn't regular gear. When we'd go out on one of the rare days it snows in the South, we'd wear whatever we had lying around. Mismatched gloves, pantyhose for warmth, jogging pants layered over jeans, and maybe Wal-Mart bags tied around our shoes so they wouldn't get wet. Governor Romney, however, was the head of the 2002 Winter Olympics and had put together quite a collection. After being outfitted in high-tech socks, pants, a jacket, and a red hat, I looked in the mirror and gasped. Practically each piece of my ensemble had the five rings emblazoned on it. I was wearing official Olympic gear from the 2002 Winter Games.

One day when I lived in New York, I was wearing one of David's Harvard Law School T-shirts running errands. A man stopped me and asked, "Did *you* go to Harvard?" When I said no, he didn't really say anything much, but the incredulity on his face said it loudly: poser. Similarly, I felt like this ski outfit belonged in an Alanis Morissette song, because it felt slightly ironic. There I was, trying not to bring attention to myself or my lack of skill, wearing Olympic ski gear from head to toe.

When we got to the lodge to get skis, I was walking behind the governor—mainly because I could barely keep up. I was wearing one of his daughter-in-laws' boots and learned a little too late that you don't tighten them up before you put your skis on. While the governor was easily going through the lodge, down the stairs, and through crowded halls of people, I was walking like an intoxicated duck, just trying not to kill myself or anyone in the vicinity. However, the vantage point of being about ten feet behind the governor allowed me to see the reactions on people's faces when they realized who he was.

First it was disbelief, followed by a loud proclamation to the person beside them, then—if we were lucky—a clever comment, such as one of the eleven variations on "Hey, Mitt! I hope these slopes aren't as tough for you as Iowa."

It also seemed that everyone had voted for him and everyone knew him . . . practically.

"My accountant knows your banker," one man explained. "Can you pose for a photo?"

I was shocked at how genuinely kind and welcoming he was, even as audacious people approached him, cell phone cameras in hand, ready for him to—at the drop of a hat—pose and engage in chitchat. He walked quickly through the crowds, because getting from point A to point B was always interrupted by people wanting a photo. Or by my *occasional* accident.

"Why don't you look where you're going?" the person I whacked with my skis would say while trying to get off the floor. That's when they'd look up and see him. "Mitt Romney! Hey, can we take a picture?" Sometimes they'd even say, "I didn't look good in that one, let me take another."

By the time we got to the top of the mountain, I was literally shaking in my boots. Or rather, their daughter-in-law's boots. I'd made a few jokes, trying to soften expectations. But nothing prepared me for that moment of looking down the ski slope and having various thoughts race through my head simultaneously . . . something about tangled webs and weaving and deceiving and how I wasn't sure how to use my new military insurance if I ended up in the emergency room.

"Go on, guys—I might be a little rusty," I encouraged Mrs. Romney and the governor, pointing to the more difficult slopes. I was standing atop a slope designated "green," apparently for the color your face turns when you look down it. Although it was supposed to be the "easy slope," it looked high to me, with the surrounding snow-capped mountains. It reminded me of the IMAX movie *Everest*, and I half expected to see frozen skeletons of skiers who had gone before me sticking out of the fluffy white snow.

"No, let's stick together," Ann said, before skiing off, cute in her little red hat and black pants. Her brother Rod and his wife, Cindy, took off after her, followed by Mitt.

And there I stood.

There are moments in life that give you pause, where you stand on the edge of the abyss and face a crucial decision. The one that faced me was particularly small—to ski or not to ski—but it felt as significant as Romeo's decision to drink the hemlock or Jean Valjean's decision to go to court at Toulon. I looked down the mountain and felt the same sensation as at the amusement park after trash-talking everyone into riding the highest and fastest roller coaster. About halfway up the steep incline, near the spot where the people on the ground look like ants, the roller coaster makes straining mechanical creaks and I wonder how many people this contraption has killed. Then I take a deep breath, pray, and regret the bravado that caused me to get in this situation. Possessing a weird combination of hubris and cowardice, I literally felt I held my life in my hands as I struggled to push off down the slope.

Then—as Mitt and Ann got farther away—some kindergartners following their instructor, skis the size of Popsicle sticks, plowed in front of me like I was the granny hesitating at the green light. I had no choice, so I took a deep breath and hoped through the power of positive thinking that I'd catch up with the Romneys and flash a winning smile as I passed them. They'd think, *I'm so glad we hired her as a writer, what with her innate athletic ability and all.* I'd realize I was a skiing savant, and Bob Costas would narrate my personal profile at the next Olympics: "She never knew she could ski, until she was thirty-three years old and finally decided to believe in herself..."

But reality is a stubborn thing.

I shot down the mountain like a bullet from a 9mm. Although I remembered I was supposed to crisscross down the slopes, I couldn't manage to change direction, making my descent a barely managed free fall. My arms flailed, I lost a pole, and I flew by Governor Romney, Ann, Rod, and Cindy like I was a thief and they were the cops.

Finally—miraculously—I turned the edge of my ski just enough to cause me to go horizontally across the slope, easing my speed just enough so I could, once again, change directions. It was a gorgeous day, and the scenery flashing by my face would've been breathtaking had fear and physical exertion not already stolen all the breath from my Olympic-clad body. Eventually, without a pole, I came to a complete stop by, well, falling on my backside and turning a flip. One ski popped off, and the other stuck out of the snow like a telephone pole. When I opened my eyes, the sun shining in my face, I saw the Romneys barely stifling laughter. There I was, like a beetle on its back, trying not to draw attention to myself as a former presidential candidate held out a helping hand.

A skier with a cell phone snapped a photo.

I imagined their conversations later that evening.

"Look who I saw on the slopes today! Here's a photo of Mitt Romney and . . . well, an Olympic athlete who must've been *really* drunk."

Apparently there's an art to getting up after having fallen down with skis on. First, you have to put the skis perpendicular to the slope so that when you do finally get up you won't just speed back down the mountain. It just so happened that I fell right beside a little cliff, and when I tried to get up I started sliding off the side. I took the governor's hand and tried valiantly again to get up. Had he won the nomination, the Secret Service would've intervened, believing I posed a threat to both of our safety. No matter how much I flailed, I only succeeded in bringing him down with me.

Miraculously, I finally made it back to a vertical position. While David was breathing the sandy remains of what could've been Nebuchadnezzar's army, I dug my ski into the soft snow and wondered what shade of red my face had become. There we were, in the middle of a run, paralyzed by my utter and complete inability to ski.

"I'm sorry," I gasped. "I lied about being able to ski because I wanted to hang out with you guys."

Cindy, stifling laughter, mustered a suggestion.

"Maybe we should take a moment to pray about this?"

We stood in silence on the side of the mountain, no one daring to say a word. First I heard Cindy giggle, then Rod. Finally, Ann broke into full-throated laughter.

"It's quite possible that you are in more physical danger right now than David."

Many Christians, after hearing about Evangelicals for Mitt and the unique relationship we had with some LDS readers, said it was a wonderful thing...what a great opportunity for them to be exposed to evangelical Christianity. After all, they explained, we could be God's chosen vessel, the face of Christianity much like Maybelline cosmetics chooses a new "face" to advertise their collagen-enhanced mascara each year. I could be the "grace not works" spokesmodel. After all, every time I met people who heard my husband was in Iraq, they invariably would tell me how awesome I was. And that many people couldn't be wrong.

However, the very idea that anyone outside traditional, orthodox Christianity would somehow be drawn to God after hanging around me was absolutely absurd. In fact, they might be suspicious of a God misguided enough to allow Himself to be publicly represented by such a buffoon.

I'd like to claim I had some sort of emotional disorder because David had gone to the front lines. Or maybe I could blame my writing for making me feel as if I'd be good at something I really wasn't. But the truth is that nothing really changes when your spouse goes to war or when you write memoirs or help political campaigns. I was still the same person with the same selfish tendencies, shortcomings usually made worse by dramatic circumstances. And standing there horrified on the side of the mountain was a pretty dramatic circumstance.

By God's provision, however, I was surrounded by understanding friends, who extended kindness and grace to their faltering, lying, lonely, uncoordinated evangelical friend. In fact, Mitt, Ann, Rod, and Cindy not only forgave me, they took turns teaching me how to ski for the rest of the afternoon.

The next time someone tells me Mormons don't understand the doctrine of grace, I'll remember that scene.

And you know what? If enough time has passed, I'll probably laugh.

19

SEND-A-BOX

Nancy

AS THE DAYS AND WEEKS passed, and as the news from FOB Caldwell grew more grim, I knew that the first part of my mission here at home—loving and supporting David—was growing more difficult. We couldn't *really* communicate...instant messages and brief, grainy telephone conversations are no way to run a marriage.

One day, in the midst of one of those maddening iChat conversations that meant so much but communicated so little, he said something that—for some reason—pierced my heart: His towels were too small. He said that the Army-issued towels were sized for preschoolers and slightly less substantial than Kleenex.

"So even after you successfully make it out of the shower, you can't even dry off," he typed.

I'm not sure if it's just a part of being a woman, but I had a strong urge to fix that problem. I couldn't do a thing about bombs buried in a road, but at least I could make sure he could dry off properly. On Sunday, I walked through the fellowship hall after church on my way to get coffee and was asked—for the tenth time that morning—the familiar question: "How's David? Is there anything he needs?"

"Towels," I said. And I kept saying it, every time I was asked. "And if you're sending a package, put some basic medicine supplies and some of that powdered drink mix stuff you can put in bottled water to make it taste better."

Four weeks later, I got a text from him: "iChat?"

I situated myself in front of my laptop and saw his familiar little icon pop up.

"I have a virtual CVS here!" David wrote. "And enough of those powdered drinks to turn the Caspian Sea into Kool-Aid."

"I don't know anything about it," I typed. "But the church put your address in the bulletin."

"And boxes and boxes of towels—some of them say, 'Turkish cotton' on the tags," he typed.

"Is Turkish cotton better than Mississippi cotton?"

"I don't know, but it sounds fancier. I got so many that I've been able to start giving them away," he typed. "And the guys appreciate it because many of them haven't gotten any packages from home."

That made me lose my breath, as images of disappointed soldiers waiting in line at mail call flooded my mind. Of course, I had no idea how mail distribution in a war zone happened, but that's how they did it at Mid South Youth Camp in Tennessee twenty-five years ago...and I could still taste the bitter disappointment on the days my name wasn't called. Skittles, melted M&M's, Turkish cotton. Somehow material items—silly cheap things—embody the notion of home. Although home is where the heart is, let's face it, it's also a collection of things—worn slippers left haphazardly near the nightstand, a dog at the foot of the bed, photos on the piano of kids missing teeth. To protect "home" is why most of the guys are over there. At the very least, when they go to the showers to wash off the dirt and blood earned from protecting these peaceful, idyllic enclaves, they shouldn't have to air dry.

"They don't get *anything*?"

"Many of them don't have strong families back home," he wrote. "They're just kids, you know."

"I'll send them boxes," I offered.

"There's a lot of guys here."

"Are you doubting me?"

"I'm talking a thousand people!"

"Oh."

We chatted back and forth about the logistics, and after a few days we made a decision to at least make a concerted effort.

We landed on the easily understood name of "Operation Send-a-Box," which would start in January and end in March. After trying to figure out an equitable way to distribute them, we asked the chaplain—a young man by the name of Benjamin Ellington—to hand them out. He agreed to distribute them to the lowest-ranked soldiers first to make sure the guys with the most dangerous jobs got taken care of.

With a name and a strategy determined, only one complication remained.

"I need a few hundred care packages," I said into my phone. On the other end of the line were our friends John and Jean, who live in Boston. David met John almost twenty years ago, when he was standing in line behind him at a bookstore at Harvard Law School. He'd been eavesdropping and heard talk of a C. S. Lewis reading group.

"Um, excuse me," David butted in. "I like C. S. Lewis too." David had come from a small evangelical college in Nashville (David Lipscomb) and was shocked to read an article in the Harvard newspaper that said, "Jesus Christ, your fifteen minutes of fame are up." When he heard the guys in front of him were reading Lewis, he knew he'd found fellow believers and invited himself to be a part of the group without hesitation.

It was a divine eavesdropping. Over the course of the last couple of decades, John and his wife, Jean, have become our dearest friends, the kind of people who don't laugh at harebrained schemes.

"Hundreds?"

"Yes, and ideally, a whole bunch of towels too. Any ideas?"

John is Vice Chairman and General Counsel of a Boston-based asset management company worth more than General Motors. Because he, Jean, and their four kids have been so blessed, they are always thinking of ways to give and serve as a family to help people in need—even going so far as to create an organization called SixSeeds that facilitates other families' desire to do the same.

"Count us in!" they both said, not exactly knowing *how* we'd pull it off but simply wanting to be a part of it. Within a month, John had the SixSeeds team design a website. With a professional-looking site—SendaBox.org—we suddenly had legitimacy and a place to direct people for details on where to send the packages and what to put in them.

"Wait," I said in the middle of the website creation phase. "What *should* we put in them?"

"We don't want some soldiers getting cheap boxes," the ever-practical Jean said. You could tell she was the mother of four and was used to seeing the emotional effects of a disparity of goods. "If some get new sheets, DVDs, and Dustbusters, we don't want others to get jilted by inexpensive boxes. And really, don't we want all of the guys to get boxes? We can't just send half of them some."

After consulting David, we made a list of much-needed and fun items for his squadron. Each box would contain a twin size sheet set, a towel, at least one new-release DVD, personal hygiene items (such as shampoo, soap, toothpaste, shaving cream, deodorant, toothbrush), reading material (such as car and motorcycle magazines, *Sports Illustrated*, paperback books), and some sort of edible treat (gum, beef jerky, energy bars, Pringles, PowerBars, anything that wouldn't melt in the desert sun).

"This is going to be expensive," I said, after mentally calculating the costs. "I don't see how you could buy all these things for less than a hundred dollars per box!"

We were on a conference call and the line was silent for a moment. We needed a lot of boxes, and therefore needed to appeal to the average American on a budget. Plus, it was right after Christmas.

"Should we cut some of the nonessentials out?" John asked.

No one answered.

Americans historically have happily and sacrificially joined the "war effort." But this war is invisible, detectable only if you're willing to dig for information in the newspaper or know someone there personally.

"I don't think we're asking too much," I said, trying not to have an edge of resentment in my voice. Everyone paused, took a deep breath, and agreed to forge ahead.

The planning was coming along nicely, until Jean went to the store and actually tried to create a box. "There's one complication...all the items will fit, just barely, but only if we leave out the towel," she explained. Flat-rate boxes cost less than ten dollars to ship, no matter how many things you stuffed in there. That's how the towels were marked off the list.

I tried not to let it bother me, because the size of the flat-rate boxes was nonnegotiable. In fact, these particular boxes actually made the whole thing possible. I'd heard that the Postal Service provides free packaging materials for military families and friends to help them send packages overseas to their loved ones. Dubious, I called the toll-free number, asked for the "military pack," and within a week was surprised to receive twenty-five boxes, tape, and packaging materials at my door.

Instead of asking a thousand of my best friends to each send one box, I decided to get "area coordinators"—people who could send twenty-five boxes—and had the post office send the military pack straight to their homes. There's nothing like twenty-five empty boxes staring at you from the front porch to make you remember your patriotic duty. And so, with all the details of the project laid out on the website, a mechanism to get packaging materials to our volunteers, and a way to distribute once the boxes got to Iraq, we were ready to launch.

The first place I went was to our website, EvangelicalsforMitt.org. Our little blog had taken on a life of its own during this hotly contested presidential race. On rare occasions, we'd ask our loyal readers to do something, like vote in an online poll, or travel to an event to vote in a straw poll for Governor Romney. Without exception, they came through in an amazing way.

But I'd never asked them for a personal favor.

"Hey guys," I began. "Soldiers in Iraq bravely fight for their country without any comforts of home (sometimes without even running water) or the ability to regularly communicate back home. For example, there are just a few phones for over a thousand soldiers, so the wait is up to two hours and frequently the person they're calling isn't home! To ease the burden just a bit, some dear friends from Boston and I are trying to send a care package to every soldier in David's squadron...Perhaps a church could adopt David's squadron...or maybe you have a 'mother's group' that gets together for playdates that could handle twenty-five? A school project? Boy Scouts?"

And so it began.

I asked interested people to email me, and within minutes my inbox began to fill. The first acceptance came from Mission Viejo, California; the next, Abilene, Texas. Then came Utah. Lots and lots of Utah. I had Mormons writing the most wonderful emails to their bishops extolling our virtues and asking for their "stakes" to adopt our cause. An evangelical church in Ohio offered to buy a hundred sets of sheets and asked their congregation to fill the rest of the boxes.

The pastor of that church called me.

"What's a sheet set, exactly?" he said.

"Well, it's a pillowcase, a fitted sheet, and a top sheet," I explained.

"I told you," I heard his wife whisper in the background.

Although the instructions on the website were pretty detailed, my phone rang all day and my inbox was filled with various questions.

"What are the restrictions on food since it's a Muslim country?"

"Can I put a religious tract in there?"

"I found great sheets at a discount, but they are pink with roses. Do you think that might get someone beat up?"

"I worked out a deal with Blockbuster for movies in bulk— perhaps you can pass this on to the other Send-a-Boxers?"

"My daughters want to send packages to the females. Are there any?"

"May I send a *Playboy?*"

I tried not to worry about quality control. With all these people shopping around for the best bargains and sending boxes that reflected their own personalities, there was no telling what would actually arrive in Iraq...if it arrived at all. I'd heard on the news that mail trucks are occasionally blown up en route. But the far more likely scenario was that these random strangers whom I'd sent twenty to a hundred boxes wouldn't actually come through. I tried not to get my hopes up. But when Kathryn Jean Lopez of *National Review Online* linked to our site (not once but twice), I started to think we just might be able to pull this off.

One day, my phone rang. "John and I are donating towels," Jean said.

"To whom?"

"To everyone!"

"But," I said as I fought back the tears, "there's a thousand guys there!"

And so, for a week or so, Jean looked for towels that could withstand the horrors of the washing machines in Diyala province. Eventually she settled on nice, strong towels that cost $25 apiece.

"Each?" I asked, aghast. I normally shopped at Wal-Mart, but we knew that we needed heftier—and consequently more expensive—towels to survive the challenges of Diyala.

"The company was willing to give us a good deal, since it was for the troops."

That night, my head raced as I drifted off to sleep, wondering if people would come through with their twenty-five-box commitment, wondering what a shipment of $25,000 worth of towels looks like, and hoping against hope that when the soldiers sponged off after a shower the plush, thick towels would also dab away just a bit of the loneliness.

But there was just no way of knowing if any of this would work, so I tried not to get my hopes up, turned over, and dreamed of the exotic fabric known as Turkish cotton.

20

DIVERSIONS

David

I'LL NEVER FORGET THE BOXES...the avalanche of boxes.

The first, small burst arrived at the height of Operation Payback. Then, week by week, they poured in. Fifty in one week. One hundred the next. Two hundred. Three hundred. Then three hundred again. And they kept coming.

Every one of them contained "good stuff" (as the guys said). Sheets, new DVDs, reading materials, food...everything a trooper needed for a nice morale boost. That's not to say some of the boxes weren't a bit quirky. I remember walking past one trooper who looked positively depressed as he examined the contents of his box.

"What's wrong?" I asked.

"Well, sir, I appreciate the box and all, but the new DVD they got me is some documentary on dolphins. He"—the trooper motioned toward his friend—"got *Transformers*. I got dolphins."

I saw one guy running past holding several rather hard R-rated movies, including the Denise Richards movie *Wild Things*. I looked at the box and saw that it also contained a virtual year's supply of *Maxim* magazines. The return address indicated that the box came from my church.

On a different occasion, I walked by and saw a trooper sitting on his bed, with pink flowered sheets bunched up at the end.

"Please tell me you didn't get those sheets from the boxes."

"Sir, they're sheets, and they're clean. So I'm better off than I was before."

Not only did we get enough boxes to supply everyone on the base, we got enough to supply everyone twice. And to supply units who came through for visits. And to supply the Ugandans who guarded our front gate. The flow eventually became so overwhelming that a Send-a-Box distribution update was added to the chaplain's brief at every weekly command update.

But not even the cumulative impact of the boxes caused as much of a sensation as the towels. One thousand towels. All Turkish cotton (whatever that is). All sent by my friends John and Jean Kingston.

First, everyone was shocked at the delivery. A thousand towels take up a lot of space in a container. Second, people were amazed at their luxury. These weren't towels, they were *bath sheets*. Baby-soft bath sheets. Like the kind you'd find at the Ritz-Carlton. Third, everyone used them. And I mean used them. Six months later, I saw one hanging outside a shower stall. It used to be blue, but it was mostly brown.

"Have you even washed that?"

"Sir, don't ask."

To this day, I fear that our guys didn't express enough appreciation. Coming when the boxes did, they arrived when men were dying, when operations were at their peak, and when we were all being run ragged. It was hard to find time to write thank-you notes. I don't even know if John and Jean, who gave so much, ever got a formal acknowledgment of their gift.

In a way, though, it was that very silence that demonstrated how much the boxes were needed. Men without time to write were given a small piece of home by people they'd never know.

As for me? I saw each one of them as a love letter—a love letter from my wife to me and to my brothers in arms.

We had so little to distract us from the war. The boxes helped, and the sheets and towels improved our standard of living, but once the granola bars were eaten, the DVDs watched (one hundred times), and the magazines passed around again and again, we were left where we started . . . with a bunch of guys in the middle of a (very) hostile desert.

As I've said before, we lived with guys—all guys—all the time. Sabre Squadron is combat arms, which means all men. Consequently, everyone lived in a constant state of starvation for any glimpse of a "real" female—an American female. (We weren't even permitted to make eye contact with the Iraqi women in black burqas who peered at us curiously from doorways and courtyards.)

In fact, it was high comedy to watch what happened when a female soldier visited our FOB. First, the rumors would start. "Sir, are some MPs coming to the FOB?" (Military Police units were legendary for their female members.) Then, as the MP vehicles actually rolled into the gate, a small crowd would gather, ostensibly to "help them with their gear." Finally, as the female soldiers walked through the dining facility, you could watch guys' heads pop up from their meals like prairie dogs across the plain.

Of course, nothing could match the sheer hysteria generated by the visit from a single—very brave—Dallas Cowboys cheerleader. For months every laptop computer on the FOB featured a desktop picture of a grinning Sabre Trooper next to a quite fetching tiny blonde woman in a tank top.

But nowhere is the deprivation more complete than at our remote combat outposts, or COPs. Stuck in the middle of the desert, far from television, unable to videoconference with girlfriends or wives, and separated even from the books and magazines that circulate the base, troopers are left with little to nothing to see or do. So it's no surprise that when one trooper's mother sent him a stack of *OK!* celebrity magazines (if you're not familiar with *OK!* think of *People* magazine without the highbrow intellectual content), they were immediately snatched up, fought over, read, and reread. Features like "Who Wore It Best?" or "Stars! Just Like Us!" sparked vicious debates about the relative hotness of Jessica Alba, Paris Hilton, and Jessica Biel.

COP Imam Mansour was the home of the *OK!* stash. The headquarters hut was full of well-read and dog-eared copies of the celebrity fanzine. I happened to be at the combat outpost because of one of the tragic accidents of war. An Iraqi man driving a truck that exactly matched a truck we were trying to locate (we were concerned that it contained explosives) sped toward one of our small outposts just as troopers on the other side of the base engaged a different threat. Concerned that the two incidents were part of one attack, a trooper fired a single round from his rifle into the engine block of the oncoming truck. That round ricocheted up from the engine and into the driver's heart.

But the driver wasn't a terrorist. He was a shepherd and father of six children. He was driving to a village with most of the family's small herd of sheep in the back of the truck. When he died, the truck flipped, killing all the sheep. At one stroke, the family lost their father and most of their worldly assets. And it was no one's fault—no one's except the al Qaeda terrorists who used identical civilian trucks as their vehicle bomb of choice.

Incidents like that, however, present huge challenges. We were living in recently liberated villages and didn't want the villagers to fear us like they feared (and hated) the terrorists. Further, there were important justice issues at stake, in Iraqi culture and our own. So I spent days carefully investigating the incident, determining the value of the sheep, obtaining condolence funds to pay the family, and providing rules-of-engagement refresher sessions for the troops in the field.

An informal lunch with tribal leaders eased the political fallout, payouts to the family took care of their financial crisis (though nothing we could do could ease the pain of their loss), and our on-ground after-action reviews were designed to prevent similar incidents. While I was out on the after-action review, my friend Jon Norquist, the officer who actually handled payments to locals, wandered over to the pile of magazines, sat down, and started flipping through. That's when he suddenly sat bolt upright and made a proclamation.

"Dude, we have to do this! Check it out." He put the magazine in my face and pointed to a picture of a guy in a hammock reading *OK!* Underneath the caption identifying him was an invitation to "submit a picture of you reading *OK!*" Apparently, if you took one of yourself reading the magazine (and you looked good enough), they would print the picture in an upcoming issue.

Jon was beside himself with excitement. "If they print that doofus in a hammock, they'll definitely print a picture of troops in the field."

I didn't hesitate. How could I pass up the chance to grace the pages of a celebrity magazine? "I'm in."

We grabbed the commander of our field artillery battery, John Romito, took three issues of the magazine, walked out to an armored personnel carrier in our full "battle rattle," and had a trooper snap our photo. The moment we finished our after-action review and rolled back to FOB Caldwell, Jon dashed up to my computer and sent *OK!* the following message:

Dear *OK!* . . .

Attached are pictures of CPT Dave French, CPT John Romito, and myself, CPT Jon Norquist . . . some of the most battle-hardened patriots this country has to offer. In the picture we are taking a much-needed break from constantly pursuing the enemy in support of a major offensive operation against Al Qaeda in Diyala Province, Iraq. It was nice to finally wash the blood off our hands and catch up on the latest celebrity child-bearing woes and get a glimpse of the red carpet glamour. Thanks for keeping us in the know!

Within twenty-four hours the reply came: "Thank You! I'm going to put this in issue 36 of picture this! :) *OK!* mag is happy we can provide you with entertainment and appreciate everything our troops do for the USA!"

And there you have it. Within days, my lawyerly face graced the same pages as beautiful people like Jennifer Aniston (she was on the cover, in fact), Angelina Jolie, and Rachel McAdams.

That's about as good as it gets in Iraq.

I say "about" because there was one diversion better than a celebrity fanzine—one diversion almost as good as the avalanche of boxes from home. Our satellite computer system did more than just connect us with our family and friends, it also opened up the possibility of late-night (when bandwidth issues weren't too severe) online gaming. In my civilian life, *World of Warcraft*—a swords and sorcery online role-playing game—is my passionate diversion and hobby. After a hard day at work and a fun evening with Nancy and the kids, I like nothing better than to crack open a cold drink, sit at my computer, and lead my elven priest named Rickybobby into combat against evil demons and dragons.

It turns out, fortunately, that I wasn't the only geek in Sabre

Squadron. In fact, our little computer cabal was full of geeks. J-Dave played a human warlock named Malefactus. Dan Driscoll ran the magical land of Azeroth as a gnome mage named Dantanimagus. And so it went. Clay Heselschwerdt's alter ego was Lunarclaw, Bob Garven's was Obregal, and even Mike Medders, the very personification of the adored athlete, got into the act.

"Lawyer," he said. "You've got me. I'm going to start playing *WoW*."

"No way."

"Yep. And I've picked out my name. I'm going to be M'Gungis."

"Muh-what?"

He parsed out the syllables. "Muh...gun...gis."

"How do you spell that?"

"M'Gungis."

"Okay."

Recruiting M'Gungis was my great and enduring coup. My favorite game was slowly but surely triumphing over "their game," *Rock Band*. Howling lyrics and wailing guitars were replaced by fireball spells and endless discussions of talent builds and spell rotations. Rarely had geekdom triumphed so completely over pop culture. It was as if the entire crowd at a cutting-edge rock concert left en masse and went across the street to a comic book convention.

I was so enthusiastic about the spread of *WoW* that I even stopped calling people by their real names. J-Dave would walk into the room, and I'd yell out, "Malefactus!" Even in (nonurgent) operational contexts I'd use character names. "Dantanimagus, when is that briefing?" "M'Gungis, are you rolling out tomorrow?"

During quiet nights we hunched over our computers, battled the evil horde in Alterac Valley, and got frustrated when the satellite signal sometimes faded and caused up to two or three seconds of lag as we directed our characters to attack our foes.

Sometimes I'd feel a little strange telling Nancy during an Internet chat that I was busy playing *WoW* rather than doing something more, well, productive and exciting. But out where we were, exciting meant deadly, and I think Nancy was more than happy to think of me having enough spare time and security to actually play a video game.

But none of our diversions was more important than dinner.

Yes, dinner. When events permitted, the staff officers put a high priority on eating together. We'd start to gather around six in the evening and then walk, en masse, to our tiny dining facility. Once there, we'd commandeer a small side room and spend the meal talking, laughing, and arguing.

As the old member of the staff, I fashioned myself the "room commander" (I also tried to get others to call me the room commander of our living quarters, but it never really stuck) and always sat at the head of the table, ready to pontificate on any topic. The pattern was always the same. We'd eat, grab a dessert, then get coffee. We'd stretch out the meal as long as we could, delighting in a small break from the war—a time when we could talk about women, video games, sports, women, or just complain...endlessly complain.

While I may have crowned myself room commander, the real star of the dinner ritual was Mike Medders, M'Gungis himself. He'd recently come over to the headquarters troop (my unit) after spending the first six months as Grim's executive officer, and—in typical Mike fashion—he immediately asserted his rather formidable presence.

A big guy with a huge smile, he would always walk into dinner like he owned the place, as if he was saying, "I'm here now, we can start." And start we would. There was always an extra energy when he was present. The jokes were funnier, the arguments louder, and the discussions about life and home always more intense.

I tried to describe Mike—and everyone—to Nancy. But it just didn't translate. The jokes—if they were printable—couldn't translate via iChat. The stories were meaningless. And there was simply no way to communicate the deep meaning of the shared experience.

It's been said so much that it's a cliché: There's no bond like the bond between brothers in arms. It's true. Indisputably true. Since I've been home, I've missed those friendships—their absence is like a hole in my heart. But I remember what it was like, when the sandstorms would rage, when operations slowed down, and we'd gather at the dining facility, laughing and talking about a life that no one but us would ever understand.

21

ILLUMINATION

David

EVERY NOW AND THEN, a plan actually works.

It all started with an air assault. The tankers and scouts of Grim Troop filed into Chinook helicopters, along with a full battalion of Iraqi soldiers, and airlifted right over the top of one of the extensive IED ambushes in Diyala. The intent was to clear al Qaeda out of a group of villages south of our FOB and to do so without taking IED casualties. If we could surprise the enemy while doing so, even better.

And it worked.

In the early morning hours of a midsummer day, an al Qaeda operative who was perhaps the highest-value target in the entire region decided to go on a drive with three members of his personal security detail. They were less than a kilometer outside their village when they were abruptly stopped by a small group of Grim troopers.

"Sir, you should have seen the looks on their faces." A Grim trooper was grinning as he stepped off the helicopter and handed custody of four miserable and defeated-looking men over to me. "It was priceless."

"I bet it was." I signed for custody of their ID cards, weapons, cell phones, and laptops, then signed over the ID cards to our intelligence shop. "Where's the rest of their paperwork?"

"No other paperwork, sir. We've got ops going right now."

"Understood." And I did understand. The last thing the troopers needed to worry about at that moment was filling out extensive forms.

"We'll fix it later. We've got three days to get these guys out of here, and we'll get it all done before then."

I knew a detainee could be released if we didn't have the paperwork in order, but at that point I had no idea that we'd captured anyone significant. I knew from their weapons and computers that we had somebody a bit unusual, but I had no clue about what would happen next.

As I was overseeing the "check-in process" (where we catalogued all the detainees' belongings, gave them physical exams, fed them, and explained the rules of behavior), a trooper from our intelligence section came running up.

"Sir, these are some huge guys we got here. Corps wants them right now and is sending a chopper to get them."

"Roger that."

Gulp. "Corps" meant the overall command of Iraq, located in Baghdad. We *never* heard from Corps. I ran back to our TOC to call the brigade provost marshal. The provost marshal essentially ran detainee ops for Diyala province, and he needed to be informed. He also needed to know about the paperwork . . . or lack thereof.

I called on the secure satellite phone. "Sir, this is Captain French with 2/3, we've—"

He cut me off. "I know all about this. The choppers are to drop them off here."

"Roger that, sir. We have a problem. I don't have paperwork on these guys. They were airlifted in here without paperwork after an overnight air assault."

"I need those sworn statements."

"Yes, sir. I don't think we have any chopper missions out to our guys until tomorrow."

"Not my problem. I need that paperwork. If it's not with them when they land here, then you've just got a few hours to get it to me. Understood?"

"Yes, sir." I hung up the phone.

Double gulp. I walked into the squadron commander's office. "Sir, I have good news and bad news. The good news is we've caught a big one. The bad news is that we don't have any paperwork on him, and Brigade has only given us a few hours to fix it."

"Well, fix it then."

"Yes, sir." I left his office and walked down to Grim Troop's TOC, where First Sergeant Adcock was preparing to leave on what I was pretty sure was his first ground mission through these IED-laden roads to resupply his troopers.

"First Sergeant, you rolling out?"

"Yes, sir."

"Can I come with you? You won't believe this, but I've got to get some paperwork done on those detainees, and your guys are the only ones who can help me."

"Sir, are you serious?"

"Very serious."

"All right, gear up." And with those words I began the most harrowing mission of my entire deployment. Now, let me emphasize that it was just *my* most harrowing mission. For the infinitely braver line troops of Grim Troop, like First Sergeant Adcock, a mission like this was just part of their lives. Roll down uncleared roads? No problem. Do it for six hours or more? Roger that.

But for me, this was new.

We left at about 1800 hours, with my heart in my throat. (Fortunately, I didn't begin this mission by breaking my own nose.) We rolled down our main supply road, past the "friendly" towns, past our most remote combat outposts, and into enemy-held territory.

The wind began to pick up. The blue sky turned brown, then orange.

A sandstorm.

"Well, there goes our air support," First Sergeant Adcock said with the same kind of tone that a man would use if he was reporting on the weather back home. Rolling out in the countryside with the air "red" was nothing new to him. It was for me.

We kept going. And going. The roads got rougher, and we passed by crater after crater—the remnants of other, less fortunate convoys from weeks, months, and even years past. We rolled past ancient villages, over irrigation canals, and looked back at shepherds who stared at us, expressionless, while they tended their tiny, scrawny herds.

This brings me to something else . . . Iraq itself.

This country is broken. There's a statement attributed to Colin Powell that's been tossed around quite a bit: "You broke it; you bought it." Well, we didn't break Iraq, but it most assuredly is broken, physically, culturally, and spiritually. Sectarian hatred didn't start in 2003. Cultural decay didn't start in 2003. The crumbling of Iraq's infrastructure didn't start in 2003. Overwhelming poverty didn't start in 2003. Shocking indifference to violence didn't start in 2003.

Iraq has a strange kind of poverty. Sitting on some of the richest resources in the world, many of the people live in conditions that would no doubt be considered disgraceful to the citizens of ancient Babylon. Mud huts and simple brick buildings dot the countryside and dominate the villages. Men dressed in flowing dishdashas (what we called "man dresses") squat in doorways and in the sparse shade, while mostly women shop in open-air markets that consist of simple carts carrying produce, meat, and other staples. Cattle graze by the road. Donkeys carrying small children trot by. If it weren't for the myriad satellite dishes and hundreds of dusty cars, minivans, and pickup trucks, the place would feel ancient.

No. "Ancient" is the wrong word. The word "ancient" can conjure up positive feelings of historical significance. I think "decayed" is the better word. After I got home, several people asked me if it was "cool" to be in a place with such a rich history. The answer is a definite no. As one friend asked me, "Do you ever think that you are walking on ground that Alexander the Great walked, where the children of Israel lived while in exile, where civilization began?"

Well, I thought about it all the time, but it never *felt* like I imagined it would feel. The following analogy comes to mind: imagine if you were walking on one of the most significant parts of American soil, like Independence Hall in Philadelphia or the site of Pickett's Charge at Gettysburg, but instead of the beautifully preserved colonial statehouse or the majestic monuments and manicured fields of the historic battlefield, there was an old pawn shop, a check-cashing emporium, a ratty trailer park, a coin laundry, and multiple overflowing Dumpsters. How "cool" would that be?

But I digress.

At that moment, my mind wasn't on the age of the villages but instead the task at hand and my own fragility. I just wanted to complete the mission and get back to my FOB "home" in one piece.

After more than an hour, we spotted our first group of Grim troopers. They emerged from the village they'd air-assaulted in just the night before—filthy, laden with weapons, and grinning from ear to ear. Our convoy wasn't just bringing the lawyer, we were bringing food and supplies—a hot meal and cold water.

I jumped out of the back of the vehicle, and one of the Grim lieutenants acted shocked.

"Sir, what are you doing out here?"

"What every lawyer does in the field...paperwork."

Fortunately, this was exactly the group of troopers I needed to see. They were the guys who'd captured the al Qaeda leader. So I set up a tiny law office in the back of our vehicle. I opened my computer, downloaded their photos onto my desktop, and then worked with them as they drafted their sworn statements and drew their diagrams of the scene. All the while, I felt faintly ridiculous. Here we were, in the middle of a major operation in a shooting war, and you've got a lawyer out in the field taking sworn statements. I'm not sure that's the right way to do things.

But what I thought (or think) didn't (and doesn't) matter. We had to do what we had to do. The entire task took about forty-five minutes, and when it was done, I became nothing more than a passenger on the rest of the mission, sitting in the back as we rolled from village to village, feeding our troopers.

It got dark.

And darker.

As the light failed completely, I heard a series of distant booms.

I turned to First Sergeant Adcock. "What was that?"

"Illumination rounds. Watch."

Within seconds, I heard a loud pop, and the entire sky lit up with a ghostly white light. From miles away, our howitzer battery was firing rounds designed to light up the night, enabling us to see any ambushes or any attempts from the enemy to sneak back into the villages we had cleared.

It was hauntingly beautiful. And the rest of the mission was conducted against the backdrop of that white light. Just as one round faded, we would hear the distant boom, the closer pop, and the sky would light up again.

Our last stop was a small, enclosed farmhouse where Grim Troop's commander, Robert Green, and the Iraqi battalion commander patiently waited for their meals. Rob invited us to eat with him. To this day, it is the most memorable meal of my life—eating (now cold) chow with a potbellied Iraqi officer while the entire night sky glowed white.

The Iraqi officer couldn't stop making jokes in broken English. He said that his drink—Gatorade—tasted like his "momma's piss," he called his "jundis" (the Arabic term for "soldier") all kinds of vile names, and he related tales of his sexual exploits. All the while laughing with a huge, jovial laugh that made us laugh with him.

The meal finished past midnight, and it was almost 2:00 a.m. by the time we rolled back "home"—almost eight full hours after we left. The squadron commander was still up. He was always up at 2:00 a.m.

"Sir, we fixed it. I'm uploading the pictures and documents now. We're good to go on the detainees."

"Good. Thanks, Dave."

I finally crashed into bed at 3:00 a.m., thanking God for my safety, thanking God that I was back, and thanking God that the next day was shaping up to be less eventful. But mostly I prayed for First Sergeant Adcock and the rest of the Grim troopers. While I was working on issues on the FOB tomorrow—and spending much of the day behind my plywood desk—he would gear up again and roll out for another eight hours. All in a day's work for the first sergeant.

Throughout the deployment, I would get emails from friends and family members with subject lines like "Can you believe this?" or "This will make you mad!" Invariably they would link to some form of radical rant that either slandered soldiers or so completely departed from the reality I experienced on the ground in Iraq that I laughed out loud. I typically read and dismissed these messages. In a nation of three hundred million, there will always be "those people"—

individuals so consumed with ignorance, dominated by hatred, and obsessed with the political cause of the moment that they lose all perspective. But I've changed my mind.

We simply cannot let lies pass unopposed. Those of us who know the truth must speak the truth. Unless we do, yesterday's slander can become today's conventional wisdom and tomorrow's history.

A couple months after my eight-hour mission to secure paperwork—during which fifteen men risked their lives to protect the due process rights of a man we knew to be a vile killer—I opened an email that linked to an insidious article not from some fringe blogger fond of words like "rethuglican" or "BuSh**ler," but from a respected member of the mainstream media, a self-described conservative who has occupied space in the most coveted perches of political commentary. Andrew Sullivan, writing for the *Atlantic Monthly*'s website, compared Russia's aggression against Georgia in 2008 with the United States Army in Iraq with the following words:

> Just imagine if the press were to discover a major jail in Gori, occupied by the Russians, where hundreds of Georgians had been dragged in off the streets and tortured and abused? What if we discovered that the orders for this emanated from the Kremlin itself? And what if we had documentary evidence of the ghastliest forms of racist, dehumanizing, abusive practices against the vulnerable as the *standard operating procedure* of the Russian army—because the prisoners were suspected of resisting the occupying power? (Emphasis added.)

I was appalled. I was enraged. My core function with Sabre Squadron was detainee operations. So I know and have lived our "standard operating procedure."

I first wanted to write to enlighten Mr. Sullivan about the way our soldiers truly behave. I wanted to tell him of the young men who risk death to capture men they could have killed. I wanted to tell him we are so careful with our detainees that the single worst injury ever suffered by any of the hundreds of men our squadron detained (even temporarily) was a scraped knee.

But I realized that all of that would be futile. I realized that Sullivan, and others like him, would slander the 99 percent of soldiers who do the right thing by reference to the 1 percent (or less) who commit crimes. And in the minds of many who inhabit Beltway coffeehouses, cubicles in Brussels, and university lecture halls, we could die doing right . . . but they will still define us by those who do wrong.

So if I can't persuade Andrew Sullivan and those like him, perhaps the Iraqis can. After all, they've lived with our "standard operating procedure" every day for more than five years. Who knows the Army better than they?

I have a few questions: If "the ghastliest forms of racist, dehumanizing, abusive" practices are our "standard operating procedure" why do the al Qaeda terrorists I've seen (and I was personally face-to-face with more than a hundred) often visibly relax when they enter coalition custody? Why do they so frequently and readily surrender rather than even try to escape our allegedly vicious detention? Why do they sometimes plead to remain in our facilities? If individuals are arbitrarily "dragged off the streets" for "torture and abuse," why do civilians, including the smallest children, pour out of their homes to see and greet American soldiers when we walk through their villages? Why do they hide behind their mud and walls only when they fear reprisals from our enemies or suspect an imminent firefight? If we are such monsters, why do sheikhs and everyday citizens beg for us to stay with them rather than live in dusty combat outposts in the heart of their communities?

Perhaps Iraqi citizens would shut their doors in fear if they learned about the Army from Mr. Sullivan's columns rather than from their personal interactions. Perhaps insurgents would fight to the death every time rather than face our "racist, dehumanizing" detention if they attended a panel discussion at your average university. Perhaps children would run screaming in fear if they saw almost any of Hollywood's recent "important" films about the war.

But they don't see any of that. Instead, they see and experience the U.S. Army as it is, warts and all. And while they chafe at the presence of foreign soldiers (as any proud people would), they are making their choice. For more than five years they have seen the contrast between our soldiers and the terrorists and militias. And unlike Andrew Sullivan, they can tell the difference.

Because nothing less than history is at stake, and so few have seen the truth with their own eyes, it's time for those of us who've been there to set the record straight. We must testify to the brutality of our enemies—al Qaeda thugs in our area of operations once shot a two-month-old infant in the face just to "send a message." More importantly, we must bear witness to the courage and virtue of our brothers and sisters in arms. Some try to define the 99 percent through the actions of the 1 percent.

We can never let that happen. And so, Captain Green, First Sergeant Adcock, and Lieutenant Colonel Calvert, this book stands as an enduring testimony that you did the right thing. That you risked more, and you gave more, than any of these critics ever will. Your "standard operating procedure" was to risk your life to protect the human rights of even your enemies.

That is the truth, and no amount of political commentary can change it.

22

FIDELITY

Nancy

I'M NOT SURE HOW SPOUSES get through long deployments without a good church family, and we live less than one mile from ours. Zion Presbyterian Church was established when Thomas Jefferson was president, seventeen states existed in the Union, and the Revolutionary War was still fresh in people's minds. By the time Napoleon was defeated at Waterloo, people had already worshipped at Zion for eight years. In fact, we'd been there eleven years when Congress decided the flag would have thirteen red and white stripes; twenty years when Beethoven died; sixty years when the United States bought Alaska; eighty years when the Statue of Liberty was unveiled in New York Harbor; and 138 years when Congress officially adopted the Pledge of Allegiance.

The sanctuary is painted a gorgeous blue. When I asked one of our historians about it, she told me that the color is in honor of our founders, who fled from the South Carolina Low Country because their new pastor denied the divinity of Christ. This traditional color can still be seen on ceilings, shutters, and walls all over the area and was referred to by slaves as "haint" blue. According to their folklore, it represented water over which spirits (called "haunts" or "haints") couldn't pass, so they painted their doorways to protect themselves from evil.

The outside of the church is redbrick, and it is tucked away under ponderosa pine trees that seem to droop in grief over the churchyard graves of soldiers from the Revolutionary War, the War of 1812, and the Civil War.

A strong sense of history emanates throughout the property. Heck, it even permeates the congregation. In a time when churches seem to outdo themselves with Starbucks coffee, JumboTron screens, and rock-style worship, our service begins with the ringing of a bell. Pastor Arch, dressed in long black robes, then reads scripture from the Old Testament, and ends by saying, "Thanks be to God."

"Thanks be to God," the congregation replies. I've gone to charismatic churches where I've heard "thank you, Jesus" shouted like someone had been on fire and God had just doused them with rain. But Presbyterians' gratitude comes in the form of a collective monotone, as spiritually infused as an obligatory "bless you" after a stranger sneezes.

But Pastor Arch, the paterfamilias of the church, is never dissuaded. He has curly gray hair that whitens just above his ears and simultaneously possesses a quick-witted levity and a spiritual sobriety that makes him very distinctive. The first time David and I visited the church, he prayed for success in the "war against Islamic jihadism," which caused David to lean over and whisper, "He had me at hello." Much to his credit, he's never asked us to hold the sweaty hand of our neighbor for a long, overly emotional prayer. Nor does our congregation project songs on an overhead screen or sing the latest choruses.

In fact, we sing hymns, which are evaluated after the service by the congregants with the fervor of a football team watching their game tapes.

One hymn aficionado is Anna, a smart Vanderbilt graduate who has a unique manner that makes people pay attention to her in spite of her petite, southern self. She seems as if she's *just about* to tell you a secret—her voice starts out at a normal volume and precipitously drops as she nears the end of her sentences. For example, she might begin, "I need to go to the store because..." But as people lean in to hear what mysterious item she needs from the store, she'll continue in a low voice, "...the cat needs milk."

She and I were tour guides for Zion's two-hundred-year anniversary. Of course, I had no business being on the historical tour committee—I could tell the church was old because the pews we sat on week after week groaned every time I moved on them. A wooden divider went right down the middle of the pews, which originally separated men from women, or slaves from masters, depending on who told the story.

That's all I knew.

Anna, however, was a great tour guide because of her genuine conservatism that lends itself to historical preservation. Whereas some churches think songs are old if they weren't thrown together at that morning's coffee hour, Anna strongly preferred hymns written *before* the Civil War. She liked the elegance of "Be Thou My Vision" over the sentimentality of "When the Roll Is Called Up Yonder." The absolute bane of her existence was the prolific hymn writer Fanny J. Crosby, who wrote three songs a week during her lifetime so that there were eight thousand possible ways to torment Anna any particular Sunday. Of course, many of these hymns are beloved by Christians across America—for example, "Blessed Assurance" and "To God Be the Glory." But this didn't matter to Anna. Nor did it matter that poor Fanny J. was blind for most of her life. Lyrics like *"Angels descending, bring from above, / Echoes of mercy, whispers of love"* felt schmaltzy, and Anna was on a one-woman war against Crosby's hymns.

Of course, this knowledge was a wonderful distraction every Sunday. When the song leader announced the page number, I didn't immediately start prayerfully preparing my mind for worship. Instead, I glanced down to the bottom of the page to determine the date the lyrics were written. If it was after 1865, I'd dart gleeful glances toward Anna to see her squirm in her creaky pew.

Another member of the Fanny J. Crosby Hate Club was Jana, an energetic jogger who had somehow convinced me to regularly run with her in the church's surrounding countryside. She pointed out that it wasn't just the sentimentality of Fanny's lyrics that bothered her. She felt they were dishonest.

"*How* are they dishonest?" I asked while we were jogging one morning. I always asked Jana questions while we ran so she would lose her breath more quickly and I could keep up better.

"*Perfect submission, all is at rest,*" she quoted from memory, speaking flawlessly even as we went up a hill. "*I in my Saviour am happy and blest?* Please. Half the time, I can't even sing that honestly. In fact, when have I *ever* been in perfect submission?"

I prayed for Jana's soul...silently, so I wouldn't have to gasp for air.

"Give me *A mighty fortress is our God, a bulwark never failing* any day over that," she said. "*Our helper He, amid the flood of mortal ills prevailing.* That'll make me *want* to submit, and it has the benefit of being true."

It was apparent that Anna and Jana had given this a tad more thought, and I realized I liked songs because they made me feel a certain way. Just as "Wake Me Up Before You Go-Go" reminds me of 1984 more than any Orwell novel, "Jesus, Keep Me Near the Cross" will forever bring up warm memories of my hometown church...of attendance cards, dropping quarters in wooden collection plates, laying my head in my mother's lap during interminably long sermons, flannelgraphs, sugar cookies, and Kool-Aid mustaches.

But I didn't tell Anna or Jana that. Basically their complaint against post–Civil War songs was that they were focused on the songwriter's moral and emotional state instead of on God's unwavering faithfulness. People, you see, are prone to sin, an easy thing to remember when you attend a church whose congregants still refer to the balcony as the "old slave gallery." Whereas all churches have baggage, ours is laid right out there on our grounds. Separated from the white folks' burial grounds by an iron fence is a slave burial ground marked with a large memorial stone whose inscription begins, "In memory and appreciation of the loyalty and service of the slaves owned by the early settlers of Zion Community buried here. Among them is Daddy Ben, a Son Royal, Prince of Africa, owned by Col. Tom Scott..."

When Anna and I were preparing for the church tours, we went into the basement to a fireproof safe that held the historical documents of the church. Carefully, we selected from the dust-covered tomes and sat at the cold rectangular table. For hours, we sat quietly under the low ceilings and breathed deeply of the aroma of history. (Although in retrospect that smell could've been the dead squirrel they later found during renovations.) With each brittle page, I began to see the truth of the old joke: "How many Presbyterians does it take to change a lightbulb?"

"The motion as to changing the lightbulb," the joke goes, "shall properly be brought under new business. When the main motion has been seconded, amendments as to the acquisition of a ladder and/or the disposal of the old lightbulb may be brought. If there is insufficient light by which the moderator may read the motion, then it fails and no action taken."

In other words, the records we found were proper and in decent order, and incredibly boring. While searching for interesting nuggets of information, Anna confided in me, "I'm glad you're on this historical committee, because I really think we have a..."

I struggled to hear the end of her sentence, due to her voice-dropping habit. In my mind, the possibilities were endless. We had an opportunity? A disaster? A tax code violation?

"A problem," she repeated herself. "How do we deal with the slavery issue when we give our tours?"

"We should be against it," I said.

But I knew what she meant. It seemed incongruous to treat the slave burial ground as if it were just another artifact of the church. "Here's the pewter communion tablets for the faithful church members, here's the hand-hewn cedar columns the men created to the glory of God, and here's the resting place of the humans they forced to build these lovely pews. These are pine, aren't they, Anna?"

"Maybe they were sorry about having them," she said hopefully as she scanned over the ornately written notes.

"We can't apply the moral clarity of today to a past we never lived in," I said.

"I'm not looking for *excuses*," she said without looking up. "I'm looking for clues. You know, to their state of mind." After an hour or so of reading, we knew how much each brick cost, what company made the pipe organ, and even discovered what years a young James K. Polk had attended our school. We found an instance where the church disciplined a member for treating his slave too harshly, and we found evidence that our congregation decided to teach our slaves to read in spite of the fact that doing so was illegal. Still, our spiritual forefathers owned and traded other human beings. It's just a fact, and a cautionary tale. Sin is and has been pervasive in the hearts of men.

And speaking of sin, it happens during long deployments.

Before David left, we sat down and had one of our worst conversations.

"I think we should have a list of rules," he said. "To make sure you avoid even getting close to an affair while I'm gone."

It was an awkward, uneasy, and difficult conversation—one I repeated to Jana on one of our jogs.

"I'm not supposed to drink at all during the deployment," I told her. "Or have phone conversations with men, or meaningful email exchanges about politics or any other subject. I'm also not going to be on Facebook so the ghosts of boyfriends past can contact me."

Even though she hates Fanny J. Crosby, she's a good friend who will tell you the truth even when you don't want to hear it.

"No Facebook?" she asked gently as we jogged.

"It's just precautionary," I huffed. "People are people, and when they're separated for a year—a full year—it's good to be on guard against temptation."

We jogged for a moment.

"Plus, he thinks I'll run into some old flame and use his shoulder to cry on."

All of this was incredibly embarrassing to admit, and it felt good to tell Jana. If I was completely honest, I resented the fact that there were occasionally women at FOB Caldwell...even if they were just "passing through" (usually). When you're constantly reminded of your husband's physical danger, you don't also want to lie awake at night, wonder about the women serving next to him, and worry about marital danger. And I don't care if it's politically incorrect to say so, but mixing men and women in combat environments just begs for drama. Since I didn't know what his day-to-day life was like, I tried to push such thoughts out of my head. But in spite of all our precautions, I worried about him and he worried about me.

Every once in a while, Jana would ask me if I was living up to my half of the bargain. "How are the rules of life?"

"Still got 'em," I'd say, and we'd keep plodding along.

One morning, I awakened early because I had to catch a flight to Washington, D.C. I was meeting a woman who wanted me to possibly ghostwrite her memoirs, and I was going up for an interview. I'd crammed for this interview like a college kid before finals—reading other books written about her and even watching a movie in which Julia Roberts played her. I grabbed my books, my laptop, and was heading out the door when I got a rather long email from David:

> Blessings on your trip! I'm thrilled for you to have such amazing adventures, and I hope that she likes you, that you get an offer, and that the offer is worth taking.
>
> I hate to write this, but it's been on my mind...As you go into what could be an amazing experience dealing with a person who has lived an extraordinary life, please be on your guard. Remember our agreements regarding alcohol, social arrangements, etc. When you do business travel with exciting people doing exciting things, it is vitally important not to make that first wrong choice.

I gulped and fought the tears. Having a relationship—a marriage—under such strained circumstances is hard. But when communication is so incredibly scarce, you don't want to use it to discuss such unpleasant topics. His letter was long and heartfelt, and it made me want to throw up. I just hated the idea that he was in a war zone worrying that I wasn't faithful.

> I hope all this makes sense. Sometimes I feel like our conversations are too dominated by things from me like "please don't do x, y, and z because they make me feel uncomfortable" rather than discussing why these things are problematic within the context of our separation.
>
> I love you so much, and you've been so amazing throughout this unbelievably trying time in Iraq. You are my best friend, my companion through the grand adventure of our lives, and the loving mother of my precious, precious children. In this fallen world, I cannot imagine a better wife and friend. Which is exactly why we should be on guard and not grow complacent.

The email was unusually long, and I could tell that he was worried that Washington would provide more temptations than tiny Columbia. He cautioned against taking the first small step toward inappropriate behavior—even used examples from our lives as to how we could've done things in the past a little more wisely. Because I had other, more pressing things to worry about—like making sure I had my driver's license and no more than three ounces of liquid in my carry-on—I tried to push his message from my head and replace it with the details of travel.

I was holding my boarding pass and looking for my gate when I ran into—literally ran into, like in the movies—a former boyfriend. We were both trying to throw away something into the same trash can when we looked up and recognized each other.

Out of all the passengers flying into and out of Nashville International Airport, garbage had brought me face-to-face with a former flame I hadn't seen in thirteen years.

And the first thing I thought of was David's email.

The ex-boyfriend, a musician, was polite.

"I'm headed to Europe for a tour," he explained.

"I'm a writer now," I replied, "and am going to Washington for an interview." (How thankful I was that I'd dressed well for the flight and had a legitimately interesting reason for flying. I always fear I'll run into old flames at the gas station in my pajamas.)

It was a brief conversation—we both had flights—but as it ended, I thought of David's admonition not to take one small step in the wrong direction. In the awkward goodbye, I made it a point not to seem interested in further contact. He didn't ask for email or phone information and I didn't ask for his, and my mind reeled as I entered my gate.

Immediately, I called my friend from church.

"Kim," I said, as quickly and quietly as I could, "you remember how David cautioned me before he left against running into old boyfriends? Well, you aren't going to believe this."

I told her the whole story, including the long email David had sent just hours before, reminding me of our commitments.

"What should I do? I *really* don't want to worry David."

Kim conferred with her husband, Paul, who was sitting right there. Before she could even get back on the phone, I heard Paul's deep voice in the background. "Email David and tell him exactly what happened."

Paul is a deacon in my church, and I resented his advice. After all, I asked his wife for counsel—not him. The last thing I wanted to do was to send an email to David and not be able to talk to him while I was in the air for the next several hours. Ever since he'd been in Iraq, David had told me awful stories about guys there whose wives had left them. I didn't want to give him any indication that there was reason to worry back home.

"I'll try to reach him when I get to the hotel," I said diplomatically.

"Do it *before* you get on that flight," Paul said adamantly. "I'm telling you—I'd want to know immediately."

And so I stood at the gate while people passed me to board, absolutely resenting my church and their advice. I typed out a simple message with the subject line "Old Flames." After explaining whom I ran into, I added:

> I just wanted to be completely honest... and quickly honest if you know what I mean. So I'm typing this out as I get onto flight. Don't be alarmed. I love you!

My stomach turned and my mind raced the entire flight. Under normal circumstances, this wouldn't have been a big deal. I'd say, "You won't believe whom I ran into," and he'd see the expression on my face, know everything was okay, and we'd share a laugh. We'd been married for years, after all, and could communicate volumes in one knowing glance.

But separated by eight thousand miles?

I asked the stewardess for Sprite, avoided eye contact with my seatmate, and tried to sip away my sorrows. When I landed, I mercifully had an email:

Dear Nancy, I had a funny feeling about this trip (for some odd reason), and I'm very happy you told me you ran into him. I don't want to be worried about chance encounters like this because they're pretty much inevitable. I'm glad you told me...things like that go a long way towards building trust. By the way, we're hitting the point where I'm seeing almost a soldier every other day whose wife is cheating on him/leaving him. It's truly astounding. It makes me appreciate your disclosure that much more.

As I tried to hail a cab, I mentally forgave Paul for rudely insisting that I email David immediately. In fact, the whole thing made me appreciate our church, as imperfect as it is, for its recognition of the dangers of being too confident in your own goodness. Pastor Arch likes to say, "You can't appreciate the good news of the gospel until you hear the bad news of the gospel. The bad news is that you're much worse than you think you are... But the good news is that God is greater than you think He is."

Within a week, I was back home in Zion, sitting on my old creaky pew under the slave gallery and singing a hymn. A pre—Civil War hymn, so instead of trying to find Anna in the congregation to exchange a sarcastic glance, I was actually paying attention to the lyrics:

O to grace how great a debtor
daily I'm constrained to be!
Let thy goodness, like a fetter,
bind my wandering heart to thee.
Prone to wander, Lord, I feel it,
prone to leave the God I love;
here's my heart, O take and seal it,
seal it for thy courts above.

Now that's an honest song, I thought as Pastor Arch approached the podium to read the scriptures like he did every week during David's deployment. He ended, as always, by holding up his Bible to us and saying in an authoritative voice, "The Word of the Lord!"

As I sat in our little country church that has been operational for two hundred years, I realized it was a testimony to God's faithfulness to us, in spite of our lack of faithfulness to Him. Which is actually quite comforting, since—as pretty as the sanctuary is—there's no paint in the world that can really keep evil from your heart and home.

"Thanks be to God," I said with my congregation, and this time I really meant it.

23

FIDELITY?

David

SHE MEANT WELL, BUT it was still wrong.

Leaving your wife for a year represents a tremendous leap of faith for both of you. She says goodbye to me wondering if she'll see me again. I say goodbye wondering—somewhere deep inside—if she'll be there when I get back.

Honestly, I think that any person who says that they've "never" had that concern is either lying or is just delusional about human nature. Human beings are imperfect. Human beings get lonely. And when a woman is lonely, there is *always* a man there to make her feel better.

Because we both understand human frailty, because neither one of us had experienced separation like this, and because both of us thought it's better to be safe than sorry, we lived by our rules.

We prayerfully considered each one and agreed, and—for month after month—everything was wonderful.

In fact, it was amazing. Nancy organized Operation Send-a-Box. She showered me with packages. She sent videos showing me the kids' daily activities. She sent me an email every night, regardless of whether I could read it. She never burdened me with too many problems from home, always listened when I spoke (as much as I could) about our pains and frustrations "downrange," and most of all, she was always loving.

Even now, as I go back and read emails from my deployment, I'm struck by their tenderness and love. It wasn't just that she related the bare facts of each day, but she seasoned her accounts of field trips, report cards, church picnics, and dinners with friends with a grace and love that always told me I was missed.

One night, in the middle of a mind-numbing series of operations, I signed on my iChat instant messenger for a final brief conversation with Nancy before bed. This was our ritual, and I loved it.

Me: Hey!
Nancy: Hey! How r u?
Me: Good. So tired.

And so it would go...in that clipped fashion that characterizes online chatting. This time, however, she started typing at length, obviously excited.

She told me about someone associated with a radio program she'd been on and how he had been intrigued by many of her references to her faith on the show. She told me about the conversations they'd sometimes had immediately after the program and the follow-up emails that would occasionally occur when discussing other business.

I could feel my stomach clenching.

She kept going. She said that she felt burdened to share the gospel with him and finally screwed up the courage to invite him to talk with her each week—to ask her any question he wanted. She said that they'd already started, and she even clipped in segments of her emails to him. They were heartfelt, warm...and full of affection. I recognized her writing style from the messages she sent me, her husband.

"Isn't that exciting?" she typed.

"You broke the rules," I typed back.

I was furious. No, I was beyond furious. As a person who's spent more than my share of time in the world of evangelical Christianity, I knew the following things: First, the *most* intimate conversations a person has are about life and faith. Second, spiritual and emotional intimacy frequently leads to physical intimacy. And third—and worst of all—I knew that we'd talked about just this sort of thing.

I had trouble containing myself. I had been gone forever, and I had forever to go. We were all in a state of mild depression on the FOB. The constant danger was exhausting, the heat crushed our spirits, and the separations from loved ones were leading to cracks (and outright fractures) in many relationships.

Men were coming home on leave to find their wives gone from their houses. Other men were getting the modern equivalent of the "Dear John" letter via Facebook message or email. Some guys discovered wives or girlfriends were pregnant, and still others were finding that their bank accounts had been looted by the very people they most trusted with their financial affairs. In fact, I would say that the ongoing betrayal of our men and women in uniform by their own family members is perhaps the most underreported scandal and toll of the war. It is an enduring symbol of the depravity of man and the fallen nature of our own culture.

So I know that I was sensitive. Too sensitive. But I couldn't help myself.

I could tell, even over instant message, that Nancy was horrified by my reaction.

"Oh no. I see what you mean. What should I do?"

But that question set me off even more. "What do you mean, 'What should I do?'" I fired back. "Isn't it obvious? End this relationship. Now."

"Okay . . . I will."

As we kept talking, I could tell that she was wounded—not by my reaction, but by her own actions—hurt that she'd hurt me, embarrassed that she hadn't spotted the problem, and eager to make amends.

But I wasn't consolable. I felt inside me something I'd never really felt before, a sense of anger that I couldn't really contain, a sense of betrayal that just would not go away. I wanted to take a step back and examine the situation rationally, to love and forgive her and move on. But I couldn't.

The next night, I began our instant messaging with words I just couldn't help but type:

"I still can't believe you did that. What were you thinking?"

"I wasn't thinking. I'm so so sorry."

But that made things worse.

"How could you not be thinking? Why would you not be thinking?"

J-Dave and Leo noticed my agitation (I couldn't keep anything from them), and they were immediately sympathetic. They knew. J-Dave had seen a previous relationship disintegrate in the strain of war, and Leo was witnessing the same strains on relationships across the FOB. Some of his own troopers—the guys he supervised in his shop— were facing the pain of betrayal. Over here, we knew the score. Back home? What did they know? How could they understand?

Even to this day, as I think about the situation, I don't know whether to feel foolish and ashamed at the extent of my reaction or to feel indignation and anger all over again. Wouldn't it have been right for me to gently remind Nancy of her promises, confident that she would be mortified by the misunderstanding? Wouldn't that have been better? Perhaps it would have been, but at that time I was utterly incapable of that kind of mature reaction.

I was incapable of the "mature" reaction because Nancy knew what was happening on the FOB, how soldiers' lives were being shattered seemingly every week by news from home. She had heard some of the worst stories—the stories that were becoming near-legend with telling and retelling. There was the trooper met at the airport when he came home for leave by his wife...and her new boyfriend. There was the officer whose wife met an older man who "knew how to be there for her." There was the sergeant whose wife said, "Three deployments are enough," and took off to her parents' with the kids. The stories were literally too numerous to tell. And Nancy knew this was all happening. She knew that it worried me. Yet she had still pressed forward with her "friendship."

The days wore on, the detainees kept coming, and I kept going out on missions. Nothing too dangerous—usually just quick trips to the local Iraqi courthouse or police station—but still, I hated rolling outside the wire with a gulf between us. I obsessed even more with the notion of the "bad goodbye." I prayed for patience, for wisdom, and just to relax.

But peace wouldn't come. The rage continued to build.

Not until days after our ordeal began, when I got the most beautiful love letter I'd ever read, delivered via email.

I don't have it anymore. My Iraq computer is long dead—killed by the abuse and sand of a year in Diyala. I don't even remember how it began or what it said, but I remember that it was perfect. That it expressed love and regret and admiration and humility—and that it was from the bottom of her heart.

I know now that it wasn't so much the words themselves as the spirit behind the words, but it broke the ice in my heart. It reminded me that this person who had filled my heart with pain and fury was the one who sat in our kitchen and—with tear-filled eyes—told me to answer the call in my heart and join the Reserves. This was the person who was filling my kids' hearts with joy in my absence... not just being mom and dad at the same time, but using our shared sacrifice to teach them to love God and their country. This was my best friend in the world.

It sounds silly that one letter could mean so much to a grown, cynical man, but it did. All was well. I could move on to the next challenge, secure that the final goodbye—if it did come while I was here—would not be dominated by the pain and regret of betrayal and misunderstanding but instead by the love of a joyful life lived together.

24

THE LOVE LETTER

Nancy

OKAY, SO MAYBE I DIDN'T actually write that letter.
The day had started normally enough. I got up, checked my email,
and scanned my inbox for the familiar message titled "Good Morning." I got one every morning, unless something bad had happened.
At least, this was what I could piece together. Sometimes, if I didn't
hear from him, he was out on a mission. I tried to search for clues
in every message, every communication. He sometimes inexplicably signed his emails "I just love you," an uncharacteristic romantic
gesture, this from a man who said that our wedding in France was
enough romance credit to last ten years. In other words, he didn't
have to prove his romantic side by doing things like, say, remembering our anniversary. So when he signed off "I just love you," it struck
me, though I wasn't sure why. I practically diagrammed his emails for
clues. Once, after he signed off that way, my friend Anna said, "Hey,
I saw David's article on *National Review*."

Having no idea what she was talking about, I went to the site and
saw an article, written by David, about a typical day in Iraq. He handled their troop's media relations and was frequently writing articles
about their activities in Diyala. The *National Review* article was well-
written, but as I read it I realized that the commander had David
delivering kerosene to villagers.

My friend sensed my anxiety. "You okay?"

I tried not to let my frustration show. He was riding outside the wire to keep America free, to help liberate Iraq, and to *deliver kerosene?* I couldn't imagine a more potentially explosive ride. "Well, at least he's getting good use out of his law school degree."

Even worse, sometimes if I didn't hear from him in the morning, it was because someone had died and they'd frozen communications until they could notify the family. I had no idea what "notifying the family" would look like. In my mind, it would be something like on *Law & Order*, where the cops would show up at the door, flash their badges, say, "We have some bad news," and the family member would faint or fall into their arms. Sometimes during church when my mind drifted, I'd wonder how I would respond to such news and what I'd do with the kids in the immediate aftermath. I had no idea what happens with servicemen who die, but I knew it would be better than Scarlett O'Hara checking the casualty list in the town square. The very fact that I didn't know—and was too paranoid to ask—made me jittery, and I'd jump when the UPS man delivered my Amazon packages or well-meaning friends just "dropped by" to check on me. The doorbell caused instant panic, and I sometimes had to will myself to walk to the door and answer.

But that morning, I was heading out the door and scanned my in-box to make sure I had an email:

THREE BEST-SELLING PACKS OF VIAGRA.

STRICTLY CONDIFENTIAL: NIGERIAN PRINCE NEED ASISTINCE
THANK YOU

I kept scanning, and finally landed on what determined if the day was going to be good or bad: "Good Morning."

I breathed a sigh of relief and clicked on it. I planned on checking it quickly before jumping in the shower and heading to the airport. In addition to writing, I had begun working for SixSeeds.tv—the organization that helped organize Send-a-Box—based out of Winchester, Massachusetts. Our good friends John and Jean Kingston started it to help parents raise kids who are generous and have less of a sense of entitlement in today's culture. When they realized they needed a writer—for their blog and other aspects—I immediately said yes. Well, "immediately" is not quite the word. John had given me a tour around town and was explaining his vision for the project. I got the feeling he wasn't going to let me out of the car until I agreed to work for them, so I ended up saying yes.

Really, it was a wonderful job for a great cause, and I frequently got to go visit with the Kingstons in Massachusetts with the kids. They were the people designated to be my "helpers" in case the doorbell indicated something much different than an Amazon delivery. John would arrange overseas travel for me, Jean would accompany me, my neighbors the Brenners would keep the kids in the short term, and my parents would keep them for a longer term. These are the things you work out in advance of deployment, along with wills and insurance information.

The kids and I were going to Boston this day for work, and I was looking forward to spending time with them. All I had to do was get out the door. I clicked on "Good Morning" and my heart sank.

We'd had a fight the day before. I'd inadvertently broken one of our "rules of life," and David had never been so angry at me. I could tell there was much more going on in Iraq than I could ever know, but I didn't know how that should affect this particular argument. Immediately, I saw him pop up on instant messenger.

"What were you thinking?" he typed.

Fighting over the course of eight thousand miles was hard enough. Plus, I simply didn't have the time to spend rehashing the same argument we had had the night before. However, I was hesitant to leave the instant messaging because it could be our last communication. I never know what the future holds, so I tried to end every communication as positively as I could. That day, however, it simply wasn't possible. We typed back and forth, iChat kicked us off, we logged back on and fought some more. Although I apologized immediately and frequently, he was still furious at me. I felt like vomiting as I got up from the computer, loaded up the kids, and headed up I-65 North to Nashville's airport.

I made my way through the airport and to the gate without the kids noticing my delicate emotional state. The whole time I drove and walked through the airport, my phone was alerting me that I had texts—"r u there?" and "can u talk?"

Normally, I wouldn't ignore the texts, but there was literally no way I could simultaneously text him, drive, walk through the airport with the kids, get them fed and then on the airplane.

After I got them situated at a restaurant near the airport gate, my phone rang. I got as far away from the kids as I safely could and put the phone to my ear, feeling like a gladiator going into the Coliseum.

"Why aren't you answering my texts?"

Actually, that's only what I guessed he said. What I heard was "Why—ans—xts?" And even though I could hear only a few syllables of his question, I knew this was not going to be pretty. My phone wasn't getting great reception, so I had to go stand in the middle of a main thoroughfare, where people dragging luggage walked slowly off their flights and to the food court.

"David, I can't hear you, but I am very, very sorry."

And I was. Because my job put me in the public eye, I frequently came into contact with interesting people in the course of the radio interviews or magazine work. I was specifically not supposed to really engage with any male in David's absence, and I did. I didn't try to hide this from David—rather, he became furious because I'd forwarded some communication I thought he'd find interesting. Instead of seeing this transparency as a lack of guilt, he was haunted by the fact that many of the wives of his friends were leaving them, and he could not be convinced that all was well.

Had we been in the same room, we could've talked it out in five minutes. But as I stood there in the airport, literally weeping on the phone, we could neither "fight it out" nor make up. Although he could hear everything I said, I couldn't hear his complete words—which may not have been a bad thing, considering the syllables I *did* hear. I could see the kids and would occasionally wave at them and paste a fake smile on my face, before turning around and continuing this awful conversation. Again, I tried desperately to smooth things over, but nothing worked.

As our flight drew near, I got more and more upset. "I think you just said you've never felt more betrayed, is that right?" I'd say, literally weeping right there near the food court, unable to move because it was the only two-foot radius in which my phone worked. A police officer eyed me from afar and gradually made his way toward me. We made eye contact and he looked at me inquisitively. "You okay?" he mouthed.

I didn't blame him. I was crying the way you would if you found out someone had kidnapped your children and were in brutal negotiations over their release. "I'm fine," I said quietly. "I'm talking to my husband, who's in Iraq."

He nodded and moved back to his position, but the weary travelers all turned and stared as they passed. I'm sure they wondered why I'd choose the middle of the airport to have a breakdown, unaware that I couldn't move to my right or left and couldn't leave my kids, who were eating obliviously within eyesight.

Having surrendered all dignity, I pled with David to forgive me so I could get on the airplane in peace.

"Y—but—me—land," I heard him say.

"I have no idea if this is right, but I think you said to text you when I land, and I will. I love you. Bye."

"—"

"I think you just said goodbye," I said hesitantly. "So . . . I'm hanging up now."

I blew my nose and took deep breaths, then went to the kids, who took one look at me and gasped. "What's wrong?" they asked, alarmed.

"Mommy's just sad that Daddy's gone," I said. "Everything's okay." We shuffled from the food court to our seats within minutes.

By the time we got into the air, however, I was seething. I'd actually been quite good during the deployment, I thought. I hadn't had a drop to drink, had taken care of the kids, hadn't spent too much money, and—in fact—had worked hard to eradicate our debt as a surprise. The fact that he couldn't forgive me gnawed at me the entire flight. By the time I got to John and Jean's house, I was livid.

The Kingstons' house is a large welcoming place with a trampoline, a play place, a Wii, and fun, energetic kids. Camille and Austin ran inside to play with the Kingston boys, and I sat down with Jean over coffee. Immediately, I told her the whole situation. Jean is the type of person who doesn't jump to conclusions and provides wise counsel no matter what problem comes your way. Temperate and insightful, she's known David for twenty years and me for fifteen. In other words, she wasn't under any preconception that either of us was faultless in this mess.

After venting for a while, Jean and I tried to work on SixSeeds projects. We sat in her living room while the kids played outside, our two white Macintosh laptops humming away. Sporadically, however, I just burst into tears. It was just too much to be eight thousand miles away from your husband and to be angry at him, especially with the knowledge that the last time we talk could really *be* the last time.

Jean's brow furrowed as she comforted me. "I have a crazy idea," she said. "This may sound counterintuitive, but what if you took a radically different approach?"

"What are you thinking?"

"It doesn't sound like you're going to be able to work this through logically."

"Or at all."

"So why don't you take a different approach and write him a love letter?"

"A what?"

"A *real* love letter. It sounds like there are so many people devastated by infidelity who are coming to him and talking about their problems that he thinks everyone is being unfaithful. Including you."

"And..."

"And you won't be able to convince him that you love him by arguing your case."

She had a point. We sat there with our hot coffee, and I looked out the window at the kids. They were jumping on their trampoline and throwing a ball at one of the Kingston boys, some sort of game they'd come up with. We had been collaborating on our first blog post. It had to be perfect, so Jean and I were sending drafts back and forth. She'd edit mine, and I'd edit hers. Blog posts, I could write in my sleep. But a love letter?

"What *exactly* do you mean?" I was skeptical. "Who over the age of sixteen even writes love letters anyway? I've never written him one in our entire marriage, so why start at the moment I'm most angry with him?"

"You can do it," she said. "You know...a passionate, I-can't-wait-to-rip-your-clothes-off love letter."

And at that time, I realized that I simply did not have it in me. I loved him, yes. Perhaps more than I'd ever loved him before. But I felt so wounded by his accusations and so hurt by the argument that I could not conjure a word. After all, *he* left *me*. It's not like I wanted him to go to war. The tears, which had been so abundant in the Nashville airport, seemed to have simply run out. "I can't, Jean," I said. "I think it's a great idea, but I just can't."

"Sure you can," she said. "Just put 'A Love Letter' in the subject line, and don't even mention the argument. Start by saying, 'My dear David, every part of me longs to be reunited with you,' and so forth."

"Go on," I urged. I was sitting in front of my laptop, but had minimized the SixSeeds blog post and started a new email I'd titled "A Love Letter." In fact, I also had the first lines, thanks to Jean.

"But it occurred to me that you are in the middle of a war zone and might need reminding of how I feel about you," Jean said as I typed her suggestions word for word.

"I love you. In fact, you are the first person I think of when I awaken in the morning..."

Jean was good. She composed and I typed and typed. By the time we were done, we had a letter that would've made Cyrano de Bergerac proud.

It was night in Iraq by the time I pressed send.

The next morning, I scanned over my inbox like I did every morning, praying that he'd gotten the love letter and that he was safe.

There, about five emails down—after that very persistent Nigerian prince who needed my help—I saw it.

"Re: A Love Letter."

It began, "I cannot wait to see you again. I cannot wait until this necessary but terrible hardship is over. Thank you for understanding all of my thoughts and feelings I expressed on the phone last night and responding in the way you did. I love you."

I breathed a sigh of relief, went downstairs to Jean, and smiled.

"It worked," I said, pouring myself a cup of coffee. That's one good thing about the Kingston home—they always have good coffee going. Then I added, with a wink, "He totally forgives you."

Sometimes, throughout the deployment, I'd find myself falling short, in need of a bit of help. Frequently, when people hear I've been a spouse left at home during deployment, they ask what they can do to help others in my situation. Honestly, I have no idea. Sometimes I'd make a list of the things that people did for me that really lifted my spirits—I had people doing everything from fixing my garage door to pulling my kid's tooth. But when Jean sat down and helped me save my marriage by ghostwriting my husband a love letter? That's *really* not something you can put in a "how to help the spouse of a deployed soldier" handbook.

I never felt like I appropriately thanked the people who lent a helping hand through that year. Specifically, I'd love to adequately express to Jean how it felt to be lifted up by such a dear friend at possibly my lowest moment. But now—as then—words fail me. Maybe one day, I'll send her a letter thanking her for her kindness...it should be easy enough.

After all, I can just have David write it.

25

THE HOT, HOT SUMMER

David

LATE IN THE SUMMER, I was almost killed.

After our air assault earlier in the summer, we just kept moving south, clearing villages all the way. The plan never changed. We never just left the villagers to fend for themselves. We stayed for days, weeks, and sometimes even months. All the while we trained Iraqi Army soldiers to take our place when we left and raised local chapters of the Sons of Iraq, citizen militias to guard their own streets.

And so it would go. We assaulted a group of villages, cleaned out the bad guys, built small outposts, patrolled the streets, trained our replacements, then moved again. And it worked. IED attacks began to taper off. Suddenly, only enemy fighters were dying. That didn't mean that our region had become safe...by no means. Simply, the enemy had lost the upper hand, and the locals were growing much, much bolder. We were on the offensive, they were on the defensive, and we could all tell the difference. The tide was turning.

One evening, a small team of al Qaeda fighters tried to infiltrate back into our zone of control. To get through, they had to get past a series of newly built security checkpoints. Some are manned by our troopers, some by Iraqi security forces (Iraqi Army or police), and some by the Sons of Iraq. Naturally, the AQI fighters picked the checkpoint manned by the Sons of Iraq as the weak point and launched a surprise attack in the middle of the night. They were able to kill one of the guards almost immediately, but the rest of the tiny band of Sons held their ground. In a short firefight, they not only fought off the attackers, they killed a local AQI leader. The villagers stood firm, and the terrorists fled. One week later, we gave a very well-deserving and humble villager an Army Achievement Medal for his bravery.

Days later, an al Qaeda terrorist tried to return to his home in a village now controlled by a large group of Sons. Keep in mind, this was a village he used to rule with an iron fist. When he snuck into his house to sleep, his own wife alerted the local men, and they armed themselves, walked to his house, and killed him when he refused to surrender. The lesson?

Hell hath no fury like a woman sick of Sharia.

To be sure, there were still armed bands lurking out there. The stillness of the night was occasionally shattered by small-arms fire, but these incidents didn't alter the fundamental reality: the Iraqi government owns the ground, and the local citizens never want to see al Qaeda return.

Across the country, the improvement was staggering. At one point in the "bad old days" of 2006 and early 2007, attacks against coalition forces could hit close to two hundred per day. Yet there was a day in July when there were only thirteen attacks against the coalition (probably half those were in our area, but that's a different story). The rate of attacks against supply convoys went down dramatically. Sectarian murders all but stopped, even in Baghdad.

I could go on and on. While we all held our breath, knocked on wood, pinched ourselves, and prayed fervently that these trends would continue, there was now an open debate as to whether Iraq was moving from a state of war to something much closer to the baseline level of violence in the country and culture.

Iraq is a violent place. It just is. And anyone who spends time there (especially if you are a member of a foreign army engaged in counterinsurgency operations) will experience that violence. One of the most eye-opening revelations of my entire tour of duty has been the discovery that not even a Stalinist genocidal maniac like Saddam Hussein had full control of this place. This was no North Korea.

While he was as brutal as he could be in pursuit of total control, he never managed to achieve it.

A combination of civil uprisings, tribal disputes, external conflict, garden-variety crime, political violence, and lively smuggling rings kept Iraq in a constant state of low- or medium-grade turmoil. In fact, any "peace" that existed in Saddam's Iraq was the product of either actual violence or the threat of it.

I have come to believe that the following statement is true, has been true, and will be true for the foreseeable future (and perhaps forever): Iraq will be far more violent than we would ever tolerate in the United States. My concern is that while we are justifiably grateful for the dramatic improvements since 2007, we don't make a major mistake in our perceptions of Iraq.

In the view of this low-ranking reservist—take what I say with a grain of salt—I fully expect that we'll see a leveling off, and as part of that leveling off, we'll still see suicide bombings, IEDs, and firefights.

But in July 2008, in Diyala we were still a long way from hitting that "baseline" level. Fighting still raged, and our missions never seemed to end. During these high-tempo operations, one of the signature command missions was the "battlefield circulation," where a commander visited the guys in the field, talked to the locals, and generally got a firsthand look at the fight. On occasion, I would go with the commander. We had launched Operation Sabre Pursuit II, the latest attack south, and our executive officer, Major Cantlon, was in command while the squadron commander was on leave. I was deployed forward at a patrol base during the first few days of the operation, and on day two he asked me to come with him as we took a look around.

We drove down the roads to link up with Fox Troop, past villages we'd already secured and into the new sector. As we drove, the villages around us all showed signs of life. Children were playing outside, small markets were functioning, and there were Iraqi Army and police checkpoints everywhere. After a few kilometers, however, that all changed. The villages went from alive to dead—literally.

These areas had been held by al Qaeda for a very long time. The people had slowly left or been killed, buildings were booby-trapped, and the countryside was littered with munitions. It was like crossing over a border from a functioning (though poor) society to the land of Mad Max, the post-apocalyptic dystopia of Mel Gibson's *Road Warrior*.

It was against this background that we approached a small village that we called "Objective Rhode Island." I don't know what the locals called it. As we walked forward, we had already heard the intelligence reports. The place was deserted.

Apparently, al Qaeda had killed every living person in the village many months ago, leaving behind only bullet-scarred walls and blood-covered floors.

From my vantage point, the place looked like any other, but with smoke curling up from small fires set in the underbrush to burn out any hidden weapons caches. I was near the back of the group, because I was one of the last out of the vehicles and because, frankly, I was struggling a bit in the heat. We'd been out all day, and the temperature was approaching 130 degrees.

We approached the village in silence, crossed through a burning canal (taking advantage of a small break in the flames) and around a corner. Most of the rest of our small group was already deep into the village.

Then...

Boom!

The canal behind me exploded. Well, the whole canal didn't explode, but a small hidden weapons cache did. The sound was loud enough to cause my ears to ring, and I could literally feel the sound in my chest. I thought, *If I'd only passed through the canal a few seconds later...*

Then my mind immediately shifted to something else. The heat. The thought process went something like this: *Wow, did I almost get blown up? Where's some shade?* In fact, the reaction of the entire group was almost casual. Guys' heads jerked up, they glanced around quickly to make sure no one was hurt, then they continued the search for shade. For the guys out there every day, an explosion was just another day at the office. For me—at the time—it was just a startling interruption in my quest for shade and a place to sit.

In fact, the heat kept dominating my thoughts even as I moved back to the FOB and talked to Nancy via instant messenger. I signed on first.

"Hey!"

She responded. "Hey! How r u?"

"So hot." (She had no sense of perspective on this response.)

"I'm sorry."

"I mean, you have no idea."

"I know. I'm sorry. How was your day?"

"Kind of interesting. I think I almost got blown up today."

I had to be under the influence of the heat when I typed those words. Nancy's reaction seemed a bit bland on my end (she said something like, "Oh my," and we went on with our conversation), but I later found out she was at our neighbor's house and burst into tears after our conversation. After months in Iraq, with vehicles getting hit by IEDs on a near-constant basis, my minor little brush with a canal explosion seemed like no big deal—just one of those things. Not so to her. To her, the incident was huge, a reminder of my mortality, that the person on the other end of the daily instant messaging session was in a war zone. But she didn't say anything. She never told me until months later that she wept the rest of that night and was shaken for days.

Me? I just went on with my life, which at that point was thoroughly, completely, and totally dominated by an overpowering desire to escape the vast oven that was eastern Diyala.

"By the way, the A/C isn't very reliable. Let's hope it works." With those words, a Sabre troop commander who shall remain nameless stepped into the vehicle, signaled the driver to start moving, and began the mission. I was in the back left seat, thunderstruck.

Keep in mind, I was already warm. The mission began in the late morning, and I'd been waiting in my body armor for thirty minutes. The temperature was at least 110 degrees—and climbing. I was soaked with sweat and clinging to my cold bottle of water with all the ferocity that a drowning man clings to his life preserver.

"It seems fine to me now." I was holding my hand over the vent, and cold air was pouring out. "When you say 'unreliable,' do you mean that it normally works or that it normally doesn't work?"

The Commander Who Shall Remain Nameless laughed. "It never works."

As if on cue, the air conditioner stopped. Well, it didn't stop entirely. It just stopped actually blowing air. I could tell that cold air was in there somewhere, it just wasn't blowing out of the tube. And so we began to bake.

As I sat there, I determined that the body goes through five stages of temperature grief. The emotional process of melting goes something like this:

Denial. This first stage was characterized by an irrational desire to mentally minimize the severity of the situation. *It's not so bad*, I said to myself. *I mean, I can still breathe.* Then, as the heat worsened, I marveled at my own toughness. *Wow, I'm a bigger man than I thought. Bring on 150 degrees!*

A sweat puddle formed under the arches of my feet, which brought me to...

Anger. Rage built. *We can put a man on the moon, but we can't build a working air conditioner? Doesn't General Motors or whoever built this horrific pile of junk support the troops? Do they even care about us?* Eventually, the fury became indescribable. I wanted to hit something.

Then I realized anger made me hotter, the last thing I wanted. So I started...

Bargaining. First with God: *Please, God, if You make the A/C work, I will never miss chapel.* Then with the driver: *I will put your children through college if you find a way to get this A/C to blow cold air.* Lastly, with the troop commander who put me in the seat: *I will let you live if you ease my suffering.*

But nothing worked because the broken air conditioner couldn't be bargained with. So then I moved to...

Depression. I plunged into deep despair. All that existed was heat, sweat, and the annoying crackling of the radio. *All that will ever exist is heat, sweat, and the annoying crackling of the radio.* The rage turned into an indescribable sadness at the injustice of the world. *Nothing will ever be good again.*

Finally, with a gigantic sigh (which caused rivers of sweat to roll down my back), I reached...

Acceptance. *It's okay. Really, it is. I can handle it. After all, I could be hotter. I could be inside an oven. I could be roasting on a spit like a rotisserie chicken. I could be sunbathing on the surface of Mercury.* And with this acceptance, an indescribable peace rolled over me.

Just then, the vehicle lurched to a stop. The door swung open and I stepped into the 125-degree heat of early afternoon in South Balad Ruz.

It felt like I just stepped into an air-conditioned building. It was all good. I was fine.

26

ALMOST HOME

Nancy

"HELLO," I SAID NERVOUSLY into my phone. "I'd like to pay off my account."

"Please enter your *nine*-digit *account* number," replied the automated voice. "Then press *star*."

I pressed the star button and listened to the melodic sound of elevator music while waiting for my "student loan consultant."

I'd done this once before, a couple of months ago when I called to pay off my PLATO loan that I got for New York University. Since I never actually graduated, it was a more manageable amount. After selling David's Land Rover, I had an extra $400 per month, which I applied to my loan. Then, after paying off my student loan, I had an extra $600 per month. Amazingly, the debt snowball seemed to be working, getting larger as it rolled to my goal of being debt-free.

It was September 2008, the deployment was almost over, and David had no idea.

I wanted to surprise him. I wanted to show him that I could survive *and* thrive as the head of the household in his absence. I wanted him to come home and find that some things were *better* than when he left.

"Name?"

"French."

"Account number?"

I repeated the number I'd just entered in the keypad. I briefly wondered why they make you enter your account number if they were going to ask you again, but nothing was going to get me down this day. When David left, we owed for his vehicle, my car, his Harvard, my NYU, and even had credit card debt—a huge total at which I was gradually picking away.

"Are you a little sad?" I asked.

If the operator was perplexed, she didn't reveal it in her expressionless response. "Why would I be?"

"I'm ending our relationship."

"You mean you're paying off your loan?"

"I mean I'm ending this relationship that lasted over fifteen years!"

"Address?"

I never finished college, but I vowed to save for it if I ever went back. My newfound reluctance to take on debt was just more evidence that I'd found my footing on the platform of adulthood. Here I was at the age of thirty-three—finally learning to take care of me, two kids, and a husband far, far away.

"I just thought you might be sad to see us go."

"Social Security number?"

I kept talking in spite of her total lack of interest because I wanted someone to share in my excitement. "I sold a vehicle to get rid of this loan, so it just feels a little intoxicating to be paying off this thing."

"Phone number, area code first?"

"My husband's in Iraq, and I'm trying to surprise him by paying off everything."

"Thank you for choosing Sallie Mae for your educational needs," she read from a script.

"Everything but the house," I amended. "I mean, I'm not Donald Trump, after all."

"Would you be interested in another of our many low-interest loans?"

"Excuse me?"

She repeated her script in a monotone.

"Haven't you been listening?" I asked. "I'm leaving you guys for good! It's over between us. We've been on the hook with you for fifteen years and I took an extra job to get rid of you."

She was silent. Then, "We have many loans to choose from that would meet your educational needs."

So maybe the loan officer wasn't proud of me, but I prayed David would be. As soon as he got over the fact that he didn't have a car.

But I didn't have time to worry about that. I had to start thinking about looking good for his return.

"We saw your husband in the magazine," my beautician Jocinda said, thumbing through the rack beside the dryers. "It's just awesome!" She always kept copies of fashion and celebrity gossip magazines on the shelf next to the dryers. David was coming home in days, and I wanted to look better than I ever had when he stepped off that plane.

"Here it is!" Jocinda said, holding up a dog-eared copy of the magazine and pointing at the photo of David and his friends sitting next to a tank or something. "He's famous!"

It's funny. David's been in countless magazine articles, newspapers, and radio spots, and we got more comments about his *OK!* appearance than his appearances on *The O'Reilly Factor*.

I sat down in her chair and slid back on the plastic seat while she put a black cape around me. "I need something dramatic," I told Jocinda, who knew "just the thing" and started giving me wispy bangs. Every time I went to get my hair cut, we'd talk about Dave Ramsey's baby steps to financial freedom, stemming from the first time I opened up an envelope marked "Hair Cuts" and paid her with cash.

"You're doing the baby steps," Jocinda surmised. Everyone in middle Tennessee knows Dave Ramsey, because he's been on the radio for years.

"I'm only on baby step number one," I told her during my first haircut after he left. Step one is saving money for a small "emergency fund."

The next time I came in, I was on baby step number two, which is when you pay off all debt except the house. For most of David's year in Iraq, I was stuck here, doing odd jobs and selling extra articles to magazines to help take a bite out of our debt.

This time, when Jocinda gave me a makeover, she asked her normal question. "Are you still doing the baby steps?" That's when I told her the news. I'd successfully paid off all our debt except for the house.

"Wonderful!" she exclaimed. "Did you do the debt-free scream?"

Dave Ramsey's radio show has a Friday tradition of taking phone calls from people who've just finished paying off all debt but the house. It's an invigorating and inspirational part of his show, as callers get the chance to announce that they are debt-free to the entire world by screaming at the top of their lungs. After their scream, the radio show plays a recording of Mel Gibson yelling "Freeeeedom" from *Braveheart*. Many callers have been paying off their debts using the debt snowball for months or even years. Frequently, they have dramatic stories of getting rid of their enormous debt by eating "beans and rice" or "rice and beans." My story, I figured, was dramatic enough to get on the air. Husband at war, extra job with presidential candidate, learning how to balance my own checkbook at thirty-three? This was going to be good!

This time, the scream would mean even more. It would be a scream of triumph but it would also be a scream of relief. Our ordeal was almost over. David was days from leaving Iraq. Soon he'd be on a plane, heading home. Soon I wouldn't be tucking in the kids by myself. Soon I would have my best friend back.

I assured Jocinda that we definitely planned on doing the scream. That afternoon, I got home from the hairdresser, gathered the kids around the phone, then dialed the show. The anticipation had built up over several months, and it was tough to take.

The line was busy. So we dialed again.

And dialed.

And dialed.

For three hours, I tried in vain to get on the show. When he took the last caller, the kids patted me on the shoulder. "It's okay, Mommy," they said. "Even though the line is busy, we know how awesome you did."

And so the kids learned that not everything ends the way you think it will. It was a lesson we'd learn again and again.

27

HOME

David

THERE ARE TIMES IN LIFE to listen to our conscience.

At some level, even as we saw al Qaeda die before our very eyes, there was a hole in our hearts. There was a feeling of unfinished business. That hole was opened on March 10, when al Qaeda killed four of our brothers. Though nothing will ever heal our wounds entirely, it was hard to have closure when you knew that our—Sabre Squadron's—highest-value target was still out there. Still alive. And enjoying the fruits of a $10,000 award that he had allegedly received from his al Qaeda paymasters for killing an American troop commander, my friend Torre.

Operation Payback had destroyed al Qaeda as an effective fighting force in that part of our battle space, subsequent raids had whittled their numbers down to a mere handful, but *he* was still out there. *He* was running free.

By the beginning of September, I was beginning to despair that we'd ever catch him. Every night, as I spoke to Nancy on our instant messenger, I'd pull up a pie graph that showed the amount of time I'd spent in Iraq compared to the amount of time left. At first, the amount of time left was enormous and the amount spent a mere sliver. Gradually, I stopped pulling up the graph—it was just too demoralizing. However, after many days and weeks, I'd pull it up to see how much of a dent I'd put into it. By the end of August, only a tiny sliver of time remained, but it was actually even less than I thought. I'd gotten the schedule for my "Freedom Flight," the flight that would take me from Balad Air Base to Fort Benning, Georgia, and I was stunned that I was leaving almost two full weeks early.

I was elated, but had a nagging feeling I shouldn't leave yet, that I had unfinished business. I kept hearing a still, small voice that seemed to be saying, *There is work yet to be done.*

"I get to leave early, but I feel like I shouldn't go," I said to Leo and J-Dave. In fact, I talked about it so much that I fear they both thought I was just seeking reassurance, probing to make sure they didn't resent the fact that my twelve-month deployment was shorter than their fifteen-month ordeal. I felt better when I heard that Sabre Squadron was being ordered off FOB Caldwell at the end of September.

Then it's time for me to leave, I thought. *If they move Sabre back to a bigger base, then I'll be pulled out to work with other JAG officers.*

So I felt better. For about a day, until that nagging feeling came back.

Too soon. Don't go.

"But the Army is giving me a gift. I should take it."

Don't go.

"But I can surprise the kids at school. It will be wonderful."

Don't go.

"There's no reason not to go! We've won. The entire region is liberated. We've paid the price, the regiment will probably pull me from the squadron anyway, and I won't be able to do much more."

Don't go.

I wasn't about to change my plans. For one thing, Nancy would never understand. "I'm sorry, I can come home early and everyone—including my commander—is telling me I'd be a fool not to go, but I kinda sorta have this feeling that I shouldn't leave." How would that go over? Just thinking through the conversation made me feel silly. But still...

Don't go.

Once, I did manage to mention this feeling to Nancy, who showed considerable composure.

"I think it's normal to feel like this when you're leaving your friends behind," she said. "But it's not like you can call Travelocity and rebook your flight."

She was right, but I still didn't have peace. One day, I was wrapping up some final administrative matters when a breathless trooper popped up in my office.

"Sir, we need you. We got him."

I felt a surge of elation. I knew who *he* was. Everyone knew who *he* was.

"Where is he?"

"On his way in, special forces got him."

And so they did. I arrived at the detention facility as the special forces detachment pulled in. They were beaming. They'd been on a roll lately, capturing a high-value target virtually every week for more than a month. But this one—while not high-value perhaps in the scheme of the war—was special.

"Sir, his own family turned him in."

This al Qaeda warrior had met a rather undignified end. As the special forces team rolled through a village, one of his uncles literally waved them down and simply pointed in his house. The team cleared the house, weapons at the ready, and found him cowering in a closet, still in his sleep clothes.

He wouldn't make eye contact with us, mumbled answers to questions the medics asked, and looked defeated—to his very core. The only thing he said (other than monosyllabic answers to medical questions) was, "I'm tired of running."

As I worked on his paperwork—which was done perfectly by the spec ops guys (it always was)—the squadron commander walked in. This was unusual, to say the least. In an entire year of operations, I'd never seen him just drop by the detention facility. There was no reason to. But there he was. Everyone snapped to attention, and I greeted him respectfully, with an inquiring tone. But he didn't say a word. He looked at the detainee. The detainee looked back at him. And then he turned and left.

I didn't chase after him. I never asked him about it. But that was one of the most meaningful moments of the entire deployment. He was acknowledging the significance—the justice—of the moment.

He wasn't leaving unfinished business. Our part of Diyala province was liberated by his men. And our worst enemy was in our hands.

At that point, I was almost overcome by a sense of gratitude. Justice is not always done in this life. Bad men go free all the time, and some deaths are never avenged. But this one was. Justice was being done, and I got to play a small part.

The circle was closed. My work was done. I was free to leave.

Three days later, the squadron commander, senior leaders, staff officers, and senior leaders of all the troops on the FOB gathered for a farewell dinner in our dining facility to say goodbye to me.

It was an emotional moment. So emotional, in fact, that I still can't bring myself to watch the video that Leo recorded. I didn't cry because, well, that wouldn't have been appropriate. But it was beyond bittersweet. When I'd arrived, I didn't know any person in that room and was a terrified rookie JAG with no idea how I could contribute. Eleven months later, these guys were my brothers and I felt like I'd done my duty.

Two days later, I did choke up when I said my formal goodbyes to my roommates. It was late at night, I'd packed up and was expecting to get up before 0500 hours the next morning. Rather than wake them up, my intention was to just roll out of my bunk and catch a ride to the landing zone. After a short Black Hawk helicopter ride, I would be in Balad. From Balad I would fly to Kuwait. From Kuwait, home.

My roommates Leo and J-Dave were very different people. One was a conservative Catholic from Alabama, the other a liberal Mexican-American agnostic who grew up in Wisconsin. I couldn't count the number of religious, political, or other arguments we'd had in the course of more than three hundred days of living together. They were my emotional lifelines. But now we were going our separate ways.

Don't go.

Suddenly, the voice was back.

I dismissed it. After all—and as Nancy and I had discussed—it's just natural to feel that way when you leave good friends. It was nothing, I told myself. Nothing but the normal regrets anyone would feel. Just before I went to sleep, I walked out into the courtyard of our

FOB, saw the clear sky, and said my goodbyes to Diyala. Tomorrow was the first day of the rest of my life.

But the skies are never clear for long in the desert. I woke up the next morning to find the whole world colored bright orange. Sandstorms had come rolling in while I slept, and no one was going anywhere. My air movement was canceled. But I didn't panic, I had a four-day window to catch my flight out of Balad.

Then the next morning was orange also.

And then the next.

So I was stuck—stuck in that awkward phase of repeated goodbyes. I kept running across people who thought I'd left already.

"Sir, aren't you supposed to be gone?"

"Yep. Sure am."

"Weather?"

"Yep. Sure is."

"That sucks."

"Yep. Sure does."

As my window of opportunity closed, I resolved to take a ground convoy out the next morning...the first ground convoy to move in days. My troop commander, Greg, was not happy to hear of my plans.

"I'm not going to tell you not to go," he said to me. "But I don't like to put guys on the road for three hours without even a basic combat load [I'd turned in my rifle and had only my sidearm and a few clips of pistol ammunition]. This will be your last mission, and I don't want anything to happen to you."

I thanked him for his concern, assured him I'd be fine, and told them that I either took the convoy or missed my flight home. I'd have to restart the whole scheduling process, and that could take—well, I had no idea how long it would take. He let me go.

Just before I jumped in the MRAP to head out, another friend called out, "See ya, Dave, I'd hate for you to die on your way home." The words stuck in me, but I honestly wasn't worried. The MRAP is an incredibly strong vehicle, and it had been months since anyone had been seriously hurt or killed on the routes I'd be traveling. In addition, I'd been on far more dangerous routes and missions than the routine run to Balad.

Just as I rolled out the gate and looked back at FOB Caldwell receding into the distance, I heard the voice again.

Don't go.

But this time, it was too late. I was already gone.

The three-hour trek to Balad happened without incident, and I overcame a last-minute snafu to catch an overnight flight on an Army puddle-jumper to Kuwait. There I was, back at Ali Al Saleem, the very base that was my initial gateway to the Middle East. But in some ways I felt like I was already home. After more than three hundred days in Iraq, I was out. Alive. I actually ate a McDonald's hamburger, drank a fountain Coca-Cola, and relaxed in an air-conditioned high-speed Internet café.

Nancy had been sending email updates to all our friends and family. They were short, but said all anyone needed to know. For three days, the message was, "Still at the FOB!"

Then the message changed. "Balad!"

Then another. "Kuwait!"

My friends back home who'd taken over the management of my longstanding fantasy baseball team in my absence changed the team's name with each move home. For almost a year, I was the "Diyala Limbaughs" (yes, Limbaughs, that's been my fantasy baseball team's name for fifteen years). Then the "Balad Limbaughs." Then the "Kuwait Limbaughs." Soon I'd be the "Fort Benning Limbaughs," and four days after that, I (and my fantasy team) would be home.

By the time we drove to our Omni Air DC-10 in the early morning hours of September 21, I was happy—but completely exhausted. Because military air travel in the theater of operations occurs mostly overnight, I was working on my third day without any real sleep, and as we boarded the plane I was looking forward to sleeping, but I was suddenly shocked into wakefulness. The plane was a complete piece of junk.

I don't know all the back story, but apparently the Air Force has entered into transportation contracts with a series of "charter airlines." One of them is Omni Air—a small company with a "fleet" of ten old DC-10s. I flew Omni Air on the way to Iraq, and the plane had mechanical difficulties in Germany. I didn't think much of it, because the flight was otherwise uneventful, but the plane was undeniably old and shabby. The plane I boarded on September 21 wasn't just shabby; it was literally falling apart.

Now I'm no big fan of flying. For completely irrational reasons, I would always rather drive than fly (that's why I felt an inexplicable sense of relief when I left FOB Caldwell in an MRAP rather than a Black Hawk even though the Black Hawk was immeasurably safer). So imagine how I felt when I walked on the plane and saw broken plastic from battered overhead compartments lying all over the floor. My overhead compartment was held shut by duct tape. When the plane's air conditioner started, condensation occasionally dripped on my head from an exposed pipe above me. If I didn't hate flying so much to begin with, the situation would have been almost comical. However, we took off without incident, and after sitting anxiously in my seat for a while, I succumbed to my exhaustion and fell into a fitful sleep.

I slept much of the way to Ireland, deplaned for an hour for refueling, a crew change, and some minor repairs, and then took off again. Two hours into the flight, just as I started to doze off again, I heard a *bang!* as the plane dropped and then swerved hard to the left. We leveled out for a moment, then began a big sweeping turn. I looked out my window and saw fuel spraying from the wingtips. The flight attendants rushed from their beverage service to their jump seats, and I saw one of them literally fall to his knees with his hands over his face.

Uh-oh. Is this what *don't go* meant?

The captain came on the intercom. "You may have felt a rather large bump a few moments ago. That was a compression failure on our number two engine. The engine is now powered down, and we are dumping fuel to prepare for a landing back in Ireland. We are not at this time declaring an emergency and can fly just fine on two engines. All of this is precautionary."

I was sitting just in front of three Black Hawk pilots. "Precautionary?" one of them snorted. "Right."

"What do you mean?" I asked.

"A compression failure means the engine is no longer air-cooled and probably melted within seconds of the failure. It just froze up. I wouldn't be surprised if we weren't spitting molten engine parts out of the back of this plane. But we should be fine so long as nothing else goes wrong."

As we descended, the plane began to vibrate...no small vibration. The overhead compartments were shaking open, and there was an audible and strange hum throughout the plane. As we descended below ten thousand feet, the vibration was too much for one of the exit doors, and one of the seals apparently gave way—causing air to come rushing through the back of the cabin. By this time the vibration and sound were almost deafening. I actually started to think the plane was crashing. It was an indescribably terrible feeling...to make it through almost a full year of war only to crash on the way home to see your family.

As we landed, I peeked out the window and saw fire trucks chasing us down the runway. Molten engine parts were, in fact, coming out of the back of the plane. When the plane careened to a stop, I became infuriated. Throughout the deployment, for almost a full year, I didn't complain. I knew that conditions would be bad. Instead, I was grateful for three hot meals and semireliable air-conditioning in a tiny base fourteen miles from Iran. Through everything, I tried to simply grin and bear it.

But not that day. That day, I was livid. It just seems so easy to give returning soldiers a decent flight home, and the Air Force had just dropped the ball by contracting with an "airline" like Omni. Seriously, spend an extra few dollars and put us on American Airlines, or Delta, or United, or Northwest...or any airline that wasn't going to throw us on thirty-year-old "retired" jets that leak, break, and almost crash.

At that point I had no options, so I fumed in Ireland while waiting for the "airline" to provide us with another plane. For almost fourteen hours we waited. Finally, another plane arrived. We took off for our first stop in America, Fort Dix, and made it there with no problems. We had only one more leg of the trip before I arrived at Fort Benning. After dropping off 150 passengers, we taxied to take off.

And then? The plane lost all electrical power.

We sat on the runway for another hour as the ground crew literally jump-started the plane. By this point, I was so nervous about flying that I was about to puke. I was working on four days without real sleep, a near plane crash, and all the emotions of returning home. When we landed at Fort Benning, I was so emotionally exhausted that I didn't feel a thing.

Well, not until I made the call.

For two days, Nancy had been sitting by the phone, waiting to hear that I was back in America. She had heard the details of the airplane malfunctions. She had agonized with me while I sat for hour after hour in Ireland. I knew that she was about as nervous as I was.

But when I landed, there was one small problem. I couldn't call her. I had no cell phone. When I left, Nancy had gone to the Verizon store and canceled my account to save money. Since she was in charge of the finances while I was gone, I didn't complain…much. Sadly, no one around me had a cell phone either, and we were bused directly from the flight to the warehouse where we'd turn in our weapons and gear.

One hour passed.

Two hours passed.

I knew she was probably in a panic by that time. There had been one incident already, and now I was hours overdue calling. Finally, I saw another soldier from our group talking on a phone.

"Sergeant?"

"Yes, sir?"

"Can I borrow your phone? I'll pay you for the time. Here's five bucks." Before he could protest I gave him five dollars from my wallet—a five-dollar bill that had been sitting there for months.

I took the phone and dialed. It rang once before Nancy answered.

"David?" She was in a store shopping for Austin's Boy Scout uniform.

"It's over. I'm home."

She started to cry. I teared up in front of everyone. I couldn't talk anymore or I knew I'd lose it. "I can't talk. This isn't my phone. I love you!"

The next few days were full of briefings and phone conversations.

I learned all the warning signs of post-traumatic stress syndrome, reported any medical problems, went to briefings telling me not to beat my wife and kids, and had final medical checkups. The entire process took slightly less than four days.

It was the early afternoon of September 25, 2008. Nancy was on her way from Tennessee to Fort Benning. I was packed and ready to go. But just before I met her, I had a few minutes to go to the Internet café, sign on, and chat with my friends back at FOB Caldwell—to tell them that my wife was coming to get me, and that we were surprising the kids at school. (Nancy had left them with friends the night before, saying that she was coming back the next day with a "gift.")

No one was online, even though it was night in Iraq, prime time for most of them to be talking to their friends and family back home.

Dread filled me. I knew what Internet silence meant.

Someone had died.

I felt my heart pounding as I sent Leo an email, knowing that he had email access even in blackouts so that he could help with the family notification process.

Moments after I sent the email, I saw Leo pop online.

"Dave?"

"It's me. What happened."

"Blackout."

"I figured that. Who was it?"

"Family notifications are complete."

"That means you can tell me. Who *was* it?"

There was a long pause, and I felt a little shaky.

"WHO WAS IT?"

"I'm sorry, Dave. It was Mike."

Mike Medders, M'Gungis. The football star from Ohio. The man who lifted our spirits every day with his irrepressible wit and spirit. My dear friend. Killed by an al Qaeda suicide bomber who blew up himself and three other al Qaeda terrorists just as Mike moved to detain them. He had been out ahead—leading from the front—and now he was gone.

At the same moment that I was getting the message from Leo, Nancy got a call on her cell—from Iraq. It was Major Cantlon, telling her to give him a call as soon as I got the message. She knew enough to know I'd lost a friend.

I knew, that instant, what *don't go* meant. I should have been there. Maybe I could have done something—after all, he was moving to detain. Maybe I could have told him it was okay to shoot. Maybe not. Probably not. But still. I should have been there. We go through these things together, not apart. You mourn together. Not apart. And I was here. They were there. And Nancy was coming in twenty minutes.

It was all too much. I broke down, weeping, in the corner of the Internet café. I dried my eyes, walked to the corner, and waited for my wife.

To this day, I can't process the mix of emotions. The horror at Mike's loss, the joy at seeing Nancy, the guilt at seeing Nancy when I felt like it was too soon, like I'd ignored God's call. On the way home, I couldn't decide whether to laugh or cry, so I did a lot of both.

The next morning, we surprised the kids, but it was too much and just felt wrong. We hadn't gauged the intensity of their emotions. Since I felt so wounded and so raw, the reunion wasn't so much joyful as tearful. It was simply too much for a nine-year-old and seven-year-old to take—and all in public.

That evening, with the kids sitting at either side while I read a book, I began to feel just a bit more peace. I was home. And my deployment was almost over.

I say "almost" because I had one more mission—to say goodbye to my friend. Mike was coming home, and I was going to be there...to stand in for those still in Iraq and to tell his parents how much we loved him.

And so, just days after I said hello to my kids, I packed my bags and said goodbye once again as Nancy and the kids drove me to the Nashville airport. This time, instead of wearing my Army combat uniform, I was wearing my service uniform, the iconic green uniform you see on television—the one soldiers wear for courts-martial, congressional testimony, and military funerals.

To get to Avon Lake, Ohio, Mike's hometown, you have to travel west from Cleveland Airport on I-90. In my rental car just a few miles outside the city, I began to see church and business marquees honoring Mike. "God bless CPT Mike Medders." "Please pray for the Medders family." "Our hero, Mike Medders." As soon as I exited from the interstate and turned on the main road leading to Avon Lake, I was overwhelmed by the tributes. Flags lined every road, and many yards featured homemade signs. This is a community that loved Mike and loves his family.

I pulled into a bank, wearing my Class A uniform. I needed directions to Avon Lake High School, where they were holding the visitation. As soon as I walked into the lobby, a teller addressed me. "Are you here for Mike?"

"Yes. I served with him in Iraq."

"I'm so sorry for your loss."

She directed me to the school, and I arrived just before the visitation began. An honor guard stood by his flag-draped coffin, and the line of mourners already snaked through the gym. My fellow Sabre Squadron captain Pat Collins—who had come home weeks before to command the squadron's "rear detachment" at Fort Hood—and I walked through the line to greet his family. His father, mother, sister, and fiancée were remarkably strong. Pat introduced me to them, and I told them I'd just returned from FOB Caldwell and served with Mike.

In the car on the way up, I'd planned to tell them we loved their son and that I was so sorry he was gone. But I could barely get a single word out before I lost my composure. His father (who is a huge man) gave me a big bear hug and just whispered, "Hang in there." I walked away, wiped my eyes, and slowly—along with Pat—saluted Mike's casket.

The next few hours were remarkable. First dozens, then hundreds, then thousands of people poured into the gym. Mike's family greeted and hugged them all. Friends, family members, Avon Lake students, members of the community, Patriot Guard Riders, the local VFW, one of Ohio's senators, Mike's friends from Officer Basic Course, other Gold Star Families—they all came. They stood together in shock and disbelief and grief, but all knew or knew of Mike and came to honor him and his family.

At 2100 hours, when the visitation ended, I drove to Mike's house. The entire way was lighted with memorial candles. At his house, his family and close friends shared stories, ate food provided by the community, and just spent some time together outside the public eye. I can't emphasize how wonderful his family is. Through their indescribable grief, they were welcoming, hospitable, and eager to meet Mike's friends. Mike was a reflection of them.

The funeral Mass was conducted in the same parish church where Mike received his first Communion, and the priest's homily was profoundly moving. Mike's mother had selected Daniel 12:1—3 as the theme of the service, and the priest weaved it throughout his remarks. The verses read:

> *At that time Michael, the great prince who protects your people, will arise. There will be a time of distress such as has not happened from the beginning of nations until then. But at that time your people— everyone whose name is found written in the book—will be delivered. Multitudes who sleep in the dust of the earth will awake: some to everlasting life, others to shame and everlasting contempt. Those who are wise will shine like the brightness of heavens, and those who lead many to righteousness, like the stars forever and ever.*

After the homily and Eucharist, Mike's four closest childhood friends paid tribute, and the Mike they described was exactly the Mike I knew: fun-loving, fearless, and a great, great friend.

The church was packed with Mike's friends and families, but the community's presence was simply overwhelming. The children from every school in the city lined the streets, hands over their hearts. Businesses closed. For miles, from the church to the cemetery, people stood to honor Mike. It was one of the most amazing things I've ever seen.

The cemetery service was brief. Under a cloudless sky, Mike received military honors, and the Cleveland Police Department's bagpipe and drum corps played a haunting and mournful rendition of "Amazing Grace." As the honor guard fired the salute, and "Taps" played, a flock of geese flew directly over us. It was simultaneously the most heartbreaking and beautiful sight I'd ever seen.

And then it was over. The funeral ended, I said my goodbyes to Mike's family, and I flew home. The last mission of my deployment was complete.

Nancy and the kids met me at the airport, and we ate at Chick-fil-A on the way home. I was still in my uniform, and the kids behind the counter thanked me for my service and gave me a free meal. It tasted wonderful.

At that instant, I was reminded of a small but telling scene at the end of Peter Jackson's remarkable adaptation of Tolkien's *Return of the King*. In a moment that seemingly takes place months after the end of their adventures, Frodo and Sam are sitting together in a tavern as the local townsfolk carry on around them. You can see in their eyes that they are glad to be home, glad to be in that spot, but they feel something different. They are no longer the same. And they'll never be the same.

I feel much the same way. After what I've seen and done and experienced, I'll never be the same person again. The person that left for Iraq is not quite the person who came back. I'm not the same father. I'm not the same husband. I'm not the same friend. I don't know if I'm better or worse. But I do know that I'm different.

But I also know—to the very marrow of my being—that it was right for me to go. It was my purpose in life, my wife's purpose, and my children's purpose that we would do all that we could do to help our country win this war.

Even if the cost was high.

EPILOGUE

Nancy

NOW THAT DAVID'S BACK and our story is almost done, allow me to uncover two very common misunderstandings about families separated by war.

People relentlessly said to me, "Thank you for *your* service. What you are doing is just as important and meaningful as what *he's* doing over there." In fact, friends so doted on me, hammering away this notion, that I started to believe I'd really done something. Even when he returned, people complimented me on having come through the year with such aplomb, carefully emphasizing the words so I'd understand that they were making a well-meaning and accurate point: deployment isn't just about the soldier. It's a family affair, and we all make very real sacrifices. It's like being at a party where everyone is explaining what they do for a living, and you come to the lady who's been dragged there by her husband.

"Do you work?" someone might ask, before correcting themselves: "I mean, *outside* the home?"

There's a strong, generous desire to make the wife feel like what she is doing is just as important as what the husband is doing. In fact, one of the reasons we wrote this book was to give a more complete picture of modern war and what it looks like from the front lines and the home front, as everyone (from the spouse to the children) decides to do their duty.

Now, as I read David's account of his months there, I feel very acutely aware that what I did was so...I guess the only word is comparatively "small." Here I am cuddled on the couch next to a sleeping Goggo, learning of some of David's adventures for the first time. Though it might not be the politically correct thing to say, our year obviously was not "separate but equal."

My travails were mere inconveniences. Even the most exciting events of my year—facing down the ski slopes in Utah, driving the renegade car in Tennessee, and slowly taking a pickaxe to our enormous debt snowball—were small events in life...challenges that happen in the wonderful luxury of America, where there are emergency rooms, mechanics, and financial advisors on the radio ready to help you through it.

And we'd always helped each other through things. Over the course of our marriage, responsibility has swung like a pendulum between us. When I'm very busy—with books or babies—he has stepped up to fill in any gaps I might have inadvertently left unattended. Then, when he's very busy—with books or Supreme Court cases—I do the same for him. It's worked out that we've rarely had big things going on simultaneously, and if we do, one of us falls back to take the role of supporting cast member until the other's drama has passed.

But with the year in Iraq, the supporting role was just that. I allowed David to walk through—to march through, I suppose—the ultimate test of character. While I'm proud of the fact that I didn't burn down the house or bounce any tithe checks, that's the least our country deserves, right? Learning to live well—within our means and with basic competence—was not the heroism that we came to sadly know over the year. While I was conjuring up the nerve to face each air-conditioned day, David was conjuring up the nerve to go outside the wire on IED-laced roads. While I was so undone over pulling my son's tooth that our church deacon had to do it, he was undone when his friends lost their lives.

So when the time came for our big reunion—when he'd greet not just his wife and kids but also new and improved, debt-free, single-car home complete with a cute and lovable dog—he was reeling from the most intense year of his life and grieving the loss of a dear friend.

He would come to appreciate the debt-free life, enjoyed picking out a used Nissan Titan truck we bought with cash, and now loves Goggo more than the rest of us love that little furball. But for days, weeks, and months, those things were just absorbed by the intensity of his emotions and the reality of the last year.

The kids, however, were always at the forefront of his mind as we tried to readapt to life as normal, which brings me to a final point...What about the kids? Why didn't I—on that fateful day when David looked at me and said he wanted to join the Reserves—put my foot down and say no for their sakes? After all, many women would have. Or so they tell me.

An exchange with one woman at a community coffee typified this second misconception. "Don't you have kids?" she asked with furrowed brow, after I was introduced with my new name for the year: "This is *Nancy-her-husband's-in-Iraq* French."

I'll never forget this day—not that it was so atypical, but it was the first of so many like it. She was dressed in sensible shoes, jeans, and a long denim shirt embroidered with cardinals sitting on a branch across her chest. Actually, a chest covered with avian embroidery should be described as a "bosom," and she readjusted the straps of her oversized quilted purse to give the cardinals more room.

It was less like a purse and more like something you might check at the airport, other than its pink quilted fabric. Although I couldn't see into it, I knew it was stuffed with Band-Aids, hand sanitizer, a pack of crayons, and Fix-A-Flat, serving as a talisman to ward off her kids' boredom at church, possible scrapes on the playground, and germs at McDonald's. She carried it under her arm like a sheriff puts a badge on his chest or a gun in his holster.

She didn't know my purse hid a driver's license from a different state that expired last November. She couldn't see that it—along with everything else—was coated with remnants of a broken cigarette from a pack I'd bought in a moment of weakness at a gas station. She didn't see me pick flecks of tobacco from sticks of gum before handing them to the kids during church.

But even without hard evidence, she crossed her arms in disapproval.

"So, when he joined the Army," she continued, "didn't he realize he'd be deployed?" What she was implying was that we'd been somehow irresponsible in this choice.

"What about your children?"

"Wars are complicated," I began, taking a sip of coffee to give myself some time. "And the government needs adults over there to run things. Frequently, by the time guys are officers, they have kids."

"Well, that's where his priority should be," she said. "His kids."

And that was that.

Sometimes in the past, during lively political conversations with friends about politics and war, we'd all get so heated that we made a rule banning the word "Hitler." If anyone mentioned the ultimate evil dictator in the argument, he'd automatically lose the debate. There's just nowhere to go conversationally after that. Similarly, invoking "the children" always ends the conversation, because you're left in the unenviable position of defending your "anti-child" policies and, frankly, you've already lost. So there I stood, looking over the chasm between me and the other mom, feeling every inch of distance.

I admit, I sometimes felt like motherhood was a giant sorority you don't automatically get invited to pledge even after childbirth. I owned strollers and sippy cups, but I didn't have a philosophy on them...nor did I want to discuss, dissect, or compare mine to others. I didn't read *Consumer Reports* before buying my kids' car seat, and quite frankly I didn't care if anyone else did. Why, some would ask, didn't I carry pictures of the kids in my purse? The truth is that their school photos were somewhere unopened in a drawer next to little cards reminding me of their dental appointments I invariably forgot. I developed a reputation with the PTA because I'd never collected box tops for education. And if anyone used the word "scrapbooking," I'd want to impale myself on the nearest Wii controller.

"Kids aren't young long, you know. He can't be a father if he's not there," the lady said, uncrossing her arms as if she realized I was not going to fight back. Her eyebrows lowered, softening her expression into something that looked like pity.

"Here, your coffee's getting cold."

I pressed the mug to my lips and gulped.

In the following days, I ran the conversation over and over in my head, regretting that I didn't defend my kids, my husband, or even myself. *What happened to me?* I wondered. *And what exactly is a bosom?*

Gradually, all the sensible things I should've said came to me. I could've explained that if the entire segment of the population called "parents" excluded themselves from military service, we couldn't have stormed the beaches of Normandy, won at Gettysburg, or even gained our independence from Britain. (Note the World War II reference *without* mentioning Hitler.)

"It wouldn't have mattered," said Anna, whose husband is a doctor who was also eventually deployed as a lieutenant colonel in the Air Force. "People like that don't get it, and no amount of explaining can make them understand. They just close their eyes and hope someone else will do what needs to be done. And you're a living, breathing 'someone else' reminding them that *somebody* has to do *something*."

Over the next few weeks and months, I had dozens and dozens of opportunities to relive the moment.

Almost everyone asked the same initial question: "Don't you have kids?"

Even though my answer got more nuanced with practice, Anna was right. In a child-centric culture that defines "good parenting" as a dad who never missed a soccer game, my explanation was as rhetorically forceful as Charlie Brown's teacher giving a homework assignment.

It wore me down. Had I been tasked with writing a research paper on the role of fathers in the military, I could've made a logical argument. Instead, I was having these conversations within the context of our new life without Dad. After months of listening to the kids' muffled tears in their pillows, I lost the ability to explain myself. I felt I was driving a damaged car, waving out the window at the people honking behind me. *Just go around*, I'd think, *we have to go at our own pace.*

And if you got right down to it, the subjects of the ubiquitous question were doing pretty well. We had a "one-year campout," deserting the upstairs and allowing the kids to sleep in my room. Left to the quietness of their thoughts at night, they'd get a bit emotional, but I'd reach over and pat them on their backs. In the morning, they fought over who could mark out the previous day on the calendar with a big X.

Occasionally, going about our business, something unexpected would throw me off my game. *What show-offs*, I thought one day at the library as I watched a dad read a book about pirates to his son while the mom entertained their younger daughter. *Who goes to the library as a family anyway, especially in the middle of the day?*

I meandered closer, pretending to look at the books, much like an insect goes instinctively to the light that'll kill it.

"Yo-ho, my friends, I have a tale to tell..."

The dad's awful impersonation and casual happiness wounded me. Even after David returned from the war, he wouldn't speak pirate.

Things were different when he returned—which, of course, is what everyone tells you but you don't believe. I figured he'd be the type of guy that would experience Iraq and come home the same guy...except with more carefully honed political positions about the war. For a year, I'd imagined what it would be like when I saw him for the first time. I settled on a new hairstyle and got a nice new outfit—he'd be incredibly impressed that I got bangs, I thought. Had I gained weight while he was gone? I wondered. My friend Rene said she'd take the opportunity to quit shaving her legs for a year and get obese, but I tried—tried—to keep it together in the looks department. As I approached Fort Benning, with much trepidation, I had butterflies in my stomach. Who has these kinds of nerves after thirteen years of marriage?

I pulled up in our now only car and saw him standing on the street with his huge camouflage bags at his feet. He looked skinny and his eyes were bloodshot from crying after hearing of Mike's death. When we hugged for the first time, he collapsed into me and wept.

If Hollywood had written this story, they would've been triumphant tears of joy. We would've gotten into the car, headed straight to the hotel in Birmingham that's connected to Ruth's Chris Steak House, and had one heck of an evening. I would've told him that the car was paid for—and by the way, we needed to think about replacing his old Land Rover—and perhaps we would've bought a

Porsche on the way home in order to romantically drive off into the sunset. My friends Tabby, Monica, and Lauren (moms of kids in Austin's class) were so certain of the "Hollywood" version of events that they threw me a lingerie shower the week before.

As frequently happened this year, things turned out differently than we'd anticipated. We had a nice romantic evening, with good food, wine that the Kingstons sent to our hotel room as a gift, and I told him about paying off all of our debt.

As I look back at the events as they unfolded, this may have been when he started walking in the "returning dad and husband" role. He was pleasantly surprised at everything, but he was different inside, and we both knew it. The "big moment" I had been building to, the moment when I unveiled all of the changes in our life, simply fizzled. The truly big thing was the change in David, not in our finances.

Other people noticed it too. David was always the life of the party, but now he had an "edge" to him that was indescribable but still very much there. He didn't sleep, he missed his friends, and he felt strange going back to a job at a desk without having his weapon with him.

It caused conflict, arguments, and misunderstandings as we learned to live together again. Once—we call it the Great Bowl-Kicking Incident of 2008—we had the strangest fight over the fact that he kicked Goggo's water bowl outside one afternoon. I can't remember why it escalated so quickly; perhaps I pointed out the bowl he'd accidentally kicked too emphatically. But within minutes a normal afternoon with the kids became a "I hope they don't repeat that word at school" and "let's pray the neighbors aren't home" debacle. When he took the kids to a movie after his return, I was annoyed that he chose a movie a little scarier than anything I'd let them see while he was gone. Once, we had gotten so irritated with each other on a drive that I jumped out of the car at the first stop sign and started walking. You've never felt like a marital failure until your husband is driving five miles per hour on an old country road, yelling out the window at you to get back in the car.

Of course, all of this is understandable, in retrospect. He came home to more social obligations than ever before—welcome-home parties, seeing family and friends for the first time in a year, and parental duties at which he'd grown rusty. He felt like a third wheel after I'd gotten used to him being gone. He couldn't sleep. But the main difference is that he was grieving. A number of his friends had been murdered—that's the right word—in Iraq, and he'd seen things that they don't even show on the old television show *24*. And then he's expected to know which kind of fake violence in a movie theater might frighten our son? Sometimes I think even our happiness at his return was irritating to him. We got to live our lives so joyfully, when he had experienced something we'd never understand.

In other words, he was home from war, but he was still paying the price.

Frequently, I'd get asked if it was worth it, if the cost to our marriage was too much, and I always told them the same thing. If David was obeying God's prompting in his life to go to war, then he's more of the true "David" now than he'd ever been in our marriage. In other words, he's more fully what God intended him to be than when he was the best conversationalist at the law firm cocktail party.

Five months after he returned, we attended a Boy Scout banquet. Before the festivities, he and Austin had to bake a father-son cake, and this time, his father was home to help bake it.

Camille and I ate cereal while we watched David piece together a cake that had fallen apart after baking. He'd used a Hershey's Kiss cake pan and Austin wrote "Troop 154" in blue ink on a white strip of paper to put at the top of the confection.

Camille played with a gift the tooth fairy had given her—a girl made of Legos—while Austin taped Iraq money to a posterboard. He was supposed to bring a collection of something—anything—and so we tried to find all the foreign money he'd collected over the years. David had brought some cool coins back from his military travels. Under money that had the former dictator's picture on it, Austin wrote "boo, Saddam" and we laughed.

This—to me—was happiness: the clank of spoons on the counter, the sound of Honeycombs being crunched by Goggo, the kids bickering over who gets to read the back of the cereal box, the hum of the freezer making ice, the drip-drip-dripping of coffee into a carafe.

"Hey, I have an idea." David smiled, put the icing-covered knife down, left the room, and returned with a bag of ornamental coins, one and a half inches in diameter, that the Army uses to commemorate a special event or unit. "You can bring these too."

The coins were those he'd picked up in Iraq, all of which told a story I knew I'd probably never know. He placed them carefully down on the table and picked one up. "Four of these ten men listed in this unit were killed."

Camille looked up from her Legos, and I felt the incongruity of the moment suck the air from the room.

In a small voice, she asked, "Are you sad?"

"I'm always sad," he said. "But I'm thankful I knew them, and I'm thankful they lived." Camille looked thoughtful, then went back to her new toy. After a moment, she responded:

"I'm proud of my daddy."

He, too choked up, didn't respond, and we made our way to the Boy Scout banquet.

"David is a graduate of Harvard Law School, and has appeared on *The O'Reilly Factor*, ABC News, and Neil Cavuto..." the scout master read from a paper that had bits of biographical information taken from the Internet.

The Boy Scouts were eating barbecue and tearing strips of table-cloth off in curly ribbons as David approached the microphone, dressed in the Army's dress blues and carrying a sabre he got for serving with the 3d Armored Cavalry Regiment.

"I want to talk to you about this uniform," he began as he walked to the podium.

The little boys sat up tall in their matching hats, kerchiefs, and navy blue shirts.

He then told stories about normal, average people who had the courage to put on a uniform and do their duty with honor. He pointed out his various ribbons—including the Bronze Star he was awarded in Iraq—and explained what they meant.

"Uniforms are a way you can actually *wear* your heart. One day, your Boy Scout uniform will tell the story of your scouting life...whether you did the minimum to get by, whether you tried new things, whether you had the courage to give a task your all," he said. "I hope your uniform tells a wonderful story."

When he was done, the room of Boy Scouts, parents, and grandparents got up from their folding chairs and paper plates of barbecue to give a standing ovation. I swallowed a lump in my throat that threatened to betray me.

As the room applauded his father, Austin stood on his chair to get a closer look. He clapped and yelled, "Daddy! Daddy!" at the top of his lungs.

Joy.

I wish I was still in contact with the cardinal lady so I could tell her that my kids learned lessons from their dad, even in his absence...perhaps because of it. Camille learned about civic duty, Austin learned to persevere. They also learned their parents' lives aren't centered around their activities, which I supposed holds a certain amount of freedom as well. Although he's not yet speaking like a pirate, David certainly has "tales to tell," little stories that come out at breakfast or on a walk that the kids will remember forever.

Just for kicks, the next time I'm at a cocktail party, I'd love to ask someone what he does for a living and respond, "An accountant?"

I'd look at him skeptically, because the deployment has made us parents who are less afraid, less skittish about duty, and even a tad more in love. I think it gave our kids an advantage.

Then my skepticism might turn to pity. "Don't you have kids?"